Case Studies on Educational Administration

FOURTH EDITION

Theodore J. Kowalski

Kuntz Family Chair in Educational Administration
The University of Dayton

PEARSON

Boston • New York • San Francisco
Mexico City • Montreal • Toronto • London • Madrid • Munich • Paris
Hong Kong • Singapore • Tokyo • Cape Town • Sydney

Senior Editor: *Arnis E. Burvikovs*
Series Editorial Assistant: *Megan Smallidge*
Manufacturing Buyer: *Andrew Turso*
Senior Marketing Manager: *Tara Whorf*
Production Coordinator: *Pat Torelli Publishing Services*
Cover Administrator: *Joel Gendron*
Editorial-Production Service: *Lynda Griffiths*
Electronic Composition: *TKM Productions*

For related titles and support materials, visit our online catalog at www.ablongman.com.

Library of Congress Cataloging-in-Publication Data

Kowalski, Theodore J.
    Case studies on educational administration / Theodore J. Kowalski.--4th ed.
        p. cm.
    Includes bibliographical references and index.
    ISBN 0-205-41208-4
    1. School management and organization--United States--Case studies. I. Title: Educational administration. II. Title.

LB2805.K63 2005
371.2'00973--dc22   2004045248

Printed in the United States of America

10 9 8 7 6 5 4   08 07 06 05

Contents

Preface   v

Matrix of Topics by Case Number   vii

Introduction   1

CASE 1   *Another Federal Intrusion*   12

CASE 2   *What Alternative School Concept Is Best?*   18

CASE 3   *A Bully's Threat*   25

CASE 4   *Lounge Talk*   33

CASE 5   *Get Rid of the Sloppy Assistant Principal*   41

CASE 6   *Let the Committee Decide*   50

CASE 7   *A Principal Clashes with the Culture*   59

CASE 8   *How about School-Based Management?*   66

CASE 9   *Getting Back to Basics*   74

CASE 10   *A Matter of Honor*   83

CASE 11   *An Invisible Superintendent*   94

CASE 12   *Captain Punishment*   103

CASE 13   *An Ambitious Assistant Principal*   112

CASE 14   *A One-Trick Principal*   118

CASE 15   *A Maverick Board Member*   127

CASE 16   *Excessive Punishment or Just Politics?*   134

CASE 17   *The Passive Principal*   141

CASE 18   *A Disillusioned Assistant Principal*   149

CASE 19   *Dissention over the Vocational School*   156

CASE 20   *In-School Suspension: An Effective Idea?*   163

CASE 21   *Let's Not Rap*   171

CASE 22   *Is the Devil Teaching Spelling?*   179

CASE 23   *Decentralization and Inequality*   187

CASE 24   *Who Creates the School's Vision?*   199

Case Worksheets   206

Index   231

Preface

Effective practice in school administration is being redefined by popular reform strategies such as state deregulation, district decentralization, school restructuring, and culture change. These tactics bring into question long-standing role expectations for both district and school leaders. To what extent do these evolving conditions move administrators away from a preoccupation with management? To what extent do they require administrators to provide leadership for changing organizational culture? How will the work lives of administrators change if teachers finally achieve the status of true professionals? Such queries are central to current efforts to ensure that the next generation of school leaders will be adequately prepared for the challenges that await them.

Case Studies on Educational Administration, Fourth Edition, is intended to help prospective administrators develop problem-solving and decision-making skills. Case studies provide an excellent venue for achieving this objective for at least two reasons. First, they infuse contemporary issues into the classroom; second, they provide a nexus between theory with practice. Addressing the problems presented in the cases encourages you to engage in problem framing, critical thinking, and reflective practice—three activities central to effective practice in school administration. Working with cases can help you learn how to use information to identify and solve problems, how to develop and evaluate alternative solutions, and how to continuously refine your professional knowledge base as a result of exposure to new knowledge, skills, and experiences.

The cases in this book present a range of problems encountered by contemporary practitioners in districts and schools. Both the matrix at the front of the book and the subject index at the back of the book can be used to identify key topics addressed in the 24 cases. None of the cases is taken to conclusion so that you and other readers can assume decision-making roles. This edition includes three new cases, one focusing on new federal legislation (the *No Child Left Behind Act*), one on alternative schooling, and one on vocational schools. In addition, more cases focus directly on principals and assistant principals than in the previous edition.

My thanks go to many individuals who helped me complete this edition. Among them are

- Administrators who provided information necessary to develop the cases
- Students in my doctoral seminars who made countless suggestions about possible improvements to the book's format

- Colleagues at other universities who shared their experiences teaching with the cases
- My office assistant, Elizabeth Pearn, and my graduate assistant, Nancy Seyfried

I am also especially grateful to the following individuals who reviewed the manuscript and provided constructive criticisms and insightful recommendations: Jits Furusawa, California State University, Dominguez Hills; Art Safer, Appalachian State University; and Rodney Stanley, Morehead State University.

Matrix of Topics by Case Number

							Case Number																	
Topics	1	2	3	4	5	6	7	8	9	10	11	12	13	14	15	16	17	18	19	20	21	22	23	24
Administrator-Teacher Relationships			•	•	•	•	•		•	•		•		•			•	•				•		•
Alternative Schools/Programs		•																		•				
Assistant Principals			•		•											•					•			
Assistant Superintendents/Central Office	•	•				•	•	•						•		•		•		•		•	•	
Budgeting, Fiscal Issues						•					•			•			•		•			•	•	
Business Manager						•					•													
Career Development				•	•		•	•			•		•	•				•		•				
Change Process	•	•		•	•	•	•	•	•				•				•			•		•	•	•
Communication Problems			•	•	•	•	•	•	•	•	•	•		•	•	•	•	•		•	•	•	•	
Community Relations (see Public Relations)																								
Curriculum and Instruction			•		•	•	•	•	•	•	•	•	•	•	•		•		•		•	•	•	
Decision-Making Procedures	•	•			•	•	•		•	•	•	•	•	•	•	•	•		•	•	•	•	•	•
Educational Outcomes	•						•	•	•	•	•	•								•		•	•	
Elementary Schools							•	•	•								•					•	•	
Employment Practices				•			•		•				•				•			•	•		•	
Employment Security/Stress					•						•	•	•	•	•	•		•		•			•	
Ethical/Moral Issues			•		•	•				•	•	•	•	•	•	•	•	•	•		•	•		
Evaluation	•			•					•	•				•	•		•		•		•	•		
Federal Programs	•																							
High Schools		•	•	•	•								•	•				•	•	•	•			
Leadership Style/Theory	•	•	•	•	•	•						•	•	•			•	•	•	•	•	•	•	•
Legal Issues			•									•	•		•				•	•	•		•	
Middle Schools																		•						•

(continued)

Matrix of Topics by Case Number

Topics	1	2	3	4	5	6	7	8	9	10	11	12	13	14	15	16	17	18	19	20	21	22	23	24
Multicultural Issues			•				•			•		•				•				•				
Organizational Theory				•	•	•	•	•	•		•	•	•	•			•	•		•	•		•	•
Philosophical Issues		•	•	•	•	•	•	•	•	•	•	•	•	•	•	•	•	•	•	•	•	•	•	•
Policy Development/Analysis		•	•	•	•	•	•			•		•	•	•	•	•	•		•		•	•	•	
Political Behavior	•	•	•	•	•	•	•	•	•	•		•	•	•	•	•	•	•	•	•	•	•	•	
Power, Use by Administrators		•	•	•	•	•	•	•		•	•	•	•	•		•	•	•		•	•		•	
Principals	•	•	•	•	•	•	•	•	•	•		•	•	•		•	•	•	•	•	•	•	•	•
Public Relations			•		•	•	•	•	•	•		•	•	•		•		•	•	•	•	•	•	•
Rural, Small-Town Schools								•					•		•								•	
School Boards			•										•		•		•		•				•	
School Reform	•	•						•						•	•		•		•				•	
Site-Based Management								•									•						•	
Student Discipline (Student Services)			•				•			•		•				•				•	•			
Suburban Schools					•	•		•		•	•				•			•				•	•	
Superintendents			•		•	•		•		•					•	•		•			•		•	
Teacher Professionalization				•			•		•	•		•				•	•					•		•
Teacher Unions (Collective Bargaining)														•		•								
Urban/Larger City Schools			•				•			•		•		•		•	•			•	•			
Visioning/Planning	•						•												•					•
Violence			•									•							•					
Vocational Schools																•			•					
Women Administrators		•		•	•					•	•			•		•	•	•	•		•		•	•

Introduction

> In the varied topography of professional practice, there is a high hard ground over-looking the swamp. On the high ground, manageable problems lend themselves to solutions through the application of research-based theory and technique. In the swampy lowland, messy, confusing problems defy technical solution.
> —Donald Schön, 1990, p. 3

Since the late 1980s, there have been many calls for sweeping changes in the professional preparation of school administrators. Demands for reform have been fueled by recent efforts to address organizational and governance issues in elementary and secondary education. But meaningful change has been elusive for a variety of reasons, including varying conditions across and within states, the absence of a standardized national curriculum, and differences of opinion about the effectiveness of public education and the nature of improvements needed.

Most students enrolled in university-based courses in school administration are either preparing to be practitioners or they already are practitioners. They are adult learners, many in the middle stage of their careers. They appropriately expect classroom learning experiences, even those involving abstract theories, to be relevant to the real world of elementary and secondary education. Consequently, effective preparation programs achieve three noteworthy objectives:

1. They provide students with theoretical knowledge that can guide practice either by predicting or describing behavior.
2. They provide students with relevant experiences demonstrating the utility of these theories; for example, application examples based on common problems of practice reinforce the teaching of theoretical knowledge.
3. They prepare students to be lifelong learners, primarily by teaching them to meld theoretical knowledge with artistry (craft knowledge) through the process of reflection.

Donald Schön (1983) aptly noted that practitioners in all professions are baffled when the technical skills they acquired during academic preparation prove to be ineffective when they are applied. Such bewilderment is especially likely when practitioners fail to consider the context in which the knowledge is applied. Human and material conditions surrounding a problem (contextual variables) can attenuate the effectiveness of theory, and for this reason, theory is not infallible. Consequently, the most successful practitioners in a profession are not those who have memorized most theories, but rather those who are able to meld artistry (developed through experiences) with theoretical knowledge in situations where theoretical knowledge alone is insufficient. Consider motivation theories and their use in teaching and school administration. In many instances, application of praise will produce expected results, but there are situations when this technique will not motivate an individual. If an administrator learns from previous experiences, he or she is better prepared to deal with the situation. Why has the technique been unsuccessful in the past? What alternative actions are available? The most effective principals, for instance, are neither those who rely entirely on theory or entirely on instincts; they are administrators who have developed the knowledge and skills to make adaptations when theoretical knowledge proves to be ineffectual.

Over the past few decades, most communities have changed demographically, economically, and politically. At the same time, advances in learning theory, technology, communication, and organizational planning have redefined the parameters of effective practice in school administration. The Internet, for instance, allows superintendents and principals to access legal information and statistical data in just minutes; communication among district and school employees can occur more rapidly and frequently because of electronic mail. Such changes, affecting both communities and schools, have heightened expectations that school administrators can make decisions and solve problems in a timely manner.

The Use of Reflection

In true professions, practitioners are expected to possess (1) a theoretical base for practice, (2) technical skills required to apply theory, and (3) the ability to engage in reflective practice—the process by which the practitioner benefits from experience by integrating knowledge, skills, and experience. Schön (1990) differentiated between "knowing-in-action" and "reflection-in-action." The former is embedded in the socially and institutionally structured context shared by members of a given profession. As an example, all physicians are expected to know anatomy and pharmacology; all administrators are expected to understand organizational and motivation theories. The latter represents a form of artistry that is especially critical when conditions are less than rational. Again, as an example, physicians develop skills and techniques learned through practice that they use to treat atypical patients; school administrators develop skills and techniques that help them deal with unusual forms of conflict or an atypical employee. If needs, motivations, and behaviors in schools were completely predictable, knowing-in-action would suffice. But in the real world, the unexpected occurs, and when it does, reflection-in-action becomes critically important.

Reflection does not occur naturally. The process must be learned and the requisite skills are usually acquired in professional preparation. Consequently, school administration professors are placing added emphasis on connecting classroom and work experiences. For instance, students are encouraged to write in journals and then discuss possible associations between course content and real work experiences. Reflection can be viewed as a form of research in which the individual tests ideas or possible decisions by applying evidence and subjective criteria, such as emotion and bias. Critiquing experience from multiple perspectives is a key element of true reflection (Kowalski, 2003).

The degree holder in educational administration should be thoroughly practiced in theoretical reflection, philosophical inquiry, research, and history, as well as prepared in the areas of administrative and technical practice. Consequently, the graduate experience for prospective school administrators typically has two basic components:

1. Emphasis on the theoretical dimensions of practice, the historical roots of school administration practice, and research
2. Emphasis on management skills, such as learning to prepare a school district budget or a high school schedule

Traditional lecture and demonstration approaches may be used for a portion of this curriculum, but other instructional approaches are needed so that students learn to gather information, observe behavior, and analyze the relationships between theoretical applications and contextual variables (Clark, 1986).

Case Studies on Educational Administration relies on one proven method of associating academic study with the real world of school administration: the case study. Many educational reform reports issued since the early 1980s have cited the need for the infusion of reality into preparation programs for educators. In an interview regarding needed improvements in the preparation of professional educators, noted researcher Lee Shulman commented:

> I'd like to see much greater use of cases, much like what is done in law and business education. That might reorient the teaching of teachers from the current model, which is either entirely field based, where you have little control over what goes on, or entirely classroom based, where everything is artificial. We have to create a middle ground, where problems of theory and practice can intersect in a realistic way. The genius of the case method, especially in business, is that you use realistic problems, but you can still deal with both the theoretical and the tactical aspects. (Brandt, 1988, p. 43)

Defining Case Studies

A case is a description of an administrative situation, commonly involving a decision or a problem (Erskine, Leenders, & Mauffette-Leenders, 1981). The terms *case study* and *case method* do not have the same meaning. A case study is the general description of a situation and may have several purposes: (1) as a method of research, (2) as a method of evaluation, (3) as a method of policy studies, and (4) as a teaching method. Thus, a case study is the narrative description of the incident, not its intended purpose. Case method, on the other hand, has specific reference to using the case studies as a teaching paradigm. More specifically, the case method entails a technique whereby the major ingredients of a case study are presented to students for the purpose of studying behaviors or problem-solving techniques.

Several other related terms may cause confusion and, thus, deserve explanation. One of these is *case work.* This term is commonly used in psychology, sociology, social work, and medicine. It connotes the development, adjustment, remedial, or corrective procedures that appropriately follow diagnosis of the causes of maladjustment. Another term is *case history.* This has reference to tracing a person, group, or organization's past (Merriam, 1988).

Unfortunately, there is no universal definition of or style for a case study; some case studies may be only a few paragraphs, while others are hundreds of pages (Immegart, 1971). As Lincoln and Guba (1985) wrote, "While the literature is replete with references to case studies and with examples of case study reports, there seems to be little agreement about what a case is" (p. 360). Variance in case length and style is often related to their intended purpose. Cases commonly fall into one of three categories: true cases (no alterations to names, dates, organizations), disguised cases, or fictitious cases (hypothetical examples to illustrate a principle, concept, or specific set of conditions) (Matejka & Cosse, 1981).

Case Method as an Instructional Paradigm

The case method has gained acceptance in professional preparation programs for business administration, law, and medicine. The best-known successes belong to Harvard University. The continued emphasis on the case method in the Harvard Business School is evidenced by publications such as *Teaching and the Case Method* (Christensen, 1987). In business courses, case studies use real incidents to sharpen student skills with regard to problem solving, formulating and weighing alternative decisions, and assessing leadership behaviors. Acclaim surrounding the effectiveness of the Harvard Business School approach has influenced the teaching methods at a number of prominent business schools.

Essentially, case studies can serve two instructional purposes. First, they can be employed to teach students new information, concepts, and theories. For example, the professor may use a case study of a grievance in a high school to illustrate that conflict in organizations is inevitable. When cases are used in this manner, the student deals with new knowledge through the process of induction. That is, by reading a case that exemplifies the concept, the student is expected to note associations between certain factors. When these associations are repeated (e.g., in other cases), the student is expected to master the concept through induction. Cases that are fact driven and taken to their conclusion are often used in disciplines such as science, where single correct answers are common (Herreid, 1997). Second, cases can serve as a vehicle for applying acquired knowledge and skills in specific situations. Application can serve several goals, such as teaching reasoning, critical thinking, problem-solving, and decision-making skills.

There are two universal aspects of teaching with cases. One is the Socratic method and the other is the presentation of selected information included in the case study (e.g., facts about individuals, facts about school districts). This information is referred to as *situational knowledge.* Each person who reads a case is exposed to the same situational knowledge but each individual often develops varying interpretations. Why? The answer is that individuals process the information in different ways. This processing is called *abstraction.* Each reader essentially filters situational knowledge through his or her own values, beliefs, experiences, biases, and acquired knowledge. Since these variables are not identical across the population, and since people differ in their ability to process information, different conclusions, and subsequently different behaviors, are usually observed.

Studying teacher decision making, Shavelson and Stern (1981) observed the following:

> People selectively perceive and interpret portions of available information with respect to their goals, and construct a simplified model of reality. Using certain heuristics, attributions and other psychological mechanisms, people then make judgments and decisions that carry them out on the basis of their psychological model of reality. (p. 461)

Output variability is a critical aspect of the case method. When making case-based decisions, students determine what they intend to accomplish, what they view as critical contextual variables, and what they frame as the central problem, all based on a combination of personal convictions and professional knowledge. Because individuals do not share the same convictions or the same level of knowledge and because the weight they give to each of these factors is not constant, their conclusions, decisions, and actions usually differ. These outputs in the case method are referred to as *specific knowledge.*

Use of Cases in Education

Within schools of education, case studies have been used most frequently as a diagnostic tool in counseling and as a research tool. Psychologists commonly employ case histories and case work in their practices. The growing acceptance of qualitative methodology in the social sciences has magnified the value of case studies in this arena. Ethnographic research is perhaps the best known of the qualitative techniques, and the work of Yin (1984) and Merriam (1988) is particularly enlightening for individuals wanting to explore case-based research. Yin's writings describe this methodology in varying contexts, including policy analysis, public administration, community psychology and sociology, organization and management studies, and public service agencies; Mirriam's work is more directly focused on education. Both terms, *ethnography* and *case studies,* have become synonyms for qualitative research (Lancy, 1993). In the past few decades, case-based research has provided richer descriptions of the work environments of professional educators (e.g., Erickson, 1986).

However, beyond its use in psychology and research, the case study has not been a conspicuous component of graduate work in education. In school administration, two similar techniques have been used occasionally: simulations and "in-basket" programs. Even back in the mid-1950s, texts were published on case studies for educators (e.g., Hamburg, 1955; Sargent & Belisle, 1955), and some leaders in the University Council for Educational Administration (UCEA) have advocated the use of case studies and simulations for over three decades (e.g., Culbertson & Coffield, 1960; Griffiths, 1963). But the case study never became an integral part of professional preparation. Research indicates that the lecture method of teaching and classroom discussion remain the dominant instructional paradigms in school administration (McCarthy, 1999).

Using Simulation and Cases

Professional schools rely on several methods to expose students to the real world of practice. The internship is one of the most common. This segment of the curriculum is typically structured as a capstone experience, and although valuable, it does not provide early and continuous experiences permitting the graduate student to integrate theory with practice. *Simulation* is one way to infuse reality into coursework.

Simulations provide vicarious experiences for students—an approximation of the practitioner's challenges, problems, opportunities, and so forth. This form of teaching can be used at all stages of professional preparation. There are two general approaches: (1) providing complete data about a given situation before requiring the student to address the problem and (2) providing basic information sufficient to permit the student to address the problem. The former is best characterized by *in-basket* techniques. In this process, the student receives detailed information about a position, problem, and so forth. Often, this approach requires the student to spend a great deal of time studying the documents (e.g., budgets, memoranda), and it is considered most effective when specific problem-solving skills are being addressed.

The other approach focuses on using only essential information related to a given situation. This situational knowledge can be effectively transmitted through a case study. This option is usually employed when general problem-solving skills are addressed, and it is advantageous when time parameters do not permit students to review mounds of data. Simulations using what Cunningham (1971) called a *nonmaterial-based approach* (i.e., using only basic situational information) were proven to be successful when used with educators at the University of Chicago in the mid-1960s. In fact, Cunningham noted that he changed his own views about the necessity of detailed information after viewing the successes with simulation under these conditions. Hence, simulations and cases such as those presented here provide a powerful combination for integrating theory and practice, teaching critical thinking, developing problem-solving skills, and refining the process of reflection.

Using Theory as a Guide

There are many misconceptions about theory. Some students define *theory* as a dream representing the wishes of an individual or group. Others perceive it to be a supposition or a speculation or a philosophy (Owens, 1998). In reality, theories are used to synthesize, organize, and classify facts that emerge from observations and data collections in varying situations (e.g., research studies). Hoy and Miskel (1987) characterized theories in educational administration as interrelated concepts, assumptions, and generalizations that systematically describe and explain regularities in behavior.

Educational leaders have the same decision-making options available to all other types of administrators and managers. When confronted with circumstances demanding action, the individual may choose one of several behaviors (Kowalski, 1999):

1. Ignore the situation (no decision is made).
2. Act instinctively.
3. Get someone else to make the decision.
4. Duplicate a decision made by some one else under the same or similar circumstances.
5. Use the professional knowledge base to formulate a decision.

Any of the first four alternatives may be effective in isolated situations, but eventually they cause problems. Use of a professional knowledge base distinguishes a professional practitioner from a trained technician. The professional gathers pertinent information and integrates that information with the knowledge base. Then he or she determines alternative decisions (contingencies), evaluates these alternatives, and selects the most prudent decision given the prevailing conditions.

Among the numerous decision-making models used in administration, the best known and most widely used is probably the *rational-analytical model*. This paradigm consists of four steps: (1) defining the problem, (2) diagnosing the problem, (3) searching for alternative solutions, and (4) evaluating alternative solutions (Romm & Mahler, 1986). The case method is an excellent format for applying this and similar decision-making models. Students can complete all four stages of the rational-analytical model by reading and reacting to cases. The advantage of the rational-analytical approach is that it permits you to apply general problem-solving skills to specific situations.

Each case in this book includes contextual variables that should affect the choices you make. The community, the school district, the challenge, and the individual personalities are examples. When you employ theoretical constructs and technical skills to analyze these conditions in relation to the challenge presented, you are using a scientific approach to decision making. Accordingly, you should become increasingly skillful in applying general problem-solving abilities to specific situations. When using cases, however, you will recognize that emotion and bias almost always temper rationality. That is, decision makers often reject, modify, or selectively accept evidence based on their dispositions toward a problem or challenge.

The evolution of literature on the topic of decision making exhibits the movement of graduate study in educational leadership from a narrow training focus on technical skills to one where behavioral studies now play a critical role. In concluding that accumulated information about decision processes was eradicating the comfort of simple solutions, Estler (1988) wrote the following:

> We might replace recipes with skills in analysis of organizational dynamics and contexts. Though the ambiguities of educational decision making cannot be eliminated, they can be made more understandable and less threatening. By understanding a variety of approaches to decision making and the range of organizational conditions under which they may be applicable, the administrator can be better prepared to respond to, and even enjoy, organizational ambiguity and complexity. (p. 316)

More than any other element of graduate study in educational administration, it is the knowledge base relative to decision making that illuminates the value of infusing case studies into graduate education. Those who still contend that there are tried-and-true recipes for leadership behavior that work in all situations under all sorts of conditions are either misguided or uninformed.

The Content of the Book

This book contains 24 cases selected to exemplify the diversity of challenges in contemporary educational leadership. You should not look at any case as having a single dimension, even though the title or primary focus of the material may lead you to that conclusion. The cases actually are quite intricate, with multiple foci—exactly the way problems exist in the real world of practice. For example, a case may involve conflict resolution, effective communication, power, participatory decision making, and leadership style.

The narrative format used in the cases is not uniform. Some cases are divided into sections with information about the community, school district, school, and the incident presented under subheadings. Other cases contain a great deal of dialogue. Information in the real world of practice is often neither predictable nor uniform. Variance in the way information is presented in the cases reflects the unevenness of communication that exists in districts and schools. Although the narratives vary, the format for presenting the material that follows the description of each case is uniform. Following each case there are four components:

1. The Challenge
2. Suggested Activities
3. Suggested Readings
4. References

In addition, a worksheet is included for each case in the appendix at the back of the book. These worksheets are often used for classroom assignments.

One of the goals of the case method is to help you become proficient at filtering information. As a practitioner, you will need to learn to separate important and relevant facts from those that have little or no bearing on the problem(s). Remember, you must determine what information is most crucial to your decisions.

Effectively Participating in the Case Method

Two extremely important factors already have been mentioned regarding the use of cases. First, *information filtering* permits you to isolate pertinent data needed for making a decision. Second, using *accumulated information and knowledge* in a systematic fashion (i.e., utilizing a decision-making model) produces more enlightened decisions. With regard to this latter point, you should constantly remind yourself of the differences between education and training. Educated persons rely on past experiences and knowledge to make behavioral choices; they interface contextual variables with knowledge before acting. Trained persons, by contrast, rely on predetermined responses; they use a manual or their memory to identify the appropriate action.

Beyond information filtering and the recognition of what constitutes an educated response, it is critical to note that the case method does not seek the "one right answer." Romm and Mahler (1986) noted that this is particularly true when the cases are used in conjunction with the rational-analytical model for making decisions:

> Basing the analysis of the case on the rational-analytical decision-making model, implicitly carries the message that there are no "right" or "wrong" solutions to the case. By applying the model to cases, students realize that a case always has many problems, and the definition of one of these problems as the "main" problem is often subjective and arbitrary. They also realize that once a problem has been defined, it can have different reasons and be solved in different ways, depending on whose interests are being served or being given priority. (p. 695)

Cases provide an open invitation to generalize (Biddle & Anderson, 1986); consequently, you are apt to observe a range of behaviors as your peers react to cases. You can learn by analyzing your own behavior, by analyzing the behavior of others, and by having others analyze your behavior. Often, when cases are discussed in group settings (e.g., the classroom), an instructor and the students are able to capitalize on all three of these opportunities.

Remember that a person's behavior is never void of values and beliefs. This reality makes the case method even more challenging and exciting. Two graduate students sharing common educational experiences may make very different decisions when responding to the challenges presented in the cases. Why? As noted earlier, each of them develops specific knowledge through abstraction. Values and beliefs, as well as one's skill level in decision making, critical thinking, and problem solving can influence the process of abstraction.

There is one additional dimension of the case method that is undervalued. You will work with these cases in a social context. The presence of others approximates the real world of practice. Superintendents and principals rarely make decisions in isolation. Their behavior is constantly influenced and evaluated by the social contexts of their work (district, school, community). Your experiences with cases permit you to grow in both the affective and cognitive domains.

Final Words of Advice

Engaging in case studies requires several caveats regarding your personal behavior. First, the process is an active one. Case analysis in a classroom environment is a form of cooperative learning. To achieve maximum benefits, you need to be an active participant. Second, you should not be afraid to be candid or to take risks. The case method allows you to learn how others will respond to your leadership style and decisions. Third, you should respect your classmates and try to understand their behavior. Your intention should be to identify how professional (constructs and skills) and personal (needs and motivations) variables influence administrative decisions.

The observations made of experiences with the case method provide a useful resource for practice. Thus, the development of a notebook in conjunction with classroom experiences is highly advised. Although no two situations are ever identical, the general principles that are addressed in the 24 cases are likely to recur throughout your career as an educational leader.

References

Biddle, B., & Anderson, D. (1986). Theory, methods, knowledge, and research on teaching. In M. Wittrock (Ed.), *Handbook of research on teaching* (3rd ed., pp. 230–252). New York: Macmillan.
Brandt, R. (1988). An assessment of teaching: A conversation with Lee Shulman. *Educational Leadership, 46*(3), 42–47.
Christensen, C. (1987). *Teaching and the case method.* Boston: Harvard Business School Press.
Clark, V. (1986). The effectiveness of case studies in training principals: Using the deliberative orientation. *Peabody Journal of Education, 63*(1), 187–195.
Culbertson, J., & Coffield, W. (Eds.). (1960). *Simulation in administration training.* Columbus, OH: The University Council for Educational Administration.
Cunningham, L. (1971). A powerful but underdeveloped educational tool. In D. Bolton (Ed.), *The use of simulation in educational administration* (pp. 1–29). Columbus, OH: Charles E. Merrill.
Erickson, F. (1986). Qualitative methods in research on teaching. In M. Wittrock (Ed.), *Handbook of research on teaching* (3rd ed., pp. 119–161). New York: Macmillan.
Erskine, J., Leenders, M., & Mauffette-Leenders, L. (1981). *Teaching with cases.* London, Ontario: School of Business Administration, University of Western Ontario.
Estler, S. (1988). Decision making. In N. Boyan (Ed.), *Handbook of research on educational administration* (pp. 305–350). New York: Longman.

Griffiths, D. (1963). The case method of teaching educational administration. *Journal of Educational Administration, 2,* 81–82.

Hamburg, M. (1955). *Case studies in elementary school administration.* New York: Bureau of Publications, Teachers College, Columbia University.

Herreid, C. F. (1997). What is a case? *Journal of College Science Teaching, 27*(2), 92–94.

Hoy, W., & Miskel, C. (1987). *Education administration* (3rd ed.). New York: Random House.

Immegart, G. (1971). The use of cases. In D. Bolton (Ed.), *The use of simulation in educational administration* (pp. 30–64). Columbus, OH: Charles E. Merrill.

Kowalski, T. J. (2003). *Contemporary school administration: An introduction* (2nd ed.). Boston: Allyn and Bacon.

Kowalski, T. (1999). *The school superintendent: Theory, practice, and cases.* Upper Saddle River, NJ: Merrill, Prentice Hall.

Lancy, D. (1993). *Qualitative research in education.* New York: Longman.

Lincoln, Y., & Guba, E. (1985). *Naturalistic inquiry.* Newbury Park, CA: Sage.

Matejka, J., & Cosse, T. (1981). *The business case method: An introduction.* Richmond, VA: Robert F. Dame.

McCarthy, M. (1999). The evolution of educational leadership preparation programs. In L. Murphy & K. Louis (Eds.), *Handbook of research on educational administration* (2nd ed.). San Francisco: Jossey-Bass.

Merriam, S. (1988). *Case research in education.* San Francisco: Jossey-Bass.

Owens, R. (1998). *Organizational behavior in education* (6th ed.). Boston: Allyn and Bacon.

Romm, T., & Mahler, S. (1986). A three-dimensional model for using case studies in the academic classroom. *Higher Education, 15*(6), 677–696.

Sargent, C., & Belisle, E. (1955). *Educational administration: Cases and concepts.* Boston: Houghton Mifflin.

Schön, D. (1990). *Educating the reflective practitioner.* San Francisco: Jossey-Bass.

Schön, D. (1983). *The reflective practitioner.* New York: Basic Books.

Shavelson, R., & Stern, P. (1981). Research on teachers' pedagogical thoughts, judgments, decisions, and behavior. *Review of Educational Research, 51*(4), 455–498.

Yin, R. (1984). *Case study research.* Beverly Hills, CA: Sage.

Another Federal Intrusion

Background Information

The governance structure of public education in the United States is truly unique. The federal Constitution does not mention education; consequently, under provisions of the Tenth Amendment ("The powers not delegated to the United States by the Constitution, nor prohibited by it to the States, are reserved to the States respectively, or to the people"), education has been treated as a state's right. Based on this legal interpretation, each state has the responsibility to establish and operate a system of public education. In all but one state (Hawaii), some portion of that responsibility is delegated to local districts.

Having separate state systems of public education may be viewed either positively or negatively depending on one's political perspectives. Those who favor liberty and competition point to the fact that this system has permitted states to develop relevant and creative organizational structures. Those who favor equality and collaboration point to the fact that this system has resulted in disparate and unequal educational opportunities (Razik & Swanson, 2001).

Despite the legal authority of states to control their public education systems, all three branches of the federal government have been able to exert influence over this domain in the past. Consider these examples:

1. *Legislative intervention.* Federal legislation passed by the U.S. Congress falls under four overriding themes: the constitutional rights of citizens, national security, domestic problems, and protection of the economy (Kowalski, 2003). Examples include the National Defense Education Act (1958), the Elementary and Secondary Education Act (1965), and the Education for All Handicapped Children Act (1975).

2. *Judicial intervention.* Legal issues can enter the federal court system in two ways: when state statutes are questioned under the federal Constitution and

when any title, right, privilege, or immunity is claimed under the federal Constitution (Alexander & Alexander, 1998). Examples of federal intervention include landmark cases affecting school desegregation (e.g., *Brown* v. *Board of Education* in 1954).

3. *Executive intervention.* The creation of a separate U.S. Department of Education in 1979 increased the likelihood of public education being affected by federal rules and regulations (Kowalski, 2003). Examples of executive interventions have included enforcement guidelines for legislation or for court decisions (e.g., rules and regulations for complying with Title I programs).

Federal interventions in public elementary and secondary education are often viewed negatively by local school district officials who believe that such actions attenuate local control. The No Child Left Behind (NCLB) Act, signed into law on January 8, 2002, constitutes another in a series of federal interventions that spawned concerns among administrators. This law, a reauthorization of the Elementary and Secondary Education Act of 1965, purportedly emphasizes local control, flexibility for local officials, and parental involvement. It focuses on raising the educational performance of all students by setting higher standards, requiring annual testing, using test data analysis to ensure progress, and imposing rewards and penalties for outcomes. All students in grades 3 through 8 must be tested each year in reading and mathematics, and in 2006, the requirement will be extended to include science. Schools must demonstrate adequate yearly progress. All special student groups (e.g., by ethnicity, socioeconomic status) must report progress separately. At least 95 percent of each of these groups must be tested, and if one subgroup fails to make yearly progress, the school as a whole fails.

The NCLB Act is a form of directed autonomy—a condition in which a centralized authority sets standards, deregulates the process allowing local agencies to determine how to meet the standards, requires that outcomes are tested, and exercises power in relation to outcomes (rewards and punishments). Scholars who have studied public policy (e.g., Weiler, 1990) warn that there is a basic tension between emphasis on local autonomy (decentralization or deregulation) and the tendency for centralized authorities to reassert control over local agencies. Stated differently, the federal government constantly experiences challenges to its need and value in relation to public education, but even so, the government cannot nationalize this vital service because of political opposition. Hence, the federal government grants leeway to states and local schools under the guise of local control and at the same time imposes standards, requires measurement of the standards, and stipulates the consequences. Such iterations of decentralization and deregulation circuitously enhance centralization.

In this case, principals in a school district voice varying opinions about implementing the NCLB Act. The division creates a challenge for the superintendent as he tries to determine the best course of action.

Key Areas for Reflection

1. Federal involvement in public elementary and secondary education
2. Administrator resistance to coercive change
3. Administrative teaming versus competition
4. Visioning and planning

The Case

Marcum County and Ridge County are located next to each other in a southern state. Each has a single public school district. The Marcum County Schools serve 16,700 students in 31 attendance centers. Billy Pratt has been superintendent for 7 years but he had been employed in the school district for 23 years, more than half of that time as a high school principal. He drives a pickup truck and wears cowboy boots, and he is fond of telling people he meets, "What you see is what you get." Behind his desk hangs a big calendar with a tag hanging below it; in big red letters it reads, "422 days to go." The number refers to the working days remaining before Superintendent Pratt retires.

The Ridge County Schools serve about 13,500 students in 23 attendance centers. Dr. Stacy Barstow became superintendent of the district after having served as an assistant state superintendent for the previous six years. Her primary interests are instructional improvement and staff development. Dr. Barstow has had to fight an uphill battle in winning support from many of her principals who were not thrilled about having a person from outside the district named to this key position.

Despite their many differences, Billy and Stacy have become friends. Billy was one of the first persons to call Stacy to congratulate her when her appointment was made public. He was acquainted with her because of her role as the top curriculum person with the state department of education, but the two had not worked together previously. The two superintendents have been meeting for breakfast the first Monday of each month. Stacy has found the meetings to be helpful, especially with respect to Billy's insights about local politics.

After the NCLB Act was signed into law, both superintendents expressed initial concern based on the sketchy details that were available to them. Their intentions to deal with new law, however, were dissimilar. Superintendent Pratt was angry about yet another government intrusion and indifferent about how the Marcum County Schools would respond. Superintendent Barstow supported the law's objectives but was deeply concerned about the Ridge County administrators implementing it.

After the principals and other administrators in Marcum County had an opportunity to learn about NCLB, Superintendent Pratt held a special meeting to discuss the issue and how it was to be handled. As usual, he was brutally candid.

"I'm not anymore thrilled about this law than you are. This act is another example of what happens when pinheaded, briefcase-toting bureaucrats have too little to do. But hell, we got to move forward. Fortunately for me, I'm not going to be here three or four years down the road. If this law remains as it is, every district and most schools in this state are going to have serious problems. There is no way we are going to be able to get all these students to pass the tests—especially the special education and bilingual students. These bureaucrats can set all the goals and targets they want. But there is no way all the kids are going to pass. At some point, the politicians are going to see this. If I had to bet, I think this law will be amended or rescinded before too long. But what do I know? I'm wrong at least 50 percent of the time."

Nervous laughter filled the room. The administrators were not especially comforted to hear their superintendent tell them that he would be retiring before the "reward/penalty" phase of the law took effect. Nor were they put at ease by his prediction that the act would probably go away, partially or totally before principals were potentially affected. One of the middle school principals was next to speak.

"Regardless of how we might feel, we have to get moving. I'd like to know whether we are going to prepare collectively or are we supposed to sink or swim on our own. The act basically puts principals on the hot seat; they are most accountable for student achievement, quality of staff, staff development, and so forth. We no longer have a choice regarding being an instructional leader and we no longer have the luxury of self-defining this role. The 'feds' have done this for us. If you take the law literally, some of us could lose our jobs three years down the road just because we didn't reach an unreachable goal."

Superintendent Pratt responded, "I suggest that the secondary principals meet with Joe Miller [assistant superintendent for secondary education] and the elementary principals meet with Bonnie Stiker [assistant superintendent for elementary education]. As groups, you should decide how you're going to move forward. I'm here to help, and I will if you call on me to do so. Otherwise, I'm going to stay out of this one."

Superintendent Pratt's comments to the school board and local media were a bit softer than those he made to his administrative staff. Yet, the general message was the same. He criticized the federal government for ignoring local control, he criticized the NCLB Act as being unrealistic, and he predicted that the law would be amended or rescinded after policymakers realized that they had set unattainable goals.

The NCLB Act was treated quite differently in Ridge County. Superintendent Barstow focused on the law's objectives and carefully avoided making negative statements. She told her administrative staff, "I know all of this is threatening, but the act can be a catalyst for positive change in our schools. Fortunately, this state has been out in front on the issue of standards-based reform and I was deeply involved with these matters at the state department of education. Think about NCLB as an extension of what we are already doing with standards-based accreditation. I realize that many of you view the goals as unrealistic and most of you are threatened by potential penalties if they are not achieved, but remember, every other district and school in the state is in the same boat. Our challenge is to be out in front of them. We will implement the law on time and we will do it better than they do it."

One of the high school principals asked, "How are we going to proceed?"

"Initially, we will be working together," responded Superintendent Barstow. "I plan to conduct several workshops to ensure that each administrator in this district understands the law, the relationship between the law and the state's standards-based curriculum, and the processes necessary to erect a successful plan. If necessary, I will commit resources to retaining consultants to assist each of you. I realize that the law creates more work and more headaches, especially for principals. We have two choices. We can complain and criticize the law or we can be upbeat and do our best to play the hand we have been dealt. Personally, I believe the latter is a better choice. Even if the law is not fully implemented, we are likely to improve the educational program for many students who are not doing well in the current system."

Superintendent Barstow followed her own advice in making comments to the school board and media. She also addressed NCLB on the district's webpage. On it, she laid out the law's basic requirements, including identification of student subgroups, expectations of teacher quality, annual testing requirements, state guidelines for measuring progress, the consequences of yearly progress reports, and the requirement for states and local districts to have staffing plans. In addition, she added information about what the state department of education was already doing to implement the law. This included providing consultants to local districts, requiring districts to develop or revise two-year improvement plans, and targeting resources to areas that are most likely to assist districts in implementing the NCLB successfully.

The Challenge

Evaluate the approaches each superintendent has taken with respect to NCLB. Determine the strengths and weaknesses of each approach.

Suggested Activities

1. Discuss the issue of federal involvement in public elementary and secondary education. Identify reasons why the federal government may set laws and policies in this area.

2. Identify what your state is doing to implement the NCLB Act.

3. Discuss what local districts in your area of the state are doing to implement the NCLB Act.

4. Invite principals from an elementary school and a secondary school to your class to discuss their views on the NCLB Act and this case.

5. Complete the worksheet for this case.

Suggested Readings

Blaney, C. J. (2002). Open arms, open records. *School Administrator, 59*(6), 24–27.

Calabrese, R. L. (2003). The ethical imperative to lead change: Overcoming the resistance to change. *International Journal of Educational Management, 17*(1), 7–13.

Children's Defense Fund. (2002). *The state of children in America's union: A 2002 action guide to leave no child behind.* Washington, DC: Author.

Colgan, C. (2002). The debate gets serious on "No Child Left Behind." *The American School Board Journal, 189*(12), 6–8.

Garcia, J. (Ed.). (2002). No Child Left Behind: Meeting challenges, seizing opportunities, improving achievement. *Achieve Policy Brief, 5.*

Hardy, L. (2002). A new federal role. *American School Board Journal, 189*(9), 20–24.

Hardy, L. (2003). Education vital signs. Main events: The year of No Child Left Behind. *American School Board Journal Supplement,* 2–5.

Harvey, T. R. (1996). Making changes: Mission impossible. *Learning, 24*(6), 58, 60.

Keegan, L. G. (2003). Help wanted. *Education Next, 3*(2), 28–31.

Lewis, A. C. (2002). A horse called NCLB. *Phi Delta Kappan, 84*(3), 179–180.

Linn, R. L., Baker, E. L., & Betebenner, D. W. (2002). Accountability systems: Implications of requirements of the No Child Left Behind Act of 2001. *Educational Researcher, 31*(6), 3–16.

Mann, D., & Shakeshaft, C. (2003). In God we trust: All others bring data. *School Business Affairs, 69*(1), 19–22.

Neill, M. (2003). High stakes, high risk: The dangerous consequences of high-stakes testing. *American School Board Journal, 190*(2), 18–21.

Paige, R., & Ferrandino, V. (2003). No principal left behind. *Principal, 82*(4), 52–55.

Rose, L. C. (2003). No Child Left Behind: Promise or rhetoric? *Phi Delta Kappan, 84*(5), 338.

Thomas, M. D., & Bainbridge, W. L. (2002). No Child Left Behind: Facts and fallacies. *Phi Delta Kappan, 83*(10), 781–782.

Walberg, H. J. (2003). Accountability unplugged. *Education Next, 3*(2), 76–79.

Wolf, D. P. (2002). When raising isn't rising. *School Administrator, 59*(11), 20–23.

References

Alexander, K., & Alexander, M. D. (1998). *American public school law* (4th ed.). Belmont, CA: Wadsworth.

Kowalski, T. J. (2003). *Contemporary school administration: An introduction* (2nd ed.). Boston: Allyn and Bacon.

Razik, T. A., & Swanson, A. D. (2001). *Foundational concepts of educational leadership* (2nd ed.). Upper Saddle River, NJ: Merrill, Prentice Hall.

Weiler, H. N. (1990). Comparative perspectives on educational decentralization: An exercise in contradiction. *Educational Evaluation and Policy Analysis, 12*(4), 433–448.

What Alternative School Concept Is Best?

Background Information

Fifty years ago, the only distinctive options to traditional public elementary and secondary education were found primarily in private schools (Deal & Nolan, 1978). During the 1960s, public alternative schools were created to serve students experiencing difficulties in traditional schools. As national and state policymakers shifted their attention from equality to excellence issues during the 1970s, growth in a number of these schools waned. The trend, however, shifted again in the late 1980s, largely because many leading reformers believed that equity and excellence could be pursued concurrently (Kowalski, 2003).

The proliferation of alternative schools over the past two decades has stemmed from the realization that traditional institutions are not effectively reducing the number of students at risk of not completing the twelfth grade. Now there are more alternative schools and alternative school principals than at any time in the past (Kowalski & Reynolds, 2003).

By 2000, over half the states had enacted some type of provision requiring alternative public schools; in addition, some states adopted legislation providing incentives for this purpose. The primary intents of both strategies have been to provide a viable option for students excluded or about to be excluded from regular programs (Barr & Parrett, 2001) and to respond to national reform initiatives such as the No Child Left Behind Act. Unfortunately, state policymakers typically have not been aware of the fact that there are three distinctive types of alternative schools, each with some capacity to improve the overall condition of public education.

1. *Type I schools* are institutions of choice that any student may attend until high school graduation. These schools are innovative and have both nontraditional organizational and administrative structure.
2. *Type II schools* are placement institutions enrolling disruptive students for a temporary period. These schools provide an alternative to expulsion, and they focus on behavior modification to reduce or eliminate problems that caused discipline concerns in traditional schools.
3. *Type III schools* are referral institutions enrolling students with academic, social, or emotional difficulties. These schools focus on rehabilitating students so that they can succeed in a traditional schools (Raywid, 1994).

Both Type II and Type III schools attempt to change the student, behaviorally in the former and behaviorally and/or academically in the latter. Type I schools, however, focus on changing the school environment. The dissimilar missions can be traced to differences in how the problem is framed. Whereas Type II and Type III schools are predicated on the belief that the student (or possibly society) is the problem, Type I schools are predicated on the belief that some students are unable to succeed in traditional schools (i.e., the school is the problem).

Clearly, then, not all alternative schools are alike. This fact is probably not recognized widely, even within the profession, because most educators are familiar with only Type II schools. Researchers (e.g., Frazer & Baenen, 1988; McCann & Landi, 1986) have concluded that the potential for Type II schools to have a dramatic effect on district-level school reform is limited either because some students never adjust their behavior or because behavioral changes produced by alternative school placement have usually been temporary. Leading alternative school scholars (e.g., Conrath, 2001; Gregory, 2001; Raywid, 1995) contend that most students who encounter difficulty in traditional schools do so because their learning styles and intellectual talents do not conform to traditional school norms. Placing these students in Type I rather than Type II schools has proven to be more effective (Wehlage, Rutter, Smith, Lesko, & Fernandez, 1989).

This case is about conflict over establishing an alternative high school in a suburban school district. Administrators first disagree over the need for such a school and then they argue over the type of school that should be established. Both the nature of alternative schools and the manner in which the administrators deal with conflict are key issues.

Key Areas for Reflection

1. At-risk students
2. Instructional leadership
3. Competing values and beliefs
4. Alternative education
5. School culture

The Case

Sharon Gonzalez sat in her car, staring at the front of South Preston High School. The building's exterior brought back fond memories of her days as a student. Now, 21 years after she had graduated from the school, she has returned as its new principal. Although the facility looked pretty much the same, the surrounding neighborhoods did not. Many of the homes had deteriorated and front yards were littered with trash and junk cars.

Coming back to South Preston was a difficult decision for Sharon. Most of her family no longer lived there and the once thriving industrial city was now a mere shell of its former existence. The steel mill and oil refinery had closed during the 1980s, and the negative impact on the economy was obvious. Enrollment in the school district had declined continuously for two decades and the once proud school system now has a reputation as one of the state's worst districts. But Superintendent Jackson Jones is a tremendous salesman and he convinced Sharon that she would be South Preston High School's perfect principal. She had been principal of an inner-city high school where she built a reputation for developing effective programs for at-risk students. Superintendent Jones actively recruited her based on her successes and based on a belief that her knowledge of South Preston would be invaluable. In her senior year of college, Sharon's parents moved to Texas. She remained in New Jersey after finishing college and began teaching in an urban district. She eventually became an assistant principal and then principal.

During her first weeks as principal, Sharon studied statistical reports detailing student performance at South Preston High School. Among the most alarming figures were the following:

DATA

- Thirty-one percent of the students who took the state's required proficiency exam for high school graduation failed.
- Forty-eight percent of the students who entered as freshmen did not graduate with their class last spring.
- Only 13 percent of last spring's graduating class enrolled in a four-year college.
- Hispanic American students were twice as likely as white students to fail the proficiency exam and to drop out of school.
- African American students were three times as likely as white students to fail the proficiency exam and to drop out of school.
- Females were just as likely to drop out of school as were males; about two-thirds of the females who dropped out of school were pregnant.
- Nearly 70 percent of the district's students qualified for free or reduced lunch programs.

Even though Sharon knew that South Preston was not the community it used to be, the statistics shocked her. When she was a student, 75 percent of the students were white; now that percentage was down to 21 percent. Hispanic American students now accounted for 33 percent of the district's enrollment.

Sharon's next surprise was discovering that no alternative school program was available for the district's students. Pregnant females were allowed to remain in school, but few elected to do so. Moreover, there were no accommodations for female students who had babies (e.g., day-care centers in the school). Sharon raised the issue of alternative education at the first principals' meeting she attended in early August. The topic received a cool reception. Despite the demographic composition of the community and school district, a majority of the district's principals and central office administrators were white males who had spent their entire careers in South Preston. Virtually all of them were opposed to creating an alternative school.

Joe Buskovich, the assistant superintendent for secondary education, was the most adamant. "This idea of creating an alternative school comes up every so often, and each time, we find out that there is little support for it. In my opinion, these schools send the wrong message to students. Symbolically they tell students that their behavior is acceptable. I don't believe this is the right message for us to be sending. Students need to learn that society has rules; if you break them, there are penalties. We've operated without an alternative school all these years, and we can continue to do so."

Sharon stated her philosophy, explaining that alternative schools have helped literally thousands of students to succeed. She detailed the purposes of these schools and argued that the dropout rate could be reduced dramatically if an effective alternative school was established. She even said she was willing to have that school operate as a "school-within-a-school" at Preston High School. Of the district's other 9 principals, 7 openly disagreed with her.

Recognizing that his new principal was seriously outnumbered, Superintendent Jones said, "We're not going to resolve anything today. Besides, it's too late to do anything for this school year. I'll put this topic on the agenda for a later meeting and we can spend more time with it."

After the meeting, Superintendent Jones told Sharon privately that he agreed with her position. He had proposed an alternative school when he became superintendent two years ago. The principals' group rejected the idea.

Over the next two months, the superintendent and the high school principal met on three separate occasions to discuss the feasibility of creating an alternative school. Dr. Jones then decided that he would raise the issue at the November principals' meeting. He told Sharon that he would give the principals one more chance to discuss the issue rationally; if they refused to do so, he was prepared to announce that he would move forward to plan the school.

As expected, most principals remained unfavorable to an alternative school. After hearing the same objections yet again, Dr. Jones lost his patience. "I've thought about an alternative school ever since becoming superintendent. I put the idea on the back burner hoping that you would change your opinions. Clearly, that has not happened. So I have decided to move forward anyway."

The principals did not expect this outcome. Dr. Jones rarely opposed them, in part because many were still well connected to local politicians. This was especially true of Mr. Buskovich; his brother was on the school board and his nephew was on the city council.

Dr. Jones appointed an ad hoc committee to study the matter and to issue recommendations regarding establishing an alternative school. The committee members were Joe Buskovich, Sharon Gonzalez, and two other principals. The superintendent said, "I don't want the committee arguing over whether we should have an alternative school—that issue is decided. The task is to determine what type of school we should open. I suggest that you visit other districts and see what has worked. Sharon has a great deal of experience in this area, and she can provide a list of effective alternative schools."

The administrators who remained opposed to the superintendent's decision predictably tried to influence the school board members. Having experienced this tactic previously, Superintendent Jones beat them to the punch. He briefed the board on the issue; five of the seven members supported the superintendent's decision.

Sharon's experience with the ad hoc committee was not pleasant. Now resigned to the fact that the district would probably have an alternative school for the first time, Mr. Buskovich and his supporters attempted to make the school plan as unattractive as possible. They did not want the school to be autonomous and they objected to serving students below the ninth-grade level. Mr. Buskovich wanted to establish a maximum enrollment period of one school year. If a student had not corrected the condition that caused him or her to be excluded from the regular program during that period, he or she would be removed from the alternative program. Sharon's position was quite different. She wanted the alternative school to be a school of choice. She framed her position as follows, "Those of you who favor a correctional-type institution see the student as the problem. Therefore, you want to change the student's behavior. In my opinion, the school environment is often the problem. That is, many of students can succeed if they are placed in the proper environment."

The other committee members concluded that Sharon was terribly naïve. Despite having lived in the community previously, and despite having worked in inner-city schools, they saw her as not understanding the problems faced by their student population.

Sharon again turned to Dr. Jones for support. This time, however, he said that he did not think that the board would support her position. "Two of the board members have already told me that they are taking a risk just supporting the school. Personally, I don't think they will favor your approach of having a school of choice. Is it better to have some type of alternative school or no alternative school at all? That's the question we have to answer. Even though I agree with your preference, I don't think a majority of the board will support it—at least not with other committee members favoring a different type of school."

The Challenge

Place yourself in Sharon's position. What would you do?

Suggested Activities

1. Evaluate the approach Sharon used to pursue an alternative school.
2. Identify and critique possible missions for an alternative school.
3. Determine if there are alternative schools in the county in which you reside and discuss the nature of their programs.
4. Discuss possible reasons why there has been a resurgence of interest in alternative schools in the past 25 years.
5. Some alternative schools are based on the premise that students who can function in traditional schools require remediation; other alternative schools are based on the premise that some students require unique schools. The former is commonly called the "fix-the-student" approach and the latter is commonly called the "fix-the-school" approach. Discuss the differences between these two strategies and identify your preference.
6. Complete the worksheet for this case.

Suggested Readings

Duke, D. L., & Griesdorn, J. (1999). Considerations in the design of alternative schools. *Clearing House, 73*(2), 89–92.

Gold, M. (1995). Charting a course: Promise and prospects for alternative schools. *Journal of Emotional and Behavioral Problems, 3*(4), 8–11.

Gregory, T. (2001). Fear of success? Ten ways alternative schools pull their punches. *Phi Delta Kappan, 82*(8), 577–581.

Griffin, B. L. (1993). Administrators can use alternative schools to meet student needs. *Journal of School Leadership, 3*(4), 416–420.

Lehr, C. A., & Lange, C. M. (2003). Alternative schools serving students with and without disabilities: What are the current issues and challenges? *Preventing School Failure, 47*(2), 59–63.

McGee, J. (2001). Reflections of an alternative school administrator. *Phi Delta Kappan, 82*(8), 588–591.

Poetter, T. S., & Knight-Abowitz, K. (2001). Possibilities and problems of school choice. *Kappa Delta Pi Record, 37*(2), 58–62.

Powell, D. E. (2003). Demystifying alternative education: Considering what really works. *Reclaiming Children and Youth, 12*(2), 68–70.

Raywid, M. A. (1994). Alternative schools: The state of the art. *Educational Leadership, 52*(1), 26–31.

Raywid, M. A. (1995). The struggles and joys of trailblazing: A tale of two charter schools. *Phi Delta Kappan, 76*(7), 555–560.

Vaughn, D. D., Slicker, E. K., & Van Hein, J. (2000). Adolescent problems and coping strategies: Alternative school versus non-alternative school students. *Research in the Schools, 7*(2), 41–47.

References

Barr, R. D., & Parrett, W. H. (2001). *Hope fulfilled for at-risk and violent youth* (2nd ed.). Boston: Allyn and Bacon.

Clark, C. (2000). Coming of age at Hippie High. *Phi Delta Kappan, 81*(9), 696–700.

Conrath, J. (2001). Changing the odds for young people: Next steps for alternative education. *Phi Delta Kappa, 82*(8), 585–587.

Deal, T. E., & Nolan, R. R. (1978). An overview of alternative schools. In T. Deal & R. Nolan (Eds.), *Alternative schools: Ideologies, realities, guidelines* (pp. 1–17). Chicago: Nelson-Hall.

Frazer, L., & Baenen, N. (1988). *An alternative for high-risk students.* (ERIC Document Reproduction Service No. ED 301 333)

Gregory, T. (2001). Fear of success? Ten ways alternative schools pull their punches. *Phi Delta Kappan, 82*(8), 577–581.

Kowalski, T. J. (2003). *Contemporary school administration: An introduction* (2nd ed.). Boston: Allyn and Bacon.

Kowalski, T. J., & Reynolds, S. (2003, April). *Alternative school principals: Career orientation, knowledge, and support of effective practice.* Paper presented at the annual meeting of the American Education Research Association, Chicago.

McCann, T., & Landi, H. (1986). Researchers cite program value. *Changing Schools, 14*(2), 2–5.

Raywid, M. (1995). Alternative and marginal students. In M. C. Wang & M. C. Reynolds (Eds.), *Making a difference for students at risk* (pp. 119–155). Thousand Oaks, CA: Corwin.

Wehlage, G., Rutter, R., Smith, G., Lesko, N., & Fernandez, R. (1989). *Reducing the risk: Schools as communities of support.* Philadelphia: Falmer.

A Bully's Threat

Background Information

Not all administrators recognize the difference between *safety* and *security*. The former addresses issues such as accident prevention, air quality, and fire or storm damage. Security, on the other hand, is concerned with preventing and responding to criminal acts and severe misbehavior (Trump, 1998). Criminal acts committed in schools, especially those that have been highly publicized over the last two decades, provide clear evidence that educational environments are not immune from society's ills. The potential for violence generates three critical questions for school administrators: How can behaviors that threaten a school's security be prevented? What measures should be taken when threats of violence are made? What measures should be taken when violence occurs?

Experts who have examined crime-related crises have concluded that many schools remain especially vulnerable to violence for the following reasons:

- Administrators are often unprepared to deal with violence, either because they have not been sufficiently educated or because they lack experiences in these situations. Kenneth Trump, one of the leading authorities on school crisis management, notes that many school officials remain unprepared to deal with most types of potential crises (Kowalski, 2002).
- School or district crisis plans are often perfunctory documents that receive little or no attention. Administrators may fear that such plans will be interpreted by parents and other taxpayers as an admission that serious security problems already exist (Moriarity, Maeyama, & Fitzgerald, 1993).
- Chaos often occurs during a crisis situation because implementation of the district's or school's plan has not been coordinated with community agencies (e.g., police, fire departments) (Seifert, 2004).
- The content of crisis plans may have been influenced by political conditions—a condition that may dissuade administrators from adopting best practices (Trump, 1998). For example, pressures to reduce expulsions may influence the types of punishment given to students who exhibit violent behavior.

This case occurs in an urban high school. A student who has a reputation as a bully threatens the life of another student. The threat is brought to the attention of the principal, and he must decide how to deal with the situation. He enlists the counsel of three of the high school's staff members. As you read the case, try to identify conditions that may have influenced the behavior.

Key Areas for Reflection

1. Dealing with threats of violent behavior
2. Political influences on crisis management
3. Racial tensions in schools
4. Principal leadership style
5. Multicultural school environments

The Case

Community

Like most urban areas in the United States, Central City has experienced considerable change in the past 30 years. The total population has declined from 325,000 in 1960 to its current level of 258,000. The property tax base has been eroded by the flight of businesses and middle-class families to the suburbs. The current mayor, now serving a second four-year term, has been slightly more successful than his predecessors in curbing the erosion of population and taxable property. Two of his initiatives, inner-city renewal and a vigorous campaign to attract new businesses, have been responsible.

Central City's crime and violence rates, however, have not been reduced, nor have poverty statistics improved. Nearly 40 percent of the school-age children live in poverty-level families, and many of them are being reared in dysfunctional families. It is estimated that as many as 15 percent of school-age children in Central City have been victims of physical or emotional abuse.

The following demographic profile developed from the most recent census reveals the city's racial diversity:

- 48 percent identified themselves as African American.
- 18 percent identified themselves as Hispanic American.
- 5 percent identified themselves as Asian American.
- 28 percent identified themselves as white (non-Hispanic).
- 1 percent identified themselves as "other."

White residents are heavily concentrated in two sections of city: Memorial Park (where virtually all of the Asian American families also reside) and Kensington.

School District

The Central City School District remains the largest district in the state; however, its enrollment has declined about 25 percent in the past three decades. Two high schools, two middle schools, and six elementary schools have been closed during that period. Most of the remaining school buildings are more than 50 years old and require extensive renovation or should be replaced.

The district is governed by a school board whose seven members are elected. Five board member positions are assigned to geographic sections of the school district; the other two are at-large positions. The following data profile the present board:

Member	Board Position	District	Occupation	Race
Venus Bronson	President	3	Lawyer	African American
Walter Sullivan	Vice-president	At-large	Plumber	White
Emily Drovak	Secretary	5	Housewife	White
Alexander Adams	Member	1	Minister	African American
James Chin	Member	4	Engineer	Asian American
Rose Ann Hildago	Member	2	Social Worker	Hispanic American
Maynard Truax	Member	At-large	Dentist	African American

Districts 1, 2, and 3 are in the city's core area; each has high concentrations of African American residents, with District 2 being almost evenly divided between African American and Hispanic American populations. District 4, known as the Memorial Park area, is located at the southern perimeter of the city. Nearly all of the district's residents are either white or Asian American. District 5, known as Kensington, is located in the northern perimeter of the city; the population here is about 60 percent white with the remainder being predominately African American.

Dr. Ruth Perkett is the district's first female and first African American superintendent. A long-time employee of Central City School District, she has been the school system's top administrator for only two years. Prior to assuming this position, she was an elementary school principal, director of federal programs, and associate superintendent for elementary education in the district. Over her long tenure in the system, she has established close ties with many government officials, including the current mayor.

Memorial Park High School

Forty years ago, Memorial Park High School was considered one of the state's finest academic schools. Although that is no longer true, the school is still considered the most academic-oriented high school in the school district. The school has an enrollment of approximately 1,350 in grades 9 to 12. Only about one-third of these students reside in the Memorial Park area of the city. The remaining students are bused to Memorial Park High School from other parts of the school district in accordance with a district-developed desegregation plan that has been in effect for 12 years.

Joseph Milhoviak has been the principal at Memorial Park High School for 14 years. He grew up in an adjacent neighborhood and graduated from the school. After college, he returned to the school as a teacher and coach. His entire 28-year career as an educator has been in this one school.

Prior to the adoption of the district's desegregation, Memorial Park High School enrolled a handful of African American and Hispanic American students. The present student profile shows how much conditions have changed in little more than a decade:

African American	40 percent
Hispanic American	10 percent
Asian American	16 percent
White	34 percent

The faculty, however, remains predominately white, despite efforts by school officials to employ or transfer minority faculty to the school; approximately two-thirds of the teachers and administrators identify themselves as Caucasians.

With the exception of the time he spent as an undergraduate student, Principal Milhoviak has never lived outside of the Memorial Park area. He is highly involved in civic activities and is considered both an educational and community leader by the area's residents. Several years ago, for example, the Memorial Park Neighborhood Association literally begged him to become a candidate for the mayor's position. He declined. Mr. Milhoviak maintains a reputation as a "tough" principal—a disciplinarian not afraid to take stern action when dealing with disruptive students. Although his approach to managing student behavior is applauded by Memorial Park parents and other taxpayers, Superintendent Perkett has a different perspective of his administrative style. She believes the principal is less than consistent when administering punishment because three-fourths of the Memorial Park High School students who either get expelled or drop out are minorities. More precisely, the superintendent thinks that Mr. Milhoviak is harsher with minority students bused to the school from other sections of the city. Since becoming superintendent, she has urged him to employ alternatives to dismissing students—options such as in-school suspension and group counseling. To date, he has not followed her advice.

Incident

Brian Isaacs entered the principal's office between the third and fourth periods and told the receptionist, "I need to see Mr. Milhoviak right now. It's an emergency!"

"What's wrong?" she inquired.

He answered, "I'm not going to talk about it with anyone except the principal."

The receptionist interrupted Mr. Milhoviak, who was meeting with a parent. She informed him that Brian was alleging an emergency situation and refused to talk to anyone but him about it. The principal knew Brian and members of his family. A sophomore, he was an above-average student academically and generally well-behaved. Upon being interrupted, Mr. Milhoviak quickly concluded the meeting with the parent and asked Brian to come into his office.

As he entered the office, the principal saw that Brian was visibly shaken. "What's the problem?" the principal asked.

The student immediately answered, "Carl Turner told me that he is going to blow my brains out. Mr. Milhoviak, he is crazy and he'll do it."

"Why is he threatening you?" the principal asked.

"This whole thing really has nothing to do with me. Carl had a couple dates with my sister, Angie, and now she doesn't want to see him anymore. He's blaming my parents and me. He said we are forcing her to not see him anymore. He told me he is in love with Angie. He said that my parents and I are racists."

Mr. Milhoviak was quite familiar with Carl Turner. He had been a football player until he was dismissed from the team earlier in the year, and he is one of the students who is bused to the school under the desegregation plan. In addition to his dismissal from the football team, he had been suspended twice for fighting. The students and faculty generally regarded Carl as a bully.

The principal also knew Brian's sister, Angie. She, too, was a senior. Somewhat introverted, she was an above-average student academically but not very involved in extracurricular activities. She recently was inducted into the National Honor Society. Mr. Milhoviak was surprised that Angie and Carl would be dating; they had such different personalities.

"What exactly did Carl say to you, Brian?" the principal asked.

"He told me that he loved Angie and he wasn't going to let my family stand in his way. He said he owned a gun and wasn't afraid to use it. He said unless we stopped pressuring Angie, he would get me and my parents."

The principal immediately asked another question, "And what does Angie have to say about this?"

"I don't know. I didn't even know that she had a date with him. I doubt that my parents knew about this either."

"Brian, I am going to alert the security officer about this threat. The officer will keep an eye on Carl. If he threatens you again, even if it is away from school, you let me know immediately. In the meantime, I'll figure out how I'm going to handle this. Whatever you do, don't agitate Carl. Don't argue with him or even speak to him."

The conversation had eliminated Brian's fear. He told the principal, "Carl said he was tired of being treated like dirt. I really think he's crazy enough to shoot someone."

After a few more minutes, the principal convinced Brian to return to class. As soon as the student left his office, the principal asked that Angie Isaacs be brought to the office. The principal immediately told her about the threat to her brother. She seemed surprised.

"I went out with him twice, and no one in my family knew about it. He had asked for a date at least six times before I finally said yes. The first time we went out, we went to a movie. I met him at the theatre. The second time, we went to a rock concert. My parents thought I was at a girlfriend's house both times. After the second date, I just decided that I didn't want to go out with him again. I told him that two days ago when he asked me out again. He got very angry when I told him," she told the principal.

"Did he ever threaten you?" asked the principal.

"No. But he scares me. He seems to be a very angry person. He gets mad easily. For example, he almost got in a fight with a guy sitting in front of us at the rock concert just because this guy wouldn't stay in his seat. Carl threatened to punch him and the guy got a security person who told Carl to cool it."

Mr. Milhoviak instructed Angie to return to class and to avoid contact with Carl. He also advised her to talk to her parents about the situation when she got home from school that day. After she left his office, Mr. Milhoviak tried to reach Angie's parents via telephone but was unsuccessful. He wanted to ensure that the parents were informed about the threat.

The principal then asked the school security officer, Carl Turner's counselor, and the assistant principal who handled much of the discipline in the school to meet with him. He briefed them on the matter, including his instructions to Brian and Angie Isaacs. The four school officials agreed that Carl should be brought to the office immediately. They wanted to hear his side of the story. The principal contacted the teacher in Carl's fourth period class via the intercom and was told that Carl was not in class. Checking the attendance records, the principal learned that Carl had been in attendance during the first three periods that day.

Carl's counselor, Mrs. Bruner, suggested that Mr. Milhoviak call the police and report the incident. Although she did not think Carl was likely to shoot anyone, she thought that he might physically attack Brian or Angie in some other manner. Riley Grimes, the assistant principal, said he thought that they should wait before contacting the police—at least until they were sure that Carl was not at the school. He commented, "What if we call the police and then find out Brian is not telling the truth? If he is not, or if he is exaggerating, Dr. Perkett may accuse us of jumping to conclusions. I say we try to find Carl first. If he is not in the school, then let's meet back here and reconsider our options."

Jamel Atkins, the school's security guard and a retired deputy sheriff, offered another recommendation. He urged the principal to locate Mr. and Mrs. Isaacs as soon as possible. He felt that they should know about the reported threat and thought that it was important to find out whether they were willing to file a complaint with the police. He assured the principal that he would protect Brian and Angie through the remainder of the school day.

Each school in the Center City district was required to have a crisis plan. The one for Memorial Park provided suggestions for handling threatened violence, but it did not require a specific course of action. Among the suggested actions were:

- Notifying the police if the incident was considered sufficiently serious
- Notifying the parents of all students involved
- Notifying the teachers of all students involved

- Suspending the student from school pending a full investigation if the incident was considered sufficiently serious

After considering the suggestions made by the three staff members and after reviewing the crisis plan, the principal decided to delay calling the police. The administrators and the security guard started searching the building for Carl, and staff in the principal's office began trying to reach the parents of the involved students. The group agreed to reconvene in the principal's office in one hour unless they asked to return before that time. Neither effort was fruitful. Carl had not been located; the parents had not been notified; the police had not been notified. When the school officials met the second time in the principal's office, principal Milhoviak again asked the staff members for advice.

The Challenge

Assume you are the principal. How would you manage this situation?

Suggested Activities_____

1. Evaluate the security guard's advice that school officials determine whether the parents are willing to file a complaint before calling the police.

2. Evaluate the school counselor's advice that school officials contact the police immediately.

3. List alternatives the principal could have used to deal with this situation and evaluate them.

4. Determine the law in your state regarding the legal responsibility of a principal (or other educators) to report students who threaten bodily harm to others to the police.

5. Complete the worksheet for this case.

Suggested Readings_____

Baker, J. A. (1998). Are we missing the forest for the trees? Considering the social context of school violence. *Journal of School Psychology, 36*(1), 29–44.

Black, S. (2003). Angry at the world. *The American School Board Journal, 190*(6), 43–45.

Bock, S. J., Savner, J. L., & Tapscott, K. E. (1998). Suspension and expulsion: Effective management of students. *Intervention in School and Clinic, 34*(1), 50–52.

Clark, C. (1998). The violence that creates school dropouts. *Multicultural Education, 6*(1), 19–22.

Constenbader, V., & Markson, S. (1998). School suspension: A study with secondary school students. *Journal of School Psychology, 36*(1), 59–82.

Edmonson, H. M., & Bullock, L. M. (1998). Youth with aggressive and violent behaviors: Pieces of a puzzle. *Preventing School Failure, 42*(3), 135–141.

Halbig, W. W. (2000). Breaking the code of silence. *American School Board Journal, 187*(3), 34–36.

Haynes, R. M., & Chalker, D. M. (1999). A nation of violence. *American School Board Journal, 186*(3), 22–25.

Johns, B. H. (1998). What the new Individuals with Disabilities Act (IDEA) means for students who exhibit aggressive or violent behavior. *Preventing School Failure, 42*(3), 102–105.

Jones, R. (1997). Absolute zero. *American School Board Journal, 184*(10), 29–31.

Kenney, D. J., & Watson, T. S. (1996). Reducing fear in the schools: Managing conflict through student problem solving. *Education and Urban Society, 28*(4), 436–455.

Levin, J. (1998). Violence goes to school. *Mid-Western Educational Researcher, 11*(1), 2–7.

Myles, B. S., & Simpson, R. L. (1998). Aggression and violence by school-age children and youth: Understanding the aggression cycle and prevention/intervention strategies. *Intervention in School and Clinic, 33*(5), 259–264.

Page, R. M., & Hammermeister, J. (1997). Weapon-carrying youth and violence. *Adolescence, 32*(127), 505–513.

Rasicot, J. (1999). The threat of harm. *American School Board Journal, 186*(3), 14–18.

Sheley, J. F., & Wright, J. D. (1998). *High school youths, weapons, and violence: A national study.* (ERIC Document Reproduction Service No. ED426 468)

Stephens, R. D. (1998). Ten steps to safer schools. *American School Board Journal, 185*(3), 30–33.

Trump, K. S. (2001). Assessing and managing student threats. *School Administrator, 58*(9), 50.

Valois, R. F., & McKewon, R. E. (1998). Frequency and correlates of fighting and carrying weapons among public school adolscents. *American Journal of Health Behavior, 22*(1), 8–17.

Will, J., & Neufeld, P. J. (2002). Taking appropriate action. *Principal Leadership, 3*(4), 51–54.

Will, J. D., & Neufeld, P. J. (2003). Keep bullying from growing into greater violence. *The Education Digest, 68*(6), 32–36.

Zirkel, P. A. (2002). Written and verbal threats of violence. *Principal, 81*(5), 63–65.

References

Kowalski, T. J. (2002). Working with the media during a crisis situation: Perspectives for school administrators. *Journal of School Public Relations, 23*(3), 178–196.

Moriarity, A., Maeyama, R. G., & Fitzgerald, P. J. (1993). A clear plan for school crisis management. *NASSP Bulletin, 77*(552), 17–22.

Seifert, E. H. (2004). Responding to crisis. In T. J. Kowalski (Ed.), *Public relations in schools* (3rd ed., pp. 274–298). Upper Saddle River, NJ: Merrill, Prentice Hall.

Trump, K. S. (1998). *Practical school safety: Basic guidelines for safe and secure schools.* Thousand Oaks, CA: Corwin.

Lounge Talk

Background Information

Role conflict is a product of incompatible job expectations. As an example, some teachers, students, and parents expect principals to be caring and loving individuals; others expect these administrators to be decisive managers; and still others expect them to be dynamic political leaders. Although role conflict always has been a concern for practitioners, the topic has assumed added importance in recent years as a result of efforts to reconstruct organization and governance in schools and districts.

Studies of role conflict and leadership styles have contributed to theory building in the areas of *transformational* and *charismatic* leadership. As Yukl noted (1989), these two terms

> refer to the process of influencing major changes in the attitudes and assumptions of organization members and building commitment for the organization's mission and objectives. Transformational leadership is usually defined more broadly than charismatic leadership, but there is considerable overlap between the two conceptions. (p. 204)

The seminal work of Burns (1978) described two contrasting administrative styles: transactional and transformational leadership. *Transactional* principals and superintendents tend to believe that people are primarily motivated by self-interests, and accordingly, they attempt to control behavior in others by providing rewards or punishments affecting those interests (Kowalski, 2003). An elementary school principal, for example, may promise a teacher financial support to attend a national reading conference if the teacher agrees to be the faculty representative on a districtwide committee. Or, a high school principal may threaten to lower a new teacher's evaluation if she refuses to be the sponsor for a student club. Bennis and Nanus (1985) concluded that the transactional style has been widely used in all types of organizations.

Transformational leaders, by comparison, hold very different beliefs about people. These administrators usually focus on higher-order, intrinsic, and moral motives and they seek to integrate individual motives toward a common goal (Kowalski, 2003). Bennis (1984) observed that transformational leaders believe in and trust people around them. They develop shared rather than personal organizational visions and then communicate and promote these visions to stakeholders once they are developed. Moreover, transformational leaders successfully engage in introspection; they know their strengths and deployed them to advance the interests of the organization, organizational members, and parties served by the organization. In the context of a school, a transformational principal is likely to exhibit these proclivities:

- Being concerned that individuals are able to grow professionally and achieve self-efficacy
- Viewing teachers as professional colleagues rather than subordinates
- Viewing the school as a learning community rather than a political battleground of competing factions

Differences between transactional and transformational leaders are especially evident with respect to dispositions on organizational change. Transactional principals or superintendents usually try to alter behavior by manipulating individuals and groups. More precisely, their actions are directed by two foundational beliefs:

1. People are motivated almost entirely by self-interests, such as personal gain and comfort.
2. The behavior of educators is affected more by political realities than professional commitment. That is, they realize that administrators do not have sufficient resources to satisfy all needs and wants presented to them. Consequently, educators are willing to compete, either individually or in groups, to satisfy their self-interests.

Because of these perceptions, transactional administrators believe that the most effective approach to influencing behavior is through the calculated use of rewards and punishments.

Transformational principals and superintendents, on the other hand, believe that the key to organizational improvement and efficacy is establishing a collective vision that melds organizational and individual interests (including the interests of individuals in the broader community served by schools). Put another way, their perspective of leadership is largely professional. Instead of trying to manipulate people to pursue personal gains, they seek to ensure that members of the organization have the requisite knowledge and commitment to implement shared goals and objectives.

In this case, four high school teachers discuss their perceptions of the school's new principal. Three of them are displeased with the school's new leader and reject her leadership style. In subtle ways, they question whether gender, age, and a lack of administrative experience are responsible for her behavior. As you read this case, focus on the differences between transactional and transformational leadership. See if you can determine why the three disgruntled teachers reject the principal's leadership style. Also, imagine that you are a teacher in the school and determine how you would react to the principal.

Key Areas for reflection

1. Transformational and transactional leadership styles
2. Principal succession
3. Role conflict
4. Teacher expectations of principal behavior
5. Leadership style and change in schools

The Case

As Peter Weller entered the teachers' lounge, the room fell silent. Three colleagues, Debra Lowler, Linda Mays, and Jake Brumwell, were seated at one of the four small round tables scattered randomly across the room. No one else was present. Having a common preparation period had caused the four teachers to become familiar with each other. Almost every school day, they spent the last 15 minutes of their preparation period having coffee together. It was not unusual for Peter to be the last one to arrive at the lounge.

Peter nodded as he sat down in the remaining chair at the table, but the silence continued. After a few seconds he asked, "Okay, what's going on here? You people look like my students when they get caught doing something wrong."

"Peter," Linda answered, "We were just discussing your favorite principal. Maybe she has a hidden listening device in this room and sent you in here to defend her! Just a joke, so don't get hostile."

Peter smiled and answered, "Don't you people have better things to discuss? Now I realize that you excel at criticizing principals. But why don't you ease up on Dr. Werner?"

Colleen Werner had been appointed principal of Drewerton South High School less than a year ago. She is only the second principal in the school's 14-year history. With an enrollment of just over 1,000 students, Drewerton South serves primarily a middle-class suburban population.

George Calbo, the school's first and only other principal had retired the previous year. He was a popular administrator, especially among teachers. He had served as a teacher and basketball coach at Drewerton High School (then the district's only high school) for 17 years before being named South's inaugural principal. His appointment, made a full year before the school opened, allowed him to personally select faculty and staff. Many of those he chose were close friends and former colleagues from Drewerton High School. Faculty at South considered Mr.

Calbo their friend and advocate. They liked the fact that he often promoted their interests to the superintendent, the school board, and the general public.

The announcement that Colleen Werner would become the second principal of South surprised many teachers and community members. She was only 32 years old at the time of her appointment and the first female administrator in one of the district's secondary schools. Her selection was even more surprising in light of the fact that four of the district's secondary school administrators (two middle school principals and two high school assistant principals) had been applicants for this position.

Differences in age, experience, and gender initially distinguished Dr. Werner from her predecessor. After a few months in the position, faculty at the school began to realize that she also possessed a very different approach to being a principal. Whereas Mr. Calbo devoted much of his time to managerial tasks, such as ensuring that the building was clean and dealing with discipline problems, Dr. Werner relegated these responsibilities to assistants so she could spend time visiting classrooms and serving on committees. Mr. Calbo spent a great deal of time in the teachers' lounge, and while there, he willingly listened to teacher concerns and complaints. Dr. Werner, on the other hand, rarely entered this room, and on those rare occasions when she did, she never stayed for more than a minute or two.

Peter Weller was one of only a handful of South High School teachers who thought that Dr. Werner was an improvement over her predecessor. Even though he realized he was in the minority on this issue, he never tried to hide his convictions and often defended the new principal to her critics. He saw Dr. Werner as highly competent, professional, and dedicated. Peter's disposition toward the new principal surprised some of his colleagues since he also had been supportive of the former principal. When questioned on this matter, Peter explained that he liked Mr. Calbo and respected his many years of service to the district and to South High School. Nevertheless, he thought that the previous principal lacked vision and had become a pawn of political factions. Since everyone knew that Mr. Calbo would be retiring, Peter concluded that there was no need to emphasize these shortcomings.

"Well, what are you crucifying Dr. Werner for today?" Peter asked the three other teachers.

"You know we have to talk about somebody," Jake answered, "and it might as well be Colleen."

"Unfortunately, you talk about her every day. You seem to be obsessed with the topic," Peter noted.

Debra Lowler, usually the quietest person in the group, spoke next. "I'll tell you what bothers me. It's her repeated comments about how teachers should behave professionally. This is just a code word for doing extra work without additional compensation. Instead of protecting teachers from being abused, she actually promotes the idea that we should be volunteering to do all kinds of extra jobs. We never got any of this nonsense from George. He knows what it is like to be a teacher in this district, and because he knows, he fought for us."

"Agree," Linda chimed in. "George defended our rights. He didn't expect us to do more work without being adequately paid. And more important, he didn't let the superintendent and school board walk all over us."

"Don't you think that Colleen cares about teachers?" Peter asked. "She was a teacher. She knows what our lives are like. Is it possible that she wants to make sure that everyone, including students, gets treated fairly? Just because she doesn't praise you every minute of the day and just because she isn't dangling carrots in front of you constantly doesn't mean she's indifferent."

Jake Brumwell, a mathematics teacher and track coach, was Mr. Calbo's closest friend and biggest defender among the group. He joined the discussion.

"Peter, Colleen still has a lot to learn, especially about working with teachers. Just last week, for example, she called me into her office and asked if I would go on a camping trip with a group of students for a weekend in June. The students who will go on this trip are involved in a dropout prevention program. She told me that two other teachers already had agreed to chaperone the trip, and she thought my presence would be good for the students. When I asked her how much I would get paid for doing this, she looked at me like I was an extortionist. I told her I was busy and couldn't go on the trip. Although she didn't say it, I could see that she thought I was acting unprofessionally. I don't like her putting me in an unfair position. Why should we do extra things on our own time and not get paid for doing them?"

Peter then asked, "Did you know, Jake, that I'm one of two teachers who has volunteered to chaperone this trip?" Not waiting for an answer, he asked another question. "Did you know that Colleen, herself, was going to go? So, it wasn't like she was asking you to do something that she wasn't doing herself."

Debra came to Jake's defense. "Sure, she's going. But she's on a 12-month contract. We're not."

"But she's not being paid for working on weekends, is she?" Peter shot back.

Linda entered the conversation again. "Look, it's more than just asking us to give up our time. Colleen's whole approach toward administration is different—she doesn't do things George's way. He made sure we got paid for extra assignments. It seems that Colleen only cares about the students—and she cares most about the students with serious problems. She should spend more time worrying about teachers. Students are not going to decide whether she succeeds in this job, but we might."

"Agree. She's going to be in trouble if she ignores the fact that administrators don't do well in this district if they lose teacher support," Jake noted. "Personally, I think she would be a more effective principal if she paid more attention to teachers and to our best students. Maybe the high achievers should be the ones who go on camping trips and get favors from the principal. Maybe Colleen is sending the wrong message to students when she focuses all of her interests on troubled students."

Peter was getting frustrated. "Do you realize that I'm not the only one in the school who supports Colleen?" he asked rhetorically. "Why don't you give her credit for some of the things she's accomplished in just a short time she's been here? What about the way she helped Deloris Hutchins? Prior to Dr. Werner working with her, she was a very poor teacher. Dr. Werner worked with her to improve her planning skills and classroom management. George Calbo never tried to help her become a better teacher; he just covered up her deficiencies and protected her. Deloris Hutchins is a better teacher now, and she openly attributes her improved performance to Dr. Werner. Now you tell me, who is the better principal—the one who made excuses for poor teaching or the one who did something about it? I'll tell you how Deloris answers that question. She thinks Dr. Werner is the best administrator she has ever known. To casually charge that Colleen doesn't care about teachers is irresponsible."

Jake responded, "See? That's what I was trying to say a minute ago. No matter if she is dealing with teachers or students, she cares a lot more about problem individuals than she does about high achievers. Shouldn't those of us who are doing a good job day after day get some recognition? Instead of praise and rewards, we get invited to spend a weekend with troubled students! And if we decline the invitation, we get labeled as uncaring teachers and insensitive human beings. Listen, Peter, I just don't like the way Werner operates. She's never going to be an effective principal unless she wises up and learns the political realties of public education."

Peter recognized that he was not going to gain any converts today. There had been a dozen or so previous conversations like this one, and each had ended without anyone changing his or her views. Yet, the four teachers always seem to feel better after venting their views about Dr. Werner. Maybe this is why the 15-minute debates did not affect their personal relationships.

"Well, colleagues," Peter said as he stood up, "time to get back to work. But before I leave, I just want to say again that you are wrong about Colleen. Why are you so unwilling to be objective? She's a bright, energetic leader. Maybe she's not perfect, but the perfect principal doesn't exist."

"Wipe that smile off your face," Linda said. "Don't you recognize that you have lost another argument? If it makes you feel better, I'll concede that Colleen has good intentions. She's just misguided."

Jake added sarcastically, "Yeah, I'll give her a B for effort and a D for achievement!"

The group always had a way of ending their discussions with a little humor. Maybe it helped ease the tension. The four teachers scattered down different hallways to their next classes and their thoughts shifted to other matters.

The Challenge

Utilize your knowledge of leadership and organizational behavior to analyze the discussion that took place. Specifically, provide an explanation of why teachers in this school react to Dr. Werner so differently.

Suggested Activities_____

1. In the case, a charge is made that Dr. Werner spends an inordinate amount of her time assisting students and teachers experiencing problems. Discuss the merits of this accusation.

2. Based on the information conveyed in the case study, describe the leadership styles of the previous principal, Mr. Calbo, and the current principal, Dr. Werner. Discuss the strengths and weaknesses of each style.

3. Based on the information provided in the case study, can you determine whether Dr. Werner is a competent principal? Why or why not?

4. Discuss the extent to which Dr. Werner is responsible for the criticism she is receiving from some of the teachers.

5. Identify actions the principals could take to reduce the criticisms and change opinions about her performance.

6. Complete the worksheet for Case 4.

Suggested Readings_____

Blase, J. (1986). Leadership behavior of school principals in relation to teacher stress, satisfaction, and performance. *Journal of Humanistic Education and Development, 24*(4), 159–171.

Bogler, R. (2001). The influence of leadership style on teacher job satisfaction. *Educational Administration Quarterly, 37*(5), 662–683.

Eden, D. (1998). The paradox of school leadership. *Journal of Educational Administration, 36*(3–4), 249–261.

Erickson, H. (1985). Conflict and the female principal. *Phi Delta Kappan, 67*, 288–291.

Foster, W. (1988). The administrator as transformative intellectual. *Peabody Journal of Education, 66*(3), 5–18.

Hallinger, P. (1992). The evolving role of the American principals: From managerial to instructional to transformational leaders. *Journal of Educational Administration, 3*(3), 35–48.

Hart, A. (1991). Leader succession and socialization: A synthesis. *Review of Educational Research, 61*, 451–474.

Hart, A. (1993). *Principal succession: Establishing leadership in schools.* Albany: State University of New York Press.

Kochan, F. K., Spencer, W. A., & Mathews, J. G. (2000). Gender-based perceptions of the challenges, changes, and essential skills of the principalship. *Journal of School Leadership, 10*(4), 290–310.

Krug, S. (1993). Leadership craft and the crafting of school leaders. *Phi Delta Kappan, 75*(3), 240–244.

Leithwood, K. (1992). The move toward transformational leadership. *Educational Leadership, 49*(5), 8–12.

Meadows, B. (1992). Nurturing cooperation and responsibility in a school environment. *Phi Delta Kappan, 73*(6), 480–481.

Ogawa, R. (1991). Enchantment, disenchantment, and accommodation: How a faculty made sense of the succession of its principal. *Educational Administration Quarterly, 27*(1), 30–60.

Peterson, K., & Kelley, C. (2001). Transforming school leadership. *Leadership, 30*(3), 8–11.

Roesner, C. (1987). Principals' leadership behavior—Do you see yourself as your subordinates see you? *NASSP Bulletin, 71*(502), 68–71.

Rossmiller, R. (1992). The secondary school principal and teachers' quality of work life. *Educational Management and Administration, 20*(3), 132–146.

Valentine, J., & Bowman, M. (1991). Effective principal, effective school: Does research support the assumption? *NASSP Bulletin, 75*(539), 1–7.

Wells, D. (1985). The perfect principal: A teacher's fantasy. *Principal, 65*(1), 27.

References

Bennis, W. B. (1984). The four competencies of leadership. *Training and Development Journal, 38*(8), 14–19.

Bennis, W. B., & Nannus, B. (1985). *Leaders: The strategies for taking charge.* New York: Harper & Row.

Burns, J. (1978). *Leadership.* New York: Harper and Row.

Kowalski, T. J. (2003). *Contemporary school administration: An introduction* (2nd ed.). Boston: Allyn and Bacon.

Yukl, G. (1989). *Leadership in organizations* (2nd ed.). Englewood Cliffs, NJ: Prentice-Hall.

Get Rid of the Sloppy Assistant Principal

Background Information

When contemplating behavior in schools, aspiring administrators often observe that assistant principals and principals are not all alike. Some are controlling, whereas others are passive. Some focus on maintaining discipline, whereas others focus on improving instruction. This individuality is explained by three realities: (1) each administrator is a unique individual who brings his or her personality, needs, and interests to the school; (2) not all schools set the same expectations for administrators; and (3) schools have unique institutional cultures that include norms to which educators are expected to conform (Hanson, 2003).

Although some variability in administrative behavior is inevitable, tolerance levels for degrees of individuality are not constant across school districts. Superintendents and school boards that attempt to limit behavioral differences often rely on policies, rules, and regulations to do so. In essence, they attempt to increase the influence of organizational expectations and restrict the influence of individual personalities. For many administrators working in these types of districts, the rewards and punishments tied to the controls are sufficient to ensure conformity to organizational role expectations. There are some practitioners, however, who are resistant, and they are almost certain to experience role conflict.

Role conflict occurs when an individual encounters opposing or competing job performance expectations (Owens, 1998). Forces that are responsible for this discord may be categorized as follows:

- *Conflict between or among administrators.* Even though role expectations may be formalized in job descriptions, administrators working together may not interpret or accept them uniformly. As an example, a principal and an assistant principal may disagree over the role responsibilities of an assistant principal.

- *Conflict between an administrator and a group.* Despite the presence of job descriptions, administrators often discover that teachers, other employees, students, and parents often ignore or do not accept these standards. As an example, a superintendent may expect all administrators to be loyal to the administrative team, whereas a teacher might expect a principal and assistant principal to be his or her advocates.
- *Conflict between role and personality.* One of the most frequent types of role conflict involves discord between an individual's personal dispositions and the formal expectations established by the organization. As an example, an assistant principal may have a high need to be liked and accepted by everyone, whereas the organization expects him to be a stern manager and disciplinarian.

Role conflict also can result from uncertainty and confusion. Consider a principal who receives mixed messages about taking risks in relation to seeking school improvement; the board and superintendent verbally urge her to be daring, but the district's policy, rules, and performance evaluation system reward failure avoidance. The principal is left wondering which message is accurate. Role conflict is a serious concern both for the employing organization and for practitioners; studies have revealed negative outcomes ranging from stress (e.g., Gmelch & Torelli, 1994) to reduced job satisfaction (e.g., Eckman, 2002).

One major reason why role conflict is prevalent in districts and schools is that administrators wear many hats. They are leaders, managers, facilitators, counselors, planners, organizers, evaluators, and even formal representatives of their employing organization (Kowalski, 2003). The knowledge, skills, and dispositions required for leading and managing, for instance, are quite different. Although many administrators obviously are capable of assuming both roles, few practitioners are equally adept and comfortable in doing so. Consequently, administrators are vulnerable to criticism when detractors focus solely on weaknesses instead of conducting a fair and balanced performance assessment.

This case is about role conflict affecting a high school assistant principal in an affluent community. The district superintendent and his associate surprise the high school principal by recommending that the assistant principal return to teaching, largely because his personal appearance does not conform to their standard. In addition to role conflict, the case includes a myriad of ethical and legal questions and demonstrates how poor communication can produce or fuel conflict.

Key Areas for Reflection

1. Relationship between organizational role and individual personality
2. Behavioral transitions between teaching and administration
3. Ethical and legal dimensions of performance evaluation
4. Community environment and influence on school culture
5. Communication and organizational conflict

The Case

Community

Thomas Creek is located approximately 12 miles from a major city in the western part of New York State. With quiet, tree-lined streets and attractive homes, it is appropriately described as an upper-middle-class suburb. Nearly two-thirds of the adult residents are college graduates, with about 15 percent being self-employed professionals (e.g., lawyers, physicians, architects).

Although two out of three Thomas Creek families have annual incomes over $220,000, the community is racially and ethnically diverse. The following population profile was developed from official census data:

Caucasian	75 percent
Asian American	14 percent
African American	7 percent
Hispanic American	2 percent
Other	2 percent

The size of the community's population is stable, because land is unavailable for new residential developments. When houses go on the market, they usually sell within two or three weeks.

School System

A brochure distributed by the local Chamber of Commerce describes Thomas Creek as "a community where cultural diversity and public education are assets." The school district is widely recognized as one of the best in the state. The high school recently received several citations from state and national groups for having excellent educational programs, and the Scholastic Aptitude Test scores for high school students have consistently been among the top 5 percent in the state. The district includes three elementary schools (grades K–5), a middle school (grades 6–8), and a high school (grades 9–12). The overall enrollment is 2,300 students. The number of students in the system declined steadily from 1976, when the total enrollment peaked at 3,150. In the past decade, however, enrollments have remained relatively stable.

There are two nonpublic elementary schools located within the district's boundaries: (1) St. Jerome Catholic School (grades K–6) and (2) Thomas Creek Academy (grades K–5). Virtually all students from St. Jerome enter the public schools after sixth grade; only about 40 percent of those attending Thomas Creek Academy do so.

Salaries in the school district are among the highest in the state and nation. Teachers at the top of the salary schedule are paid approximately $83,000. The superintendent's salary is over $190,000. The five members on the school board are elected to three-year terms. The central office professional staff includes the superintendent, an associate superintendent, a business manager, and a director of special services. Central administration is housed in a relatively new office building that is located near the high school.

High School

All school facilities in the district are excellent, but Thomas Creek High School is clearly the "centerpiece" of the community's commitment to education. Although the building is nearly 45 years old, it has been recently renovated and kept in perfect condition. With its ivy-covered brick exterior and spacious park-like setting, the facility looks like it should be located on a college campus.

Very few TCHS employees leave before they retire. Consequently, the average age of the faculty is 53. In the past five years, only three new teachers have joined the faculty. Largely because of the excellent employee compensation program, fewer than 40 percent of the Thomas Creek teachers belong to the teachers' association; historically, relationships among the school board, administration, and teachers have been collaborative. Approximately 90 percent of the school's approximately 700 pupils enter a four-year institution of higher education within two years after graduation.

Principal

Allen Miller became the principal of Thomas Creek High School four years ago. Prior to this assignment, he was the principal of a larger suburban high school near Cleveland. Energetic and enthusiastic, he frequently spends 10 to 12 hours a day at school or attending to school-related matters. Most parents, students, and district employees describe him as competent, caring, and patient. They also see him as being people oriented, devoting much of his time to meeting with students, parents, and community leaders. Each week, for instance, Allen invites approximately 15 parents to have coffee with him so that they can exchange information. He has a similar type of meeting twice a month with students. Allen also spends a considerable amount of time communicating with teachers. He frequently visits classrooms, involves himself in curriculum projects, and attends department meetings as often as possible.

In contrast, Allen spends very little time with routine management responsibilities such as supervising lunch programs, dealing with discipline problems, and managing the maintenance staff. These responsibilities have been relegated to the assistant principal. Having greater opportunities to do what he likes best was one of the primary reasons Allen accepted his current position. Although he views himself as being a capable manager, he finds this role to be boring; he believes he can contribute much more by working directly with people in areas such as planning, programming, and evaluation.

Assistant Principal

George Hopkins has worked at Thomas Creek High School for 27 years. He coached football and taught physical education for 22 of those years. He is quite popular with students who affectionately refer to him as "coach" or "the enforcer." The latter title reflects his role as the school's disciplinarian.

George and Allen are often referred to as an odd couple because their personalities and leadership styles are so different. George prefers management roles and he particularly enjoys being in charge of student discipline. He views the assistant principalship as his terminal position in school administration. Allen, on the other hand, prefers leading and facilitating activities such as vision, planning, and instructional improvement. His career goal is to become a superintendent. The two administrators also are quite dissimilar with respect to personal appearance. Allen always wears a coat and tie while at school, whereas George dresses casually.

George and Allen's predecessor, John Sturby, were close friends. Mr. Sturby had persuaded George to accept the assistant principal's position even though George had no desire to be an administrator. When Allen Miller became principal, George requested to return to a teaching assignment. After meeting with faculty, Allen asked George to continue in his administrative capacity, largely because he had been highly effective in dealing with troubled students. George agreed to remain assistant principal for at least one year. During that period, the two men developed a positive relationship and continued to work together. During the four years they have worked together Allen consistently has recommended George for merit salary increases.

Key Central Office Administrators

Both the superintendent, Dr. Ronald O'Brien, and the associate superintendent for instruction, Dr. Valerie Daniels, came to work in Thomas Creek just two years ago. They had worked together previously in an affluent suburban school district in another state. Two other administrators were assigned to the district's administrative office and each has been employed in Thomas Creek school system for more than 15years.

All of Dr. O'Brien's administrative experience has been in affluent suburban school districts. He became a superintendent when he was 33 years old, and Thomas Creek is the fourth district in which he has held this post. During his tenure in Thomas Creek, the school board members have been very supportive of him. Dr. O'Brien is an effective public speaker and projects an executive image. He is able to spend most of his time outside of his office because he delegates virtually all management responsibilities to Dr. Daniels. The other two district-level administrators report directly to her. Since coming to Thomas Creek, he has become active with the Chamber of Commerce and has been appointed to the city's planning council.

Relationship between the High School
Principal and Superintendent

When he first arrived in Thomas Creek, Dr. O'Brien was concerned that Mr. Miller did not have a doctoral degree. In the district where he previously served as superintendent, five of six principals had completed this level of education. Shortly after arriving in Thomas Creek, he told Allen that he should consider pursuing a doctorate because doing so would enhance his credibility in this upscale community. As they became better acquainted, Dr. O'Brien became less insistent because it was apparent that Allen already had established credibility and trust and he was widely supported by parents and the faculty.

Dr. O'Brien's confidence in his high school principal became evident to everyone when he nominated Mr. Miller for the state's outstanding principal award. In his letter of nomination, he wrote, "Allen Miller is an outstanding leader. He is a dedicated professional who provides a positive role model for the teachers and students. He represents the values and beliefs that make Thomas Creek High School one of the best secondary schools in the nation." Despite this high praise, the administrators have not had a great deal of direct contact with each other over the past two years. The principals also report directly to the associate superintendent, Dr. Daniels. She visits schools weekly and conducts staff meetings with the principals on a biweekly basis. Dr. O'Brien only occasionally attends these meetings; he was present at five of them in the past year. In two years, Allen has met alone with the superintendent on just three occasions.

Evaluation Procedures

The associate superintendent evaluates the performance of the principals. The results are presented and discussed in conferences typically held in March. The conferences are held in Dr. O'Brien's office and he is always in attendance. After Dr. Daniels completes her evaluation and the principal has had an opportunity to respond, the superintendent discusses his recommendation for a merit salary increase. The compensation of all the district's administrators is based solely on merit, an employment condition that has been widely supported by the school board and the administrators.

The administrative evaluation system is sequenced. First, principals are required to evaluate their assistant principals and to formulate a preliminary salary recommendation for them. The principals then hold a conference with their assistants and present the outcomes to them. Evaluation and salary decisions for assistant principals, however, are subject to the superintendent's approval. After these conferences are completed, principals attend their own evaluation conferences and present recommendations pertaining to their assistants. The salary recommendation is made by checking one of four options: high, average, low, or none.

Incident

Allen assumed that this year's evaluation conference with Dr. Daniels and Dr. O'Brien would be routine. After all, the superintendent had just recommended him to be Principal of the Year. His conference was scheduled for 9:40 in the morning and he told his secretary he expected to be back in his office by 11:00.

Allen entered the superintendent's office and took his customary seat at a small round table. The three administrators exchanged greetings and then Dr. Daniels asked him to share his evaluation of George Hopkins. The district's rating instrument contains 24 items that are rated as excellent, above average, average, or below average. George received 19 excellent ratings, 4 above average ratings, and only 1 average rating. The lowest assessment was for personal appearance.

"You know former coaches," Allen commented with a smile, "they never seem to stop looking like coaches."

Allen expected the other two administrators to laugh at his comment—they did not. Noticing this, Allen quickly retracted his grin, and then there was an awkward moment of silence. Allen sensed that something was wrong. He became uncomfortable, but he wanted someone else to break the silence.

Dr. Daniels was the first to speak. Looking directly into Allen's eyes, she said, "This community is a special place to live and work, and one reason is the reputation of Thomas Creek High School. We believe that your leadership has enhanced that reputation and we don't want anything to move the school in a different direction. When the school's number-two official looks more like a custodian than an assistant principal, we get concerned. You obviously see this same problem, but you're being very generous by rating his appearance as average. I've never seen him wear a coat and tie at work, and quite frankly, he just isn't very well groomed."

Allen was staggered by her harsh words. George had never dressed like the other administrators and everyone knew that. But why had this issue suddenly become such a concern? He asked Dr. Daniels, "George has always dressed the same way. If his appearance is unacceptable, why did you approve my recommendation to give him a high merit raise last year?"

Although the question was directed to him, Dr. O'Brien answered. "We did it for you, Allen. We felt it was more important to build your confidence than to attack this issue. If we had not supported your recommendation, you may have interpreted our action incorrectly. Now, however, we are confident that you can separate our support for you from our dissatisfaction with your assistant. We were still trying to learn about the district last year. Overturning your recommendation after being here just seven months could have been awkward for all of us. Things are different now."

"I'm not sure what you are telling me," Allen responded. "I again have recommended George for the high merit category. I think his overall performance has been outstanding. "

"This matter goes beyond a merit salary decision," Dr. Daniels answered. "To be blunt, we believe George should be replaced as assistant principal. He can return to teaching at the high school or he can be assigned to teach at the middle school. He will have the option of teaching driver education during the summer, so he won't have much of a salary reduction. We understand that he never wanted to be an administrator in the first place. Returning to teaching may be just what he wants."

Allen stared across the table in disbelief. He tried to collect his thoughts. "I had no idea you felt this strongly about George, and to be equally blunt, I don't agree that he should be reassigned. George is an effective assistant principal. In fact, he probably has not received the recognition he deserves. If he is reassigned, my work may be affected negatively. I may have to refocus my work. George is as loyal and dedicated as any person with whom I have been associated. He doesn't deserve to be reassigned."

Dr. O'Brien again spoke. "Allen, please listen. We are not asking you to change your recommendation or your evaluation. I will explain to the board that Valerie and I decided to not accept your recommendations and we will argue that George be reassigned. Neither George nor the faculty will blame you. We just don't want you fighting us publicly on this issue."

"He's right, Allen," Valerie Daniels interjected. "You have provided excellent leadership at the high school, but with an assistant who projects a proper image, you could be doing even more. Believe me, Dr. O'Brien and I have given this much thought. There are many administrators who can be as effective as George in handling discipline and management responsibilities. We simply don't want you taking sides publicly on this issue. You and the other principals know that we have the authority to accept or reject your recommendations."

Dr. O'Brien reached over and put is hand on Allen's shoulder. "We want your assurance that you will accept this decision and not create problems."

The Challenge

Place yourself in Allen's position. After identifying alternative courses of action, select the one that you believe is most effective.

Suggested Activities_____

1. Discuss the extent to which school districts in your state maintain dress requirements for administrators and the extent to which those requirements are evaluated.

2. When teachers become administrators, they typically experience socialization to their new role. Discuss the process of socialization and its purposes.

3. Debate the merits of having uniform dress norms for teachers and administrators.

4. Discuss the process of conducting performance evaluations for administrators in this district. Compare opinions regarding the extent to which the process contributed to the problem.

5. Complete the worksheet for Case 5.

Suggested Readings_____

Calabrese, R., & Tucker-Ladd, P. (1991). The principal and assistant principal: A mentoring relationship. *NASSP Bulletin, 75*(533), 67–74.

Duke, D. (1992). Concepts of administrative effectiveness and the evaluation of school administrators. *Journal of Personnel Evaluation in Education, 6*(2), 103–121.

Goodson, C. P. (2000). Assisting the assistant principal. *Principal, 79*(4), 56–57.

Hess, F. M. (2001). The priest and the pit bull. *School Administrator, 58*(10), 36–39.

Hoy, W., Newland, W., & Blaxovsky, R. (1977). Subordinate loyalty to superior, esprit, and aspects of bureaucratic structure. *Educational Administration Quarterly, 13*(1), 71–85.

Johnston, D. L. (1999). The seven no-no's of performance evaluation. *School Administrator, 56*(11), 47–48.

Lang, R. (1986). The hidden dress code dilemma. *Clearing House, 59*(6), 277–279.

Marshall, C. (1992). *The assistant principal: Leadership chores and challenges.* Newbury Park, CA: Corwin.

Marshall, C., & Greenfield, W. (1985). The socialization of the assistant principal: Implications for school leadership. *Education and Urban Society, 18*(1), 3–8.

Michel, G. J. (1996). *Socialization and career orientation of the assistant principal.* (ERIC Document Reproduction Service No. ED 395 381)

Norton, M. S., & Kriekard, J. (1987). Real and ideal competencies for the assistant principal. *NASSP Bulletin, 71*(501), 23–30.

Peterson, K. (1984). Mechanisms of administrative control over managers in educational organizations. *Administrative Science Quarterly, 29,* 573–597.

Weller, L. D., & Weller, S. J. (2002). *The assistant principal: Essentials for effective school leadership.* Thousand Oaks, CA: Corwin Press.

References

Eckman, E. W. (2002). Women high school principals: Perspectives on role conflict, role commitment, and job satisfaction. *Journal of School Leadership, 12*(1), 57–77.

Gmelch, W. H., & Torelli, J. A. (1994). The association of role conflict and ambiguity with administrator stress and burnout. *Journal of School Leadership, 4*(3), 341–356.

Hanson, E. M. (2003). *Educational administration and organizational behavior* (5th ed.). Boston: Allyn and Bacon.

Kowalski, T. J. (2003). *Contemporary school administration: An introduction* (2nd ed.). Boston: Allyn and Bacon.

Owens, R. C. (1998). *Organizational behavior in education: Instructional leadership and school reform* (8th ed.). Boston: Allyn and Bacon.

Let the Committee Decide

Background Information

During the typical work day, administrators are required to make dozens of decisions. Some are simple and nonthreatening, such as deciding what to wear to work or what to eat for lunch. Others, however, involve complex and high-risk choices, such as adjudicating conflict between two teachers. The actual behavior of practitioners is determined by an intricate mix of variables that include philosophical dispositions (personal values and beliefs), personal bias, and leadership style.

Choices made in relation to management and leadership activities revolve around three critical factors (Kowalski, 1999):

1. *Standards for acceptable outcomes.* These are criteria used to evaluate alternative actions. As an example, a superintendent may decide that her decision must be acceptable to the faculty and parents.
2. *Alternative courses of action.* These are alternative actions that are considered. As an example, a superintendent may identify six possible choices for using a vacant school building.
3. *Methods for evaluating alternatives.* These are approaches to determining which alternative will be selected. As an example, a superintendent may decide to use a democratic approach by allowing a committee representing the school district's various publics to make the choice.

Judgments about the quality of administrative decisions are made by using constructs or models. These paradigms may be either *normative* (i.e., they prescribe acceptable behavior) or *descriptive* (i.e., they detail what administrators actually do). Four decision models have been especially prevalent in the literature on school administration (Estler, 1988):

1. *Rational-bureaucratic.* This normative paradigm emphasizes problem analysis, data collection, alternative choices, and the objective selection of the ideal decision.

2. *Participatory.* This normative paradigm is nested in beliefs that participation increases productivity, morale, and the quality of information.
3. *Political.* This normative and descriptive paradigm relies on reaching compromises among vested interest groups.
4. *Organized anarchy.* This descriptive paradigm reveals that many decisions are made through a mix of changing participants, opportunities for change, and predetermined preferences.

Studying various models used by district and school officials, Tartar and Hoy (1998) concluded that none was universally superior. Nevertheless, these paradigms facilitate an understanding decision-making behavior, especially in relation to answering two essential questions about criteria, alternatives, and the evaluation of alternatives: Were these activities completed? How were they completed?

Scholars have long recognized that personal, social, and political variables produce behavioral inconsistencies among administrators. In many organizations, these discrepancies are viewed negatively because they contribute to uncertainty. Consequently, rational and easily understood decision-making models intended to control individualism and errors were widely promoted. Drucker (1974), for instance, reduced the act of organizational decision making to five steps:

1. Defining the problem
2. Analyzing the problem
3. Developing alternative solutions
4. Selecting a best solution
5. Taking action

Rational models stem from classical theory and cast decision making as an administrative activity. The involvement of others is viewed as unproductive, both because subordinates are considered to lack appropriate knowledge and skills and because their involvement is likely to produce conflict and, ultimately, inefficiency. Researchers studying district and school administrators (e.g., Crowson, 1989; Walker, 1994), however, have found that rational theories have had only a limited effect on behavior, largely because education institutions are sociopolitical systems in which power and authority is distributed among formal and informal groups. In real districts and schools, power is actually distributed among various groups and individuals.

Participatory models, by comparison, have their origins in the human relations movement that began in the 1930s. Individuals and groups in organizations were viewed as having a right to be involved in critical matters (especially in democratic societies and in public institutions), and participation was viewed as a way to increase employee morale and productivity (Kowalski, 2003). A resurgence of interest in participatory models has occurred since the mid-1980s in the context of school reform; site-based management, for example, is a manifestation of participatory decision making (Anderson, 1998).

Approaches to decision making, especially in public schools, also are influenced by political realities. Competing interests often prompt administrators to place more importance on political acceptance than on the professional appropriateness (Kowalski, 1999). Consider a superintendent, for example, who is faced with conflicting proposals for the configuration of a new middle school. The principal and faculty want to include three grades (6, 7, and 8); most parents want the school to include only two grades (7 and 8). The educators' proposal is grounded in the middle school literature and is consistent with decisions made in most other districts in the same state. The parents' proposal is based on personal fears that sixth-grade students will be influenced negatively by the older students. Fearing political repercussions from parents and the school board, the superintendent recommends including only two grades.

This case describes a new superintendent's decision to address a controversial issue by appointing a special committee having representatives of various stakeholder groups. The issue (having petty cash funds) and the superintendent's preference for a participatory approach raise jurisdictional questions between high-ranking school district officials. When a decision is reached, some key figures are critical and raise questions about the superintendent's motives.

Key Areas for Reflection

1. Decision-making models
2. Conflict and conflict resolution
3. Use of committees
4. Subordinate expectations of a new superintendent
5. Leadership style

The Case

The Community

Fullmer, a city of 45,000 residents, is the county seat of Oxford County (population 78,000). Located in the western part of a mid-Atlantic state, it is known for its scenic beauty. In recent years, the population has increased about 1 percent every two years. The growth is largely attributable to the development of condominiums and apartment complexes designed for retirees.

Over the past 20 years, most of the counties in this part of the state developed industrial parks, enterprise zones, and tax abatement programs in an effort to attract both foreign and domestic companies. Oxford County, however, is an exception. Many residents fear that increased industrial development would change the character of the community and harm the environment. There are a handful of small companies scattered across the county, and executives at several of them are considering relocating to other counties that have developed industrial parks and highways.

In addition to the natural beauty of Oxford County, three factors have been influential in attracting retirees to relocate there. They include reasonable real estate costs, low taxes, and above-average health care. Six years ago, a new hospital, costing nearly $90 million, was built in Fullmer and it is one of the most modern health facilities in the state.

The School District

The Oxford County School District serves the entire county population. It has a current enrollment of 19,700 students and operates the following attendance centers:

- Two high schools, grades 9–12
- Four middle schools, grades 6–8
- Thirteen elementary schools, grades K–5
- One vocational school (also includes an alternative program for secondary students not enrolled in a regular high school program)

Enrollment in the school system has declined just about 1 percent over the past decade, but in the last two years, kindergarten enrollments have declined by 5 percent.

The district's central office staff has remained very stable over the past 10 years. The following data below the position title and length of service in present position and in the school system.

| Name | Position | Length of Service | |
		Position	District
Bob Andrevet	Assistant superintendent—curriculum	18	24
Pamela Davis	Assistant superintendent—business	12	15
Jake Barnes	Director of personnel	10	27
Neil Vickers	Director of transportation	17	17
Iran Sults	Director of maintenance	21	26
Anne Major	Director of federal programs	19	16
Margo Jasik	Director of special education	16	16

The superintendent, Rudy Quillen, is in his first year with the school district, having replaced Orville Cruthers, who retired after having held the position for the previous 18 years.

The Incident

Dr. Quillen arrived in Oxford County in mid-July. For the past three years, he had been superintendent in a much smaller district (enrollment 2,400) in a neighboring state. Several Oxford County school board members met Dr. Quillen when they attended a presentation he made on goal setting at a national convention. Impressed with the topic and delivery, they encouraged him to apply for the impending vacancy in their district. At age 38, Rudy Quillen was in good health, experienced (he had already accumulated 12 years of administrative experience), and eager to provide leadership for a much larger school system.

A controversy that faced Dr. Quillen when he arrived in Oxford County involved the use of petty-cash funds by principals. These funds had existed for as long as anyone could remember. Recently, however, Dr. Davis, the assistant superintendent for business, recommended that they be discontinued. Her proposal was openly opposed by the principals, who argued that petty-cash funds allowed them flexibility to purchase small-cost items without having to file mounds of paperwork.

Dr. Davis has been in her current position for five years. As a former principal in the district, she was well aware of how the petty-cash funds could be used. On several occasions, she tried to persuade the previous superintendent to discontinue them, but he was unwilling to do so. Knowing he was going to retire shortly, Mr. Cruthers told Dr. Davis that this was a matter that she should discuss with his successor. Dr. Davis, however, decided to plant a seed with the school board before Dr. Quillen arrived. At the last meeting at which Mr. Cruthers served as superintendent, Dr. Davis publicly told the board members that she wanted to discontinue the petty-cash funds. Her rationale was that the funds presented risks in the area of financial management. She added that new procedures could be instituted to accelerate the purchase order process. Mr. Cruthers was surprised that Dr. Davis addressed this issue with the board after he had suggested that she discuss the matter with the new superintendent. He told the school board that Dr. Quillen should be given an opportunity to hear both sides of this conflict and to study the matter. Although the board members refused to take action on the matter that evening, two of the seven voiced support for the elimination of the funds.

Dr. Quillen was familiar with the arguments for and against petty-cash funds; they had been used in the district he had just left. Within a few days after assuming his new position in Fullmer, Dr. Davis addressed this issue with him. After listening to her concerns, he concluded that her fears were based on potential rather than actual problems. Even so, he agreed to take the matter under consideration. He first talked with the school system's attorney and subsequently with one of the attorneys employed by the state school boards' association. Both confirmed what Dr. Quillen already knew; such funds were legal and the decision to use them was a management issue.

Dr. Quillen established monthly administrative meetings that were attended by all principals and central office administrators. He mentioned that he was examining the issue of petty-cash funds at the September meeting and invited all interested parties to provide input. Several principals sent him e-mail messages voicing support for continuing the funds. The item was brought up for discussion at the November administrative meeting. Dr. Davis was permitted to speak first, since she had initiated the recommendation. She outlined her concerns and suggested how the purchasing process could be streamlined if the funds were discontinued.

Then Dr. Quillen shared the information he had received from the two attorneys. After he finished, nearly all of the principals spoke in opposition to the business administrator's recommendation. They argued that eliminating the funds would be another step toward centralizing administration in the district.

Dr. Davis was not intimidated. "Allowing so many separate petty-cash funds is not a good idea. Maybe we can reach a compromise on this matter. If you agree to give up the individual funds, we will maintain one petty-cash fund for the entire district. This arrangement still allows you to buy things immediately but we would have improved management control."

"That's just the problem," one of the high school principals answered. "More control. Every time we turn around, things are being centralized in this district. What makes you think mistakes cannot be made in your office?"

Judging that the discussion was not going to resolve the issue, Dr. Quillen announced that he was tabling the matter.

"Clearly, we have different opinions on this matter. We have a long agenda today, so let's move on to the next item. We'll revisit petty-cash funds at a later date."

Pamela Davis concluded that the superintendent was trying to avoid the issue. So she responded immediately.

"There are some serious management questions surrounding this practice, and we accomplish nothing by pretending that problems cannot occur," she said with emotion. "Just because I may stand alone on this issue doesn't mean that you are right and I am wrong. At the very least, we need to study this issue objectively."

Sensing that the tension in the room had escalated, Dr. Quillen responded.

"First, I want to make it clear that I'm not ignoring this issue. I appreciate the fact that Pamela is being conscientious. Second, I agree with her that we should study this matter objectively and in greater detail. But who among us is able to look at this matter objectively? Anyone who has a suggestion, please share it with me. I promise to return to this matter at our next meeting."

As pledged, Dr. Quillen revisited the petty-cash fund controversy at the December administrative meeting. The level of interest was heightened by a realization that the importance of the superintendent's decision on this matter extended beyond the issue at hand. His decision would reveal how he would handle conflict, especially when there was a disagreement between central office and school administrators. Some skeptics predicted that Dr. Quillen would find a way to sidestep the issue; others feared that he would support the compromise suggested by Dr. Davis at the last meeting. Everyone listened attentively as the superintendent began to speak.

"I have heard from many of you since our last meeting and I have weighed your comments carefully," he said. "Valid points have been raised by individuals having different perspectives. Some of you see this as an organizational issue—a matter of jurisdiction between the district and individual schools. You have urged me to delegate this matter to Bob Adrevet, since principals are the ones who will be most affected by the outcome. Others see this as management issue—that is, as an effort to institute appropriate fiscal controls. Those holding this view, and that includes at least two of the school board members, believe that Pamela should be delegated the responsibility to make the decision. Last, several of you see this as purely a political matter—a battle between the central office and schools over power. These individuals have urged me to support a compromise. After weighing all of these perspectives, I have decided to appoint an ad hoc committee to study the issue and to recommend a resolution. The committee will include two teachers, a parent who is an accountant, a district resident who is an attorney, and Ann Major [director of federal programs]. Ann will chair the committee. Bob and Pamela will be nonvoting advisors to the committee."

The room fell silent. After about 30 seconds, one of the principals asked, "How can you appoint a committee without any of the principals being involved? We're the ones most affected by outcome."

Dr. Quillen answered. "If we want an objective analysis, we can't have people who already have their minds made up serving on the committee. No doubt, principals will be asked to meet with the committee to share their views. Every person on this committee is sufficiently detached from the issue to ensure that he or she will be objective."

Immediately after the meeting, Dr. Davis spoke with Dr. Quillen in his office. She expressed disappointment with his decision. She was convinced that because of their numbers, the principals would influence the committee members and persuade them to support their position.

"I'm beginning to think that I should not have raised this issue. There are two things that really bother me," she told the superintendent. "First, and most importantly, I believe my legitimate authority has been undermined. This clearly is a fiscal matter and I should have been the one to make a decision. Second, by creating the committee, you are reducing an important management issue to a political disagreement. If we retain these funds, we will eventually have a fiscal or legal problem. And then, Bob and the principals will be pointing a finger at us suggesting that we should have prevented it."

Dr. Quillen recognized that Dr. Davis was upset, so he decided not to take issue with her comments. He simply asked her to be patient and to delay judgment until the committee had concluded its assignment.

Bob Andravet also visited the superintendent after the meeting to express displeasure with the decision to appoint the committee. He feared that Dr. Davis would influence the committee by scaring the members with possible legal problems and by pointing out that two members already supported her view.

The Challenge

Place yourself in the superintendent's position. Knowing that most of your administrative staff members oppose your decision to appoint an ad hoc committee, what would you do?

Suggested Activities_____

1. Discuss the three different ways in which the problem in the case has been framed (an organizational problem, a management problem, and a political problem). Try to identify factors that contribute to each perspective.

2. Critique each of the three perspectives and determine which perspective is most accurate.

3. Discuss the advantages and disadvantages of centralizing control in a school district that spans an entire county.

4. Complete the worksheet for Case 6.

Suggested Readings_____

Brost, P. (2000). Shared decision making for better schools. *Principal Leadership (Middle School Ed.), 1*(3), 58–63.

Brunner, C. C. (1997). Exercising power. *School Administrator, 54*(6), 6–9.

Conway, J. (1984). The myth, mystery and mastery of participative decision making in education. *Educational Administration Quarterly, 20*(3), 11–40.

Cunningham, W., & Gresso, D. (1993). *Cultural leadership: The culture of excellence in education.* Boston: Allyn and Bacon (see Chapter 9).

Estler, S. (1988). Decision making. In N. Boyan (Ed.), *Handbook of research on educational administration* (pp. 305–320). New York: Longman.

Feld, M. (1988). The bureaucracy, the superintendent, and change. *Education and Urban Society, 47*(8), 417–444.

Grier, T. B. (2000). Preventing project teams from developing committee-itis. *NASSP Bulletin, 84*(616), 97–100.

Ives, R. (1993). Shared decision making improves staff morale and efficiency. *NASSP Bulletin, 77*(550), 107–109.

Jackson, J. L. (2001). Politically competent decision making. *Principal Leadership (High School Ed.), 2*(4), 25–28.

Kessler, R. (1992). Shared decision making works! *Educational Leadership, 50*(1), 36–38.

Lakowski, G. (1987). Values and decision making in educational administration. *Educational Administration Quarterly, 23*(4), 70-82.

Meadows, B. (1990). The rewards and risks of shared leadership. *Phi Delta Kappan, 71*(7), 545–548.

Meadows, B. J., & Saltzman, M. (2002). Shared decision making: An uneasy collaboration. *Principal, 81*(4), 41–48.

Negroni, P. J. (1999). The right badge of courage. *School Administrator, 56*(2), 14–16.

Rieger, B. J. (1995). Boundary realignment in the eye of the storm. *School Administrator, 52*(2), 24–26.

Tarter, C. J., & Hoy, W. K. (1998). Toward a contingency theory of decision making. *Journal of Educational Administration, 36*(3–4), 212–228.

Wertz, D. C. (2002). The resilient superintendent. *American School Board Journal, 189*(7), 21–25.

References _____

Anderson, G. L. (1998). Toward authentic participation: Deconstructing the discourses of participatory reforms in education. *American Educational Research Journal, 35*(4), 571–603.

Crowson, R. L. (1989). Managerial ethics in educational administration: The rational choice approach. *Urban Education, 23*(4), 412–435.

Drucker, P. (1974). *Management: Tasks, responsibilities, practices*. New York: Harper and Row.

Estler, S. (1988). Decision making. In N. Boyan (Ed.), *Handbook of research on educational administration* (pp. 305–320). New York: Longman.

Kowalski, T. J. (1999). *The school superintendent: Theory, practice, and cases*. Upper Saddle River, NJ: Merrill, Prentice Hall.

Kowalski, T. J. (2003). *Contemporary school administration: An introduction* (2nd ed.). Boston: Allyn and Bacon.

Tarter, C. J., & Hoy, W. K. (1998). Toward a contingency theory of decision making. *Journal of Educational Administration, 36*(3–4), 212–228.

Walker, K. D. (1994). Notions of "ethical" among senior educational leaders. *Alberta Journal of Educational Research, 40*(1), 21–34.

A Principal Clashes
with the Culture

Background Information

Evidence gathered from effective schools indicates that principals are key figures in these institutions. Their precise role in producing positive outcomes, however, has often been misconstrued or exaggerated. Contrary to popular belief, the most effective principals are neither saviors nor dictators. Rather, they are individuals possessing a leadership style centered on collaboration, facilitation, and professionalism (Foster, Loving, & Shumate, 2000). Reviewing research spanning 15 years, Hallinger and Heck (1998) concluded that principals influence school effectiveness and student achievement in measurable but indirect ways. Their influence is often discernible in areas such as visions and goals.

Principal role expectations are not static, largely because communities and schools are not identical. Even in a given school, the parameters of ideal roles become altered over time. A recent Ohio study, for example, found that certain elements of educator perceptions of highly effective principals had not changed since the 1980s; these elements included being supportive, fair, friendly, considerate, and organized. Two other characteristics, however, had become much more important over that period—being a strong disciplinarian and being visible in the school (Quigney, 2000). Such findings reveal how social and institutional conditions influence perceptions of effectiveness.

When the school reform agenda began focusing on school restructuring circa 1990, many scholars began questioning traditional definitions of outstanding principals. Michael Fullan (2002), for instance, noted that being an instructional leader was laudable but insufficient in contemporary contexts. He argued that principals must be change agents capable of leading others in collective efforts to rebuild teaching and learning cultures. Leadership style reflects deeply held personal or organizational values (Goldman, 1998). As an example, a principal who believes that most teachers are lazy and uninformed is apt to be autocratic. The nexus between leadership style and values helps explain why many principals fail in their efforts to change schools. When a principal's values are incongruous with the underlying values of a school's culture, those who embrace the culture reject the principal's leadership style and resist his or her ideas (Kowalski, 2003). And the stronger the culture (i.e., the more individuals and groups embrace the same values) the stronger the resistance.

This case is about an experienced urban elementary school principal who has a reputation as an effective leader. Wanting new challenges, he volunteers to transfer to a troubled school. Once there, he enacts a number of new rules concerning discipline and student retention in grade. The rules are predicated on values inconsistent with the prevailing school culture. As resistance intensifies, some teachers lead an effort to have him removed from office. As you analyze this case, pay particular attention to how the principal attempted to implement change as well as his specific initiatives.

Key Areas for Reflection

1. Principal as change agent
2. Values and beliefs as a determinant of leadership style
3. Social and political dimensions of schools
4. School culture and its effect on change initiatives
5. Resistance to change

The Case

Oliver Wendell Holmes Elementary School is the third-oldest facility in this California city. Located in a neighborhood that has deteriorated substantially in the past three decades, the drab brick building and its rectangular shape exemplify the unimaginative nature of school facility design in the 1940s. The sidewalks around the school are cracked and soiled with endless works of graffiti, written in English and Spanish and displaying different bright colors. The playground is strewn with weeds and litter, and the broken swings and teeter-totters suggest that school officials no longer attempt to keep the area functional.

John Lattimore has been the school's principal for the last 3 years. A veteran administrator, he previously served in the same capacity at three of the district's other elementary schools. He has been an educator for 31 years and a principal for 22 of them. When the position at Holmes became vacant, John was the district's only sitting principal who applied. Administrators who knew John were baffled by his decision. Why would an experienced principal leave one of the district's best schools to go to arguably the district's worst school? Why would he leave a school where he was admired and respected to go to a school that has had six principals in the last 15 years?

Central office administrators conducting the principal search also were stunned when they received Mr. Lattimore's application. During an interview with the superintendent and assistant superintendent for elementary education, John gave the following brief and direct answer regarding his interest in becoming the principal of Holmes Elementary School: "I'm ready for a new challenge. I think I can make a difference at Holmes."

Initially, the superintendent, Dr. Ernest Gray, was not supportive of transferring Mr. Lattimore. He was highly successful as principal in his current assignment, and the superintendent did not like tampering with good situations. But after reviewing the applicant pool with the assistant superintendent, he realized that there were only two choices—approve Mr. Lattimore's request or employ another inexperienced principal for Holmes. He chose the former.

The three years at Holmes Elementary School passed quickly for John. During the first year, he adjusted to his new position. He met with parents, got acquainted with students, and tried to develop a positive working relationship with the school's staff. The second year was marked by substantial changes in rules and regulations. In particular, John revamped the school's discipline program, one that had relied heavily on corporal punishment and suspensions, and altered the criteria for retaining students in first grade. (Holmes had the highest percentage retention rate of any school in the district.) Initially, Mr. Lattimore sought teacher support for his changes, but the faculty resisted. Most were convinced that his ideas would only worsen conditions at the school. Concluding that the teachers would not be flexible on these matters, he implemented the new rules without their support.

The new discipline and student retention rules took effect in Mr. Lattimore's third year at Holmes. By that time, many of the school's faculty already had lost confidence in his ability to provide appropriate discipline. But after he imposed his new rules, the teachers now labeled him a dictator. One teacher summarized her feelings thusly, "Sure, he is friendly and cares about the students, but he is misguided. In the end, his soft approach to discipline does more damage than good. I argued with him about these matters, but as we found out, our opinions don't matter. We were hopeful when he came to Holmes. At last we had an experienced and supposedly successful principal. But he has been a disaster."

Dissatisfaction with Mr. Lattimore intensified as the new rules were used to adjudicate discipline problems. The teachers began criticizing the principal openly and they made a concerted effort to win support from parents. In early November, 70 percent of the teachers and 42 parents signed a petition demanding that the school board remove Mr. Lattimore from his position. The petition and a cover letter were sent to the assistant superintendent for elementary education, Dr. Roshanda Danton. The letter read as follows:

Dear Dr. Danton:
    Over the past two and one-half years, the teachers at Oliver Wendell Holmes Elementary School have observed the leadership style of Mr. John Lattimore. Although he is a friendly, caring, and intelligent

person, his approach to student discipline and student retention simply will not work at this school. Most of the children who attend Holmes are from families living below the poverty level. Many receive little or no direction with regard to their personal behavior outside of school. Even the parents and guardians of the students recognize that the school must be a major source of discipline. Since becoming our principal, Mr. Lattimore has weakened discipline rules and regulations, prohibited the use of corporal punishment, discouraged student suspensions, and encouraged social promotions.

We share Mr. Lattimore's conviction that many of our students are being reared in less than stable families, but we reject his solutions. The school cannot be parent, psychologist, social worker, and friend to every student. Allowing disruptive and emotionally unstable children to remain in a classroom deprives other students of their learning opportunities.

Mr. Lattimore may argue that he gave us an opportunity to participate in changes. On the surface, that may appear to be true. In truth, he ignored our input and did what he wanted to do. He has been intolerant of different beliefs, as evidenced by the fact that he has changed some very important rules without faculty support.

It is with heavy hearts that we tell you that we have no confidence in Mr. John Lattimore to be principal of Oliver Wendell Holmes Elementary School. Perhaps his talents can be utilized more productively in another assignment. He is a good person who means well. He cannot, however, effectively lead this school. We ask that he be removed as principal as soon as possible.

Respectfully,

(signed by 70 percent of the teachers and 42 parents)

cc: Dr. Gray, superintendent

School Board members

Ms. Hutchins, president of the local teachers' union

A copy of the letter was not sent to the principal; he learned about it when Dr. Danton informed him that she had received it. His initial response was disbelief. He immediately drove to her office so he could see the letter and petition. As he read the signatures, his disbelief turned to anger. Some of signers had been warm and friendly to his face; until now, he considered them to be supporters.

The school district has 87 elementary schools, most in inner-city neighborhoods. Complaints about principals were not uncommon, but this type of petition was rare. Dr. Danton asked John to meet with her the next day to discuss the matter. She wanted him to collect his thoughts and calm down before the issue was pursued. John returned to school but remained in his office with the door closed. He waited until all the teachers had left for the day before going home.

The next morning, Mr. Lattimore left to see Dr. Danton as soon as the buses unloaded and school started. The two administrators had been friends and colleagues for many years. They were fellow principals for nearly a decade, and when Dr. Danton applied to be assistant superintendent for elementary education, John wrote a letter of support for her. Their personal relationship, however, did not reduce the tension in the room. John was still angry and said that the teachers had acted unethically, first by involving parents and then by taking this action without informing him.

"You mean you had no idea that the teachers were this dissatisfied and that they were involving parents?" Dr. Danton asked.

"No," John answered. "I tried to do things correctly. I could have imposed change immediately after arriving at the school three years ago. The school was a mess. But I elected to give the faculty a chance to be part of the change process. I tried to get them to look at these issues. They refused to be open-minded. All they did was resist. No change was acceptable to them. The fact of the matter is that a small group of teachers has been running this school for a long time. No principal is going to succeed as long as that group keeps proving that it is stronger and more powerful than the administration. Quite frankly, I got to the point where I asked myself, Who is more important: the students or the teachers? My answer was the students. Did I know that some of the teachers disagreed with what I was doing? Yes, I knew that. But I never thought they would stoop to involving parents and drafting this petition."

"John, did you allow them to have input before you made changes?" Dr. Danton inquired.

"The changes were discussed in faculty meetings. We never voted on them, but I explained the changes and my reasons for them. Some teachers voiced opposition but most remained silent. I told teachers they could see me privately if they felt uncomfortable discussing the issue in faculty meetings. Only two teachers did so and they both supported my ideas. Listen, I've been around these children for a long time—and so have you. Their lives are filled with grief and disappointments. Why should school be another unpleasant experience? Maybe, just maybe, by showing some love and compassion we could turn a few lives around. Maybe we could convince a few children that someone cares. Isn't that important? What do we accomplish when we suspend and fail children? We're punishing the parent, not the child. How will we ever teach these children to be responsible for their own behavior if we constantly rely on negative reinforcements?"

"What about social promotions? Are you really telling teachers not to fail students at any grade level?" asked the assistant superintendent.

"Failing children who are already at risk simply does not work. They prefer to say that I favor social promotions. I prefer to say that I condemn failing children when it just makes it more likely they will never succeed as students; they will never graduate from high school."

Dr. Danton looked at him and asked, "John, would you consider another assignment at this time? I can arrange for you to be in the central office. Dr. Gray and I discussed this matter last night. He already has gotten calls from two board members about the petition. We are willing to assign you as assistant director of pupil personnel services immediately. This spring, Sheila Macey is retiring and you would then move up to become the director. You would get a salary increase and we would have a solution to this conflict. Dr. Gray has said he would approve if you agree to accept the reassignment. I want to be clear, however, that we are not trying to remove you from the school. If you decide to stay at Holmes, we will work with you to try to resolve these problems. What do you think?"

"Roshanda, you should already know my answer. I've had other opportunities to work in the central office. I like being around students. No, I'm sorry. I'm not going to cut and run. I'm right and if you give me time, I think I can turn the parents and teachers around."

"But John, I don't know if we have time. Dr. Gray doesn't want more political problems. One of the parents who signed the petition has a brother-in-law on the school board and he is an influential minister in Holmes area. And if the union jumps into this matter, we could really have trouble. Dr. Gray doesn't want to go to war on this issue."

John got up from his chair and nodded that he understood. He shook Dr. Danton's hand and left her office. As soon as he departed, Dr. Danton was disappointed because she anticipated he was not going to accept her offer to change positions. In addition, Mr. Lattimore was a member of a union also, the district's principals' union. John was highly respected, and if he convinced other principals to support him, the fire could become even more intense. She began to think that she was in a no-win situation. If John didn't leave the school, Dr. Gray would probably be upset with her for not brokering a compromise. If John stayed and fought, she could be blamed by the principals' union for trying to remove him.

The Challenge

Evaluate the conflict in this case. How would you propose that the situation be resolved?

Suggested Activities _____

1. Evaluate the principal's approach to pursuing change and identify strengths and weaknesses.

2. Explain the relationships between teacher resistance and the school's culture.

3. The conflict in the case can be framed as a political problem or an ethical problem. Describe the differences between these two frames.

4. Evaluate the changes the principals made regarding student discipline and retention in grade.

5. Complete the worksheet for Case 7.

Suggested Readings

Copland, M. A. (2001). The myth of the superprincipal. *Phi Delta Kappan, 82*(7), 528–533.

Emmons, C. L., Hagopian, G., & Efimba, M. O. (1998). A school transformed: The case of Norman S. Weir. *Journal of Education for Students Placed at Risk, 3*(1), 39–51.

Firestone, W. A., & Louis, K. S. (1999). Schools as cultures. In J. Murphy & K. S. Louis (Eds.), *Handbook of research on educational administration* (2nd ed., pp. 251–276). San Francisco: Jossey-Bass.

Fullan, M. (2002). The change leader. *Educational Leadership, 59*(8), 16–20.

Hartzell, G., & Petrie, T. (1992). The principal and discipline: Working with school structures, teachers, and students. *The Clearing House, 65*(6), 376–380.

Houston, W. R. (1998). Innovators as catalysts for restructuring schools. *Educational Forum, 62*(3), 204–210.

Hoy, W., Tarter, C., & Witkoskie, L. (1992). Faculty trust in colleagues: Linking the principal with school effectiveness. *Journal of Research and Development in Education, 26*(1), 38–45.

Johnson, P. E., Holder, C., Carrick, C., & Sanford, N. (1998). A model for restructuring governance: Developing a culture of respect and teamwork. *ERS Spectrum, 16*(2), 28–36.

Johnston, G., & Venable, B. (1986). A study of teacher loyalty to the principal: Rule administration and hierarchical influence of the principal. *Educational Administration Quarterly, 22*(4), 4–27.

Marriott, D. (2001). Managing school culture. *Principal, 81*(1), 75–77.

Menacker, J. (1988). Legislating school discipline: The application of a systemwide discipline code for schools in a large urban district. *Urban Education, 23*(1), 12–23.

Menacker, J., Weldon, W., & Hurwitz, E. (1989). School order and safety as community issues. *Phi Delta Kappan, 71*(1), 39–40, 55–56.

Prestine, N. (1993). Shared decision making in restructuring essential schools: The role of the principal. *Planning and Changing, 22*(3–4), 160–177.

Rosen, M. (1993). Sharing power: A blueprint for collaboration. *Principal, 72*(3), 37–39.

Sikes, P. (1992). Imposed change and the experienced teacher. In M. Fullan & A. Hargreaves (Eds.), *Teacher development and educational change* (pp. 36–55). Bristol, PA: Falmer.

Slavin, R., & Madden, N. (1989). What works for students at risk: A research synthesis. *Educational Leadership, 46*(5), 4–13.

Smylie, M. (1992). Teacher participation in school decision making: Assessing willingness to participate. *Educational Evaluation and Policy Analysis, 14*(1), 53–67.

Thomas, C., & Fitzhugh-Walker, P. (1998). The role of the urban principal in school restructuring. *International Journal of Leadership in Education, 1*(3), 297–306.

Thomas, W. (1988). To solve "the discipline problem," mix clear rules with consistent consequences. *American School Board Journal, 175*(6), 30–31.

Wager, B. (1993). No more suspension: Creating a shared ethical culture. *Educational Leadership, 50*(4), 34–37.

Wilmore, E., & Thomas, C. (2001). The new century: Is it too late for transformational leadership? *Educational Horizons, 79*(3), 115–123.

References

Foster, E. S., Loving, C. C., & Shumate, A. (2000). Effective principals, effective professional development schools. *Teaching and Change, 8*(1), 76–97.

Fullan, M. (2002). The change leader. *Educational Leadership, 59*(8), 16–20.

Goldman, E. (1998). The significance of leadership style. *Educational Leadership, 55*(7), 20–22.

Hallinger, P., & Heck, R. H. (1998). Exploring the principal's contribution to school effectiveness: 1980–1995. *School Effectiveness and School Improvement, 9*(2), 157–191.

Quigney, T. A. (2000). Effective school administration in an age of educational reform. *Mid-Western Educational Researcher, 13*(4), 21–27.

How about School-Based Management?

Background Information

Toward the end of the twentieth century, education reformers were recognizing that much of the change pursued after 1983 had produced only slight improvements. In particular, policymakers were abandoning two assumptions: relying on top-down generic strategies imposed through state reform programs and making students do more of what they were already doing could produce dramatic improvements (Kowalski, 2003). Nearly two decades of attempted reforms had led education reformers to believe that visioning and planning should be conducted at the school level so that the real needs of students would be properly addressed. In addition, the organizational climate of schools, including culture, became a primary reform target. These transitions explain why state deregulation, district decentralization, and school restructuring have become dominant change strategies.

The concept of school-based management (SBM) has become the most popular approach to school district decentralization. Although the concept has multiple iterations, it basically entails creating school councils as a means of increasing community and teacher involvement in shared decision making. Trust among administrators, teachers, and parents becomes essential if the three groups are to work collectively to improve the school (Henkin & Dee, 2001). Not all administrators and teachers, however, have been enthusiastic about SBM. Their apprehensions range from philosophical objections, such as moving away from uniform programming in a school district, to personal insecurity, such as fearing a loss of authority and power. Almost every school superintendent who pursues SBM can expect to encounter opponents who will do everything possible to derail change (Brown, 1995).

Arguments against school-based management have been strengthened by selected studies that indicate the concept has not lived up to its potential. As examples, Reitzug and Capper (1996) concluded that empirical data on SBM indicate that the strategy has not produced radical changes in schools, and based on their qualitative study of several elementary schools, Seitsinger and Zera (2002) concluded that involving parents in governance (a core function of SBM) was not an effective reform strategy.

This case involves a superintendent who wants to decentralize governance in the school district. Influential staff members resist. The objective, institutionalizing SBM, and the process used to pursue it generate conflict. As you read this case, try to identify elements of organizational life that either encourage or discourage change. Try to understand why some of the administrators resist even the prospect of studying the need for change or the feasibility of proposed changes.

Key Areas for Reflection

1. School-based management
2. Organizational change
3. Resistance to change
4. The role of organizational climate in change
5. Change processes

The Case

Lora Mipps has been secretary to the superintendent of the Lewis Public Schools for 31 years. In that period, she has outlasted eight superintendents, all of whom brought unique personalities and leadership styles to the school district. She thought about that fact as she listened to loud conversation taking place behind the closed door of the superintendent's office. As the voices became louder, she started to wonder if yet another superintendent would depart during her tenure.

Dr. George Pisak arrived in Lewis, a quiet community of 18,000 located in the "sunbelt," just 15 months ago. When he became superintendent of the local public schools, he was seeking new challenges and professional growth opportunities. Before this job, he was the assistant superintendent for instruction in a large urban school system. George recognized that being a superintendent meant less job security, but now that his two children had finished college, he and his wife, Estelle, decided they were willing to assume the risk.

Dr. Pisak was well aware of the history of leadership instability in the Lewis Public Schools before he accepted his position. The longest tenure of a superintendent in recent times was five years; in the past six years, three different individuals occupied this post. In part, the instability was linked to turnover on the school board—no incumbent has been reelected in the past three elections. Typically, there have been three or more candidates for each seat on the school board.

When George was contacted by a former professor, Ken Hollman, about the Lewis superintendency, he said he was not interested. He wanted to be a superin-

tendent, but not if it meant assuming one of the state's most precarious superinten-
dencies. Dr. Hollman explained that he had been retained by the Lewis school
board as a consultant and he encouraged George to think about the job. A week
later, he called George a second time and asked him to have lunch with him so that
they could discuss the Lewis position in greater detail.

During their luncheon, Dr. Hollman outlined five reasons why George should
pursue the Lewis suprintendency:

1. The school district desperately needs a creative and visionary leader. Three of
    the four most recent superintendents had been promoted from within the dis-
    trict, and each attempted to defend the status quo rather than pursue change.
2. The current board members recognize that they desperately need leadership
    stability if meaningful change is to occur.
3. The board members recognize that because of the district's history with
    superintendents, they must offer a high salary and attractive fringe benefits
    to find a person with the qualifications they are seeking.
4. During the past 12 years, school board elections have reflected economic and
    political divisions in the community. During that period, the board was
    always divided into two- or three-member factions—one representing the
    more affluent white-collar and basically Republican population and one rep-
    resenting the more blue-collar and basically Democratic population. Power
    between the two factions was constantly shifting because neither faction was
    able to gain more than three seats on the board. In last year's election, how-
    ever, the Republican-leaning faction captured both open seats; that group
    now holds four of the five board positions and enjoys political support from
    the mayor and the Lewis Chamber of Commerce.
5. The current board members are willing to let the new superintendent have
    considerable discretion with regard to administrative staffing.

George weighed each of points and then told Dr. Hollman that he remained
concerned about possible negatives. In particular, he mentioned that friends familiar with Lewis had warned him that most of that district's principals were
entrenched in local politics. Moreover, their resistance to change had been reinforced by the revolving door on the superintendent's office.

Dr. Hollman knew George quite well having served as his advisor and disser-
tation director. Thus, he expected his former student to be cautious. If he was going
to persuade George to apply for the Lewis position, he had to counteract his negative thoughts. Over the next two hours, he convinced George that the next Lewis
superintendent would have the power to get rid of obstructionists on the administrative team. George finally agreed to at least submit his application.

Dr. Hollman described Dr. Pisak to the Lewis school board members as a
"perfect candidate." Nothing that occurred during the first interview with the
board members altered the image that the consultant had shaped. The board members were impressed and invited George to return for a second interview.

The initial interview also had a positive effect on George. The board members seemed very astute and committed to improving the school district. They even suggested that they would be willing to negotiate a four- or five-year employment contract if they found the right individual.

Three days after the second interview, the board president called George and offered him the position. Before answering, George asked if the board was united in its decision to hire him. He was told that one member would probably not vote to approve his or any other candidate's appointment; this board member who was not aligned politically with the others had opposed the dismissal of the current superintendent. George was pleased that the board president was candid on this matter. George then asked him about salary, fringe benefits, and the length of the employment contract. The board member said all three factors were negotiable. George indicated he would return the telephone call later that day.

When George later called the board president, he said he would accept the position with an annual salary of $122,000, an initial four-year contract with a provision for annual renewals, and an automobile in addition to the fringe benefits provided to other administrators. Although the salary was $27,000 higher than the previous superintendent's compensation, the board president never hesitated. He told George, "Welcome to Lewis. We have a deal."

As expected, one board member, Dan Foster, voted against the motion to employ Dr. Pisak. In an interview with the local newspaper reporter following the board meeting, Mr. Foster called the new superintendent's salary and contract "outrageous." He said, "We have families in Lewis who cut every corner just to pay property taxes. Yet, we pay a school superintendent well over $100,000. I don't think voters in this district will approve of this decision. As you know, I think we should have kept our current superintendent. He knows the community and he had the support of most of the principals. He would have stayed in the job for a lot less money. I think that Mr. Pisak is probably a fine person, and I'll do everything I can to work with him. But I hope he realizes that the current majority on the board may hear from the voters in the next election."

After Dr. Pisak became superintendent, he was invited to speak to local service clubs and civic groups. He met many of the community leaders in the first few months and he quickly realized that Lewis was an economically segregated community. In addition, the high school boundaries clearly separated the two subgroups. The district's northern half was almost entirely residential, consisting of newer subdivisions. The southern portion included most of the city's businesses and all of the industry. The neighborhoods in the south consisted of older and much less expensive homes, trailers, and apartments. School board members were elected at-large and all four of those who voted to hire Dr. Pisak resided in the northern half of the district.

Lewis North High School was constructed 12 years ago and enrolls about 1,200 students. Approximately two-thirds of its graduates attend college. Lewis South High School, housed in a much older building, was originally the district's only high school. Located near the city's business district, it serves about 1,300 students. Only about 20 percent of the Lewis South graduates enter college. The two high schools always have been bitter rivals.

Dr. Pisak thought that the economic division in the community would be a barrier to meaningful reform because residents in the southern portion of the district probably viewed him and the four board members who supported him as political adversaries. This perspective was a primary reason why he elected not to pursue districtwide changes. Instead, he promoted school-based management.

Superintendent Pisak first shared his intention to move toward decentralization with the board members. He met with them individually, explained school-based management, and asked them to react. All reactions were positive. Next, he met with the administrators and cited three reasons for his decision to investigate school-based management:

1. Most Lewis citizens identified with and were loyal to individual schools.
2. Centralized reforms, even if defensible from a professional perspective, would probably experience considerable political resistance due to the community's bifurcation.
3. Faculty, students, and parents would be more likely to support change if they were involved in vision and planning activities.

Reactions to his proposal were mixed. Basically, the comments could be separated into three groups: those who supported the proposal, those who opposed the proposal, and those who were neutral. Not all administrators spoke, but Dr. Pisak sensed that there was considerable division among the administrators. Principals, however, seemed to be more opposed than others.

Despite the obvious differences of opinion among administrators, Dr. Pisak felt confident because all five board members appeared to be supportive. In the weeks following the March meeting, he requested and received board approval to employ two school-based management consultants. He sent administrative staff copies of journal articles favorable to school-based management and provided a list of schools that he encouraged the administrators to visit.

At the May staff meeting, Dr. Pisak engaged the administrators in another conversation about school-based management. He discovered that many of them had not read the articles he provided, and only four principals had visited schools using the concept—and all four were initially supportive. The principals who previously voiced opposition to school-based management did so again. Dr. Pisak told them, "I appreciate your candor but I still plan to pursue school-based management. My intention is to recommend to the school board that we begin an implementation study. This study will be conducted by the two consultants and they will work in conjunction with an advisory committee appointed by me. After they conclude their work, I will make a final decision on school-based management."

Many of the administrators, including all of the secondary school principals, spoke against conducting the study. Dr. Pisak, however, was not dissuaded. He told them that he would present the recommendation to commence the study at the next board meeting.

Keeping his word, the superintendent prepared the following recommendation that he sent to board members and administrators several days prior to the board meeting:

Topic: Feasibility Study for the Implementation of School-Based Management

Superintendent Recommendation: A special committee, consisting of three administrators, three teachers, and three district residents, should be formed to study the feasibility of implementing school-based management. The committee shall work with Dr. Jane Jones and Dr. Milton Brown, the consultants who have been retained by the school district. The committee shall present a report to the superintendent and school board within 10 months.

Background Information: I have concluded that school-based management offers the greatest promise for achieving school improvement in this district. The approach permits schools to pursue their own reform agendas, and to do so with the active participation of taxpayers, teachers, and students. The feasibility study will better prepare you to make a final decision on this critical matter. The committee will be looking at potential policy changes, structural changes, and resources. I want to stress two points. First, you should know that a significant portion of the administrative staff—maybe as many as 60 percent of them—do not support my recommendation. Second, I want to stress that you will be voting to approve the study and not to implement the concept. If the study produces a recommendation to implement school-based management, that matter would require a separate vote.

After having received a copy of the recommendation, the principal at Lewis South High School telephoned the other district principals and invited them to attend a meeting at his house. All but two of them attended. A petition was circulated at the meeting asking the superintendent to withdraw his recommendation before the board meeting. It read as follows:

Dr. Pisak,

We respectfully request that you reconsider your recommendation regarding a feasibility study for implementing school-based management. We believe that school-based management could seriously diminish administrative control in our schools and there is little evidence that this strategy has resulted in real improvements in teaching and learning. In addition, we believe that the money and human resources required for this study should be used for real needs. Nearly all of the principals oppose the study: therefore, we request that you withdraw your recommendation and consider other alternative approaches to school improvement in this district.

The petition was signed by 11 of the district's 14 principals.

After receiving the petition, Dr. Pisak asked the two assistant superintendents to join him in his office. He showed them the letter and asked if they knew anything about it. They said that the letter had been circulated at a meeting organized by the principal at South High School. Dr. Pisak immediately called the principal and asked if he had circulated the petition. The principal said that he had, but pointed out that he was encouraged to do so by at least six other principals. Dr. Pisak then told the principal he wanted to see him in his office at 5:00 that afternoon. The principal asked if other principals could come with him; the superintendent said no.

Superintendent Pisak knew that the Lewis South High School principal had been a staunch supporter of the previous superintendent and a close friend of board member Foster. When he arrived at the superintendent's office, he took the offensive. He said that the superintendent was being dictatorial and noted that prohibiting other principals from attending their meeting was not in the best spirit of team management. The encounter between the two men deteriorated from that point. Their voices became progressively louder and more hostile. Sitting outside the closed door to the superintendent's office, Mrs. Mipps, the secretary, thought, "Here we go again." Would yet another superintendent be leaving after only a year or two?

The Challenge

Critique the superintendent's decision to move forward with studying the implementation of school-based management.

Suggested Activities

1. Identify factors that influenced Dr. Pisak to accept the superintendency in Lewis.

2. Discuss contextual variables that are relevant to this case. Determine if these variables are positives or negatives with respect to school improvement.

3. Discuss Dr. Pisak's approach to implementing change. Identify the positive and negative aspects of his behavior.

4. Evaluate Dr. Pisak's decision to pursue school-based management after having been in the school district for only about six months.

5. Discuss why economic and political divisions in the school district have contributed to leadership instability.

Suggested Readings

Brandt, R. S. (2000). A boost for school-based management. *Principal, 80*(2), 50–51.
Brubaker, D. L., & Coble, L. D. (1995). The derailed superintendent. *Executive Educator, 17*(10), 34–36.

Caldwell, S. (1988). School-based improvement: Are we ready? *Educational Leadership, 46*(2), 50–53.

Caldwell, S., & Wood, F. (1992). Breaking ground in restructuring. *Educational Leadership 50*(1), 41, 44.

Cawalti, G. (1989). The elements of school-based management. *Educational Leadership, 46*(8), 46.

David, J. (1989). Synthesis of research on school-based management. *Educational Leadership, 46*(8), 45–53.

Davis, S. H. (1998). Why do principals get fired? *Principal, 28*(2), 34–39.

Guthrie, J. (1986). School based management: The next needed education reform. *Phi Delta Kappan, 68*(4), 305–309.

Hallinger, P., et al. (1992). Restructuring schools: Principals' perceptions of fundamental educational reform. *Educational Administration Quarterly, 28*(3), 330–349.

Haynes, E. A., & Licata, J. W. (1995). Creative insubordination of school principals and the legitimacy of the justifiable. *Journal of Educational Administration, 33*(4), 21–35.

Herman, J., & Herman, J. (1992). Educational administration: School-based management. *The Clearing House, 65*(5), 261–263.

Holloway, J. H. (2000). The promise and pitfalls of site-based management. Educational Leadership, *57*(7), 81–82.

Sackney, L. E., & Dibski, D. J. (1994). School-based management: A critical perspective. *Educational Management and Administration, 22*(2), 104–112.

Sorenson, L. D., & Evans, R. D. (2001). Superintendent use of site-based councils: Role ambiguity and accountability. *Planning & Changing, 32*(3/4), 184–198.

Trachtman, R., & Fauerbach, E. (2001). The limits of within-school governance reform. *Educational Horizons, 79*(3), 110–114.

References

Brown, D. J. (1995). The sabotage of school-based management. *School Administrator, 52*(3), 8–12, 14.

Henkin, A. B., & Dee, J. R. (2001). The power of trust: Teams and collective action in self-managed schools. *Journal of School Leadership, 11*(1), 48–62.

Kowalski, T. J. (2003). *Contemporary school administration: An introduction* (2nd ed.). Boston: Allyn and Bacon.

Reitzug, U. C., & Capper, C. A. (1996). Deconstructing site-based management: Possibilities for emancipation and alternative means of control. *International Journal of Educational Reform, 5*(1), 56–59.

Seitsinger, R. M., & Zera, D. A. (2002). The demise of parent involvement in school governance. *Journal of School Leadership, 12*(4), 340–367.

Getting Back to Basics

Background Information

The term, *teacher empowerment,* is interpreted in several different ways. Definitions typically are anchored in the concept of professionalism; that is, they focus on a professional orientation to teaching (Ponticell, Olson, & Charlier, 1995). Some reformers believe that meaningful school improvement requires an intricate combination of state deregulation, district decentralization, and teacher empowerment. Such strategies have become more popular as policymakers recognize the needs of students are not constant across local districts, schools, or even classrooms. Empowerment, however, adds risk and responsibility to teaching because teachers become accountable for what they elect to do in their classrooms.

Some apprehensions about deregulation and decentralization are related to tensions between liberty and equality—two values that historically have guided public policy in the United States (King, Swanson, & Sweetland, 2003). For example, decentralization often increases liberty by allowing those associated with an individual school to have greater autonomy. Such independence, however, can lead to unequal educational opportunities in a single school district and among districts in a state. In addition, decentralization can lead to interschool competition and political strife among school employees that eventually involves the broader community (Jackson, 1999). For this reason, total empowerment—granting teachers absolute and total control over their practice—is highly improbable. Rather, sociopolitical arrangements that represent compromises between liberty and equality are more likely to determine the boundaries of empowerment.

Administrators who always have worked in traditional schools often are apprehensive about giving teachers free reign to determine what they do in the classroom. Their trepidation is often associated with these beliefs:

- Administrators will be held accountable for teachers who fail to comply with state laws and regulations.
- Administrators will be criticized for not exercising control by parents and students who disagree with the decisions teachers make.

• Teachers who prefer not to take risks or assume added responsibility will blame principals for the changes that are imposed on them (Kowalski, 1995).

Because of the nature of public schools, administrator and teacher decisions are judged in political contexts; even the most prudent professional decision may be rejected if it is incongruous with the beliefs, interests, or needs of the majority or influential individuals who control the majority. Even in a homogeneous community, residents rarely share identical values of beliefs. Thus, any decision is apt to produce criticism or more direct forms of opposition (e.g., defeating incumbent school board members or getting an administrator dismissed). Administrative control is one of these areas. Whereas some taxpayers expect principals to be efficient and demanding managers, others expect them to facilitate and encourage the professional work of teachers. Role expectations help determine leadership style. Principals are often described as either *transactional* or *transformational leaders.* The former style involves an exchange between leader and follower for purposes of achieving personal objectives; it often entails a bargaining process focused on self-interests (Sergiovanni, 2001). The latter style involves attempts to influence behavior by appealing to higher ideals and moral values; the leader and followers share common goals, are guided by ethical and moral principles, and are motivated by higher-order needs (Burns, 1978). In essence, transactional leadership is a political process involving a quid pro quo, and transformational leadership is an ethical/moral process involving commitments to personal and organizational growth (Kowalski, 2003).

Conflict emerges in this case when a principal convinces a first-grade teacher to take a third-grade assignment. Her philosophy about homework, which was not a problem previously, is challenged by a group of parents. The principal is asked to take control but is apprehensive, partly because he is responsible for transferring the teacher to a new grade assignment. As you read this case, consider both the political and ethical issues associated with the conflict.

Key Areas for Reflection

1. Teacher empowerment
2. Principal role conflict
3. Political dimensions of public education
4. Ethical decision making
5. Transactional versus transformational leadership

The Case

Ocean County

Ocean County is large geographical area and has a diverse population. About 20 percent of the families live at or below the poverty line, but about 10 percent have annual incomes in excess of $370,000. Racial minorities constitute about 35 percent of the district's population, and nearly half of these families immigrated to the United States in the past two decades, mostly from Latin America and the Caribbean. Economic segregation in housing is very evident. Most low-income families reside in Rio Del Mar, the county seat; most high-income families live on or near the oceanfront; and most middle-class families reside in one of the more than 80 subdivisions scattered across the county.

School District

The Ocean County School District serves the entire county. Enrollment has doubled since 1975, requiring the construction of 12 new schools in the past decade. About half of the district's schools are in Rio Del Mar.

A seven-member school board, representing various geographic sections of the county, governs the school system. Four of the seven board members are from Rio Del Mar. Board members are elected to four-year terms in nonpartisan elections. With approximately 75,000 students, there are 83 attendance centers that include:

1. Twelve high schools
2. Twenty-eight middle schools
3. Forty -two elementary schools
4. One alternative high school

The central office staff consists of over 100 professionals.

Since 1982, the school system has implemented an in-district, one-way busing plan to improve racial balance. Approximately 25 percent of the minority children who live in Rio Del Mar are bused to district schools located outside the city.

Dr. Elizabeth Eddings has been the district's superintendent for the past two years. Since coming to Ocean County, she has promoted decentralization and teacher empowerment as school reform strategies. The school board and the media have been supportive of her ideas. She has encouraged principals to attend workshops on these topics and she has offered incentives to those who embrace aspects of these strategies.

School

Seminole Elementary School, enrolling just over 800 students in grades kindergarten through 5, is one of the newest attendance centers in the district. Opened just four years ago, it is located about four miles north of Rio Del Mar. Three of the district's most expensive subdivisions are within this school's attendance boundaries. About one-sixth of the students are bused to Seminole from Rio Del Mar.

Seminole has six sections per grade level in kindergarten and first grade, and five sections in each of the remaining grades. Overall, the faculty members at Seminole Elementary School are young and inexperienced. Their average age is only 31 and the average level of teaching experience is just five years.

Principal

Howard Carlsburg has been the principal of Seminole Elementary School since it opened. Prior to receiving this assignment, his professional experience included 2 years as an assistant principal and 11 years as a fifth-grade teacher. As principal, his performance evaluations have been consistently above average and he is viewed by Superintendent Eddings as one of the district's most competent elementary school principals.

Teachers view Mr. Carlsburg as a "hands-on" leader who visits classrooms regularly and talks to teachers almost daily. He dislikes managerial work and delegates much of this responsibility to his assistant principal, Betty Jenson. Her responsibilities span attendance records, the lunch program, bus loading and unloading, student discipline, and facility maintenance.

When Dr. Eddings arrived in Ocean County, Mr. Carlsburg became one of her most vocal supporters. He, too, thought that decentralization and teacher empowerment were effective reform strategies, and volunteered to attend workshops on these topics. He pledged to the superintendent that he would make Seminole the most effective elementary school in the district.

Teacher

Alicia Comstock, age 29, has been a teacher for five years, the last two at Seminole Elementary School. She is an even-tempered, positive person who is liked by other teachers and the principal. People who walk into her classroom generally experience a warm feeling; the walls are covered with the students' work and the bulletin boards are brightly decorated. She is always upbeat and appears to like being around children.

Prior to this year, Alicia had always taught first grade. She enjoyed the assignment, and after five years, she had become a confident instructor. Her performance evaluations, including those in her first year of teaching, were consistently high.

Grade Assignment Change

Mr. Carlsburg's primary plan for improving the school was to employ the absolute best teachers he could find. Under Superintendent Eddings, principals were given considerable freedom to recruit applicants, and none did so more aggressively than Mr. Carlsburg. He visited seven Florida universities in the past year to interview students who were about to graduate. On one of these trips, he met a woman who impressed him more than any candidate he had met previously. However, there was a problem. She would accept only a position teaching first grade and there were no first-grade vacancies at Seminole that year. Mr. Carlsburg needed to employ four new teachers, but the vacancies were at the third- and fifth-grade levels. He told the applicant that he would see if one of the first-grade teachers was willing to move to a different grade level. If so, he would offer her a position.

The next day, Mr. Carlsburg talked to each first-grade teacher individually, and none was willing to transfer. The last person with whom he spoke was Alicia Comstock. She had the least seniority and he considered her the most likely to accept a different grade-level assignment. When she said she was not interested in teaching either third or fifth grade, he began pleading with her. He indicated that he would see that she got the best classroom and any equipment she might want. He also said he would find money for her to attend summer courses related to her new assignment.

"Why do you want me to take a new assignment?" she asked.

"I asked all the other first-grade teachers if they would be willing to take a new assignment, and they all said no," he answered.

"Well, I also said no. I have always taught first grade."

"Alicia, I'm asking you to do this for the school. As principal, I have to look at the big picture. I have a chance to employ a terrific teacher. You have the least seniority teaching first grade. If you move to another grade, I promise you that you can go back to teaching first grade if another assignment becomes vacant. The way we are growing, that could be as soon as next year."

Alicia already felt uncomfortable having said no to the principal twice. She enjoyed teaching at Seminole and did not want to jeopardize her job or her relationship with Mr. Carlsburg. She reluctantly told him she would teach third grade next year. She left their meeting, however, feeling that she was not treated fairly.

Problem

Two months after Mrs. Comstock started teaching third grade, three parents called Mr. Carlsburg to register concerns about her. The first was from a mother who complained that her son was not being given homework.

"My daughter was in third grade last year and she had homework almost every day. My son is in Mrs. Comstock's class and she never gives him homework. I'm very concerned. Do you know about this?" she asked the principal.

Mr. Carlsburg answered her question with a question. "Have you talked to Mrs. Comstock?"

The mother said that she had not because she had not met her. The principal then encouraged her to meet with the teacher and he assured her that he would look into the matter. Over the next week, Mr. Carlsburg did not speak to Mrs. Comstock, hoping that the problem would rectify itself when the mother talked to her. It did not. He received calls from two other parents voicing the same concern. After receiving these calls, he talked to Alicia about the matter.

When told about the three parents who had voiced concerns, she told the principal that she did not think that homework was appropriate for third-grade students.

"My students have a long school day, and we work hard during that time. I don't think that giving them more work to do at home is a good idea at their age."

After talking to Alicia, Mr. Carlsburg met individually with the other third-grade teachers and asked about homework. They all indicated that they assigned homework but the frequency and length of assignments varied. One teacher made assignments twice a week and she estimated that a student would spend about 45 minutes completing each of them. Another made assignments four times per week and she estimated that a student would spend about 20 minutes completing each of them. The remaining three teachers said their homework assignments fell somewhere between these two.

After talking to the other third-grade teachers, the principal met with Alicia again. He suggested that she adopt the practice of assigning homework twice a week and the assignments would require only about 20 to 30 minutes to complete. He said that this action would probably mollify the parents; however, he did not know that.

Again, Alicia found herself in a position where being obedient seemed to be the prudent action. Although she was not convinced that homework was effective for third-grade students, she agreed to follow his advice.

About six weeks later, Mr. Carlsburg again received two telephone calls complaining about Mrs. Comstock. One of the calls came from a parent who had voiced concern previously. Both parents said that they were disappointed with the low expectations she had for students. They also said that she did not impose sufficient structure in her classroom. One the parents put it this way, "My son has never been happier about school. But why shouldn't he be? He's never had a teacher who lets him set the agenda."

Over the next 10 days, the principal received six more complaints about Mrs. Comstock. Several parents threatened to take the matter to the superintendent and school board if something was not done to improve conditions in her classroom. Mr. Carlsburg told them he was dealing with the matter. He suspected that someone was orchestrating these telephone calls but he realized that the issue could get out of hand. Over the next week, he made three unannounced visits to Mrs. Comstock's classroom. Each time, he stayed in the room at least 30 minutes. He told her he was making the visits as part of her annual performance evaluation; he did not tell her about the most recent phone calls from parents. His observation led him to conclude that Mrs. Comstock was structured and that she was doing a good job.

None of the complaining parents knew why Mrs. Comstock had been moved to teach third grade. The principal did not mention this issue to the parents, partly because he did not think it was relevant and partly because he felt responsibile for the transfer. After observing Alicia's teaching, Mr. Carlsburg concluded that the complaining parents either had a very narrow perception of schooling or a hidden agenda. Regardless of their motives, he thought they were being unfair.

The holiday vacation was near, and the principal called each of the parents involved and indicated that he would meet with them when school resumed in January. He noted that he would be inviting all parents, not just those who had complained. He had hoped that many of the parents would defend Mrs. Comstock, thus demonstrating that only a minority were concerned. On the last day of school before the holiday break, the principal finally told Alicia about the additional phone calls he had received, fearing that she might hear about them from someone else. He also told her that he disagreed with the parents and would be inviting the parents of all her students to attend a meeting with him when school resumed. She asked if she should attend the meeting, and he said he did not think that her attendance was advisable.

The meeting with the parents was held three days after school resumed in January. It was not well attended; parents of only 11 of 24 students were there. The principal began by saying that he wanted the meeting to be positive and told them that Mrs. Comstock was not there at his request. He then emphasized the following points:

- Initially, two parents had complained that Mrs. Comstock was not assigning homework; since October she has been doing so.
- He had observed her teaching five separate times during the first semester, three of the observations being completed between Thanksgiving and Christmas. On each occasion, he said that he judged her to be an effective teacher.
- He explained that all teachers had to be evaluated formally in accordance with district policy. He noted that although the results of the five observations were positive, he had not yet completed her annual evaluation.

"In my opinion," he told the parents, "Mrs. Comstock is a competent, sensitive, and caring teacher. She tries to meet all the needs of her students. This includes social adjustment, development of a positive self-image, and, of course, educational progress. She believes that students who like school will be productive. So she does try to make school an enjoyable experience. Doing this does not mean she ignores the basics."

His comments were not received well by Ben Rodius, a stockbroker and a parent who had complained about Mrs. Comstock. When he spoke, he said he was speaking on behalf of the concerned parents who had contacted the principal previously.

"Mr. Carlsburg, let me first say that I returned from a business trip a day early to be here today with my wife. So I obviously think this is a serious issue. When we moved here from Vermont two years ago, I put my children in the public schools because I was told they were very good. My daughter, Betsy, who is in Mrs. Comstock's class, attended a private preschool program when she was 3 years old. By the time she entered kindergarten she could read. When we attended the parent-teacher conference in early November, Mrs. Comstock said virtually nothing about Betsy's academic progress but she kept assuring us that she was a happy child. Mrs. Comstock doesn't need to tell us she is happy, and making her happy is not her job. My wife and I believe it is her job to set high expectations and to challenge our daughter. Public schools that try to solve social issues are often ineffective schools. I want my daughter to receive a good education. Keeping her happy and seeing that she acquires the right kinds of values is a family responsibility. You and the teachers should concentrate on what you are supposed to do."

The principal responded that it was unfair to characterize Mrs. Comstock as unconcerned about academic progress. He pointed out that her students were not all alike. Some of the students had difficulty adjusting to school.

After listening to the principal's comments, Mr. Rodius asked, "Do you think it is unreasonable for parents to expect a teacher to challenge students to do the best they can?" Before the principal could answer, he asked him another question,

"Well, forget that. Just tell us if our concerns will influence this teacher's final evaluation?"

"It is inappropriate for me to discuss Mrs. Comstock's evaluation. The process will not be completed until March. If you are asking me whether I think she is doing a good job given what I know now, I already told you my answer is yes."

At that point, one parent defended Mrs. Comstock. She said, "My son has never shown interest in school before. He talks about Mrs. Comstock all the time. I don't want to argue with others, but I think she is a great teacher. I'm pleased Jarrod is in her class." Two other parents voiced agreement with the comment.

The principal concluded the meeting by saying that the purpose was not to have a referendum on Mrs. Comstock. He told the attendees, "I don't believe that Mrs. Comstock sets low expectations for students, nor do I believe that she lets students do whatever they want. Perhaps she doesn't push her students as hard as some other teachers, but that does not make her incompetent. I encourage you to visit her classroom and observe her teaching. I encourage you to talk to her directly about your expectations. I think everyone will benefit. Unfortunately, the efforts of good teaching may not be visible in students for a long time. But I can assure you, if my son or daughter was in third grade, I would be delighted with Mrs. Comstock as the teacher."

Based on nonverbal behavior and seating patterns, Mr. Carlsburg guessed that only five or six of the parents in attendance were sympathetic with the views expressed by Mr. Rodius. He felt better as he left the meeting. As he walked down the hall toward his office, Mr. Rodius tapped him on the shoulder. "You need to know that I and the other concerned parents are not satisfied. We will be taking this matter to the school board."

The Challenge

Determine what the principal should do at this point.

Suggested Activities_____

1. Discuss possible personal and organizational motives related to the principal transferring Mrs. Comstock to the third grade.

2. Identify the variables that may have influenced the principal's behavior in this case.

3. Develop a list of alternative actions the principal could have pursued to deal with this matter. Identify the strengths and weaknesses of each alternative.

4. Discuss policy and procedures used in your school district (where you work or reside) to deal with parental complaints about teachers.

5. Interface the demographic nature of Seminole Elementary School and the differing expectations of parents.

6. Complete the worksheet for Case 9.

Suggested Readings

Cascadden, D. S. (1998). Principals and managers and leaders: A qualitative study of the perspectives of selected elementary school principals. *Journal of School Leadership, 8*(2), 137–170.

Goldring, E. (1990). Elementary school principals as boundary spanners: Their engagement with parents. *Journal of Educational Administration, 28*(1), 53–62.

Johnson, P. E., & Short, P. M. (1998). Principal's leader power, teacher empowerment, teacher compliance and conflict. *Educational Management and Administration, 26*(2), 147–159.

Kohn, A. (1998). Only for my kid: How privileged parents undermine school reform. *Phi Delta Kappan, 79*(8), 568–577.

Kowalski, T. J. (1995). Preparing teachers to be leaders: Barriers in the workplace. In M. O'Hair & S. Odell (Eds.), *Educating teachers for leadership and change: Teacher Education Yearbook III* (pp. 243–256). Thousand Oaks, CA: Corwin.

Madsen, J., & Hipp, K. A. (1999). The impact of leadership style on creating community in public and private schools. *International Journal of Educational Reform, 8*(3), 260–273.

Margolis, H., & Tewel, K. (1988). Resolving conflict with parents: A guide for administrators. *NASSP Bulletin, 72*(506), 26–28.

McEwan, E. K. (1998). *How to deal with parents who are angry, troubled, afraid or just plain crazy.* (ERIC Document Reproduction Service No. ED 422 639)

Ribas, W. B. (1998). Tips for reaching parents. *Educational Leadership, 56*(1), 83–85.

Sagarese, M. M., & Giannetti, C. C. (1998). Turning parents from critics to allies. *Educational Leadership, 55*(8), 40–41.

Shen, J. (1998). Do teachers feel empowered? *Educational Leadership, 55*(7), 35–36.

Short, P. M. (1998). Empowering leadership. *Contemporary Education, 69*(2), 70–72.

Short, P. M., & Short, R. J. (1998). Teacher empowerment and principal leadership: Understanding the influence process. *Educational Administration Quarterly, 34*, 630–649.

Tschannen-Moran, M., Hoy, A. W., & Hoy, W. K. (1998). Teacher efficacy: Its meaning and measure. *Review of Educational Research, 68*(2), 202–248.

Turner-Egner, J. (1989). Teacher discretion in selecting instructional materials and methods. *West's Education Law Reporter, 53*(2), 365–379.

Watkins, D. (1993). Five strategies for managing angry parents. *Principal, 72*(4), 29–30.

References

Burns, J. M. (1978). *Leadership.* New York: Harper and Row.

Jackson, D. (1999). Westchester County, New York: Harnessing micropolitics in a learning community. *School Leadership and Management, 19*(2), 205–207.

King, R. D., Swanson, A. D., & Sweetland, R. A. (2003). *School finance: Achieving high standards with equity and efficiency* (3rd ed.). Boston: Allyn and Bacon.

Kowalski, T. J. (1995). Preparing teachers to be leaders: Barriers in the workplace. In M. O'Hair & S. Odell (Eds.), *Educating teachers for leadership and change: Teacher Education Yearbook III* (pp. 243–256). Thousand Oaks, CA: Corwin.

Kowalski, T. J. (2003). *Contemporary school administration: An introduction* (2nd ed.). Boston: Allyn and Bacon.

Ponticell, J. A., Olson, G. E., & Charlier, P. S. (1995). Project MASTER: Peer coaching and collaboration as catalysts for professional growth in urban high schools. In M. J. O'Hair & S. J. Odell (Eds.), *Education teachers for leadership and change: Teacher Education Yearbook III* (pp. 96–116). Thousand Oaks, CA: Corwin.

Sergiovanni, T. J. (2001). *The principalship: A reflective practice perspective* (4th ed.). Boston: Allyn and Bacon.

A Matter of Honor

Background Information

Contrary to values expressed in some normative theories, administrators rarely can be trained to make rational, objective, and predictable decisions consistently. Those who have studied administrative behavior (e.g., Begley, 2000; Willower, 1994) have commonly found that emotion, personal values, and political contexts contribute to subjectivity in decision making. Writing about the decision-making process, Sergiovanni (1992) identified three dimensions of leadership that may influence behavior. He labeled them the heart, the head, and the hand. The *heart* pertains to personal beliefs, values, dreams, and commitments; the *head* pertains to theories of practice that evolve by integrating theoretical and craft knowledge; and the *hand* has to do with the actions and behaviors used as strategies that become institutionalized in policies and procedures. When these dimensions are discordant, administrators almost always experience personal conflict. Often, administrators must choose between ethical decisions and politically expedient decisions.

In this case, a minority student is caught plagiarizing a book report in her English class. The teacher, invoking school district policy, recommends that the student be given a failing grade for the semester. The magnitude of the problem is exacerbated by the fact that the student is a gifted athlete and good student who has recently accepted an appointment to one of the service academies. A failing grade in English would almost certainly mean that her appointment to the military academy would be rescinded.

As the case unfolds, the principal finds that he must choose between enforcing the district's policy, as demanded by the teacher, and forging a political compromise, as suggested by the attorneys representing the school district and the student. Although the principal favors the compromise, he fears possible repercussions from the teachers' union if he fails to support the teacher by enforcing the policy.

Decisions, such as the one confronting the principal in this case, have moral and ethical implications. Hodgkinson (1991) noted that "values, morals, and ethics are the very stuff of leadership and administrative life" (p. 11). Morality focuses on "right" and "wrong" and may or may not involve illegalities. Ethics, however, "begin where laws and doctrines of right and wrong leave off" (Howlett, 1991, p. 19) and these standards are commonly encapsulated in codes of conduct for professions.

Matters of student discipline often are demanding for principals because they involve an intricate mix of political, professional, moral, and ethical issues. Often, policies and rules are promulgated to ensure consistency and efficiency in discipline decisions; zero-tolerance policies are prime examples. Eliminating administrator discretion in decision making presents two potential problems: (1) the principal is unable to use his or her professional knowledge to judge a case independently and (2) the principal is unable to inject moral and ethical considerations (Kowalski, 2003). For example, some principals would weigh a student's total record in determining a punishment for cheating rather than treating first and third offenders identically. Think about the need for administrators to exercise discretion in discipline decisions as you read this case.

Key Areas for Reflection

1. Rational versus subjective decision making
2. Ethical and moral dimensions of student discipline
3. Zero-tolerance policies
4. Political contexts for administrative decisions
5. Plagiarism and appropriate penalties

The Case

Community

Newton, Michigan, has fallen on hard times in recent years. The local economy was devastated when two automobile-related factories, a transmission plant and a battery plant, closed. Union strife, lower domestic automobile sales, high labor costs, and automation contributed to their demise. The parent companies diverted much of the work from Newton to new operations they opened in Mexico—a pattern that had become all too common and exasperating for Michigan residents.

Newton had grown rapidly after World War II. High salaries in emerging industries attracted a steady stream of new residents who came from very different cultures. One group included individuals of eastern European extraction; previously they had resided in large industrial cities such as Chicago, Detroit, and Pittsburgh. The other group included individuals who had migrated from southern states such as Tennessee and Alabama; nearly all were African Americans. A third ethnic group, Hispanics, came to Newton approximately 25 years later. Most of them were previously seasonal migrant farm workers.

Union Influence

Most factories in Newton used to be associated with the automobile industry, and those who worked in them were loyal members of local autoworkers' unions. In the mid-1960s, these unions were the most powerful political, social, and economic force in this community. Union leaders, either by virtue of holding public office or by virtue of exercising power over those who did, essentially controlled the local government. When a resident wanted a pothole fixed or some other improvement to city property, he or she was more likely to call a union official than to call the appropriate city administrator. Everyone knew how things got done in Newton.

Local union officials also assumed an important community social role that was instrumental in building racial harmony. The union halls were a hub of activity and special events, such as the annual Christmas party and the Fourth of July picnic, attracted virtually all union members and their families.

Economic and political conditions began to change in Newton circa 1980. Jobs in the auto-related factories were reduced, causing the unions to lose membership—a trend that had negative economic and political repercussions. In 1985, the two largest factories closed completely and union membership dropped to its lowest point since 1948. The once-a-month socials at the union halls featuring free beer and music were cancelled and major annual events were either curtailed or discontinued.

New Mayor

The 1990s were a difficult time for Newton residents. The city had lost about 20 percent of its population and property values had declined. In the midst of these problems, Newton residents looked to the past when they elected a new mayor. Stanley Diviak, a 65-year-old retired tool-and-dye maker, was a folk hero. He had been president of the largest local union from 1968 to 1978—years that many residents fondly remembered as the very best.

Stanley Diviak is a shrewd and capable politician. During his tenure as union president, he wielded more power than anyone in town and he had few enemies. He personifies the values that many residents still hold important. He keeps his word, he helps his friends, he is a devoted father and grandfather, and he goes to church regularly.

During the election, Stanley faced only token opposition from the Republican candidate, a 28-year-old lawyer. The election outcome was never in doubt. Rather than comparing the merits of the candidates, residents who routinely gathered at Gloria's Diner and Kelsey's Bar reminisced about the good old days when Stanley Diviak "got things done." Many deluded themselves into believing that Newton's fate would had been different had he remained in office as a union president. Discussions about the global economy or America's transition to becoming an information-based society were not tolerated, especially after everyone had had a few beers.

Following his election, Stanley appointed former union associates to key administrative positions in city government. He took special care to select a diverse group of individuals who represented the various publics being served. He also appointed a special committee to examine prospects of attracting new industry to the town, noting that efforts made by the local Chamber of Commerce had been insufficient. His most popular act after becoming mayor, however, was the reestablishment of the annual Fourth of July picnic, which would be co-sponsored by the local unions and the city.

Newton High School

Ask a Newton resident about the local public schools and chances are great that he or she will talk about former athletes or athletic teams. The high school is located just four blocks from the center of town in a two-story building now nearly 50 years old. As you walk through the front entrance, the first thing you see is a huge trophy case overflowing with tarnished cups and plaques. Pictures of athletes from years past line the hallways.

The school's principal, Nick Furtoski, attended Newton High School and returned there as a teacher after graduating from college and serving two years in the military. He and his family occupy the house his parents had built prior to World War II. While a Newton High School student, he played on a state championship football team and was captain of the baseball team. In addition to being principal, he is considered the authority on Newton High School history.

Principal Furtoski loves Newton High School and he enjoys reminiscing about past athletic victories. Visitors to his office rarely leave without being told about past championships or former student-athletes who brought recognition to his beloved Newton High School. Despite having lost nearly one-third of its enrollment since 1975, the school's athletic teams remain successful; last year, 13 students received full or partial athletic scholarships from colleges. But even Mr. Furtoski knows that the best days of Newton High School are probably in the past.

Newton School District

Overall, the school district's enrollment has declined from about 8,500 in 1975 to a present level of just over 6,000 students. Superintendent Andrew Sposis has survived seven difficult years in office. During his tenure, two schools have been closed and over 25 teaching positions and four administrative positions eliminated. He also has weathered three employee strikes, two involving the teachers' union and one involving the custodians' union.

Historically, the Newton school board has had a preference for selecting internal candidates for administrative positions. Superintendent Sposis, for example, has never worked in another school system. Over 29 years, he has been a teacher, elementary school principal, assistant superintendent for business, and superintendent in the school system.

The school board is composed of five members selected through nonpartisan elections. Members serve three-year terms. In the past 10 years, the entire board has changed. Only one member who was in office when Superintendent Sposis was named superintendent remains on the board. The current board consists of the following members:

- Casmir Barchek, a postal worker
- Yolanda Cody, a nurse
- Matthew Miskiewicz, a mechanic
- Angela Sanchez, a housewife
- Darnell Turner, a dentist

Mr. Miskiewicz is president of the board and Dr. Turner is the vice-president. Both Mrs. Cody and Dr. Turner are African Americans; Mrs. Sanchez is an Hispanic American. Matt Miskiewicz is married to Mayor Diviak's sister.

Incident

Nancy Allison, a senior at Newton High School, is a B student, an outstanding athlete, one of the most popular students in the school, and an African American. By the end of her junior year, she had been named to the all-state basketball team and was inundated with scholarship offers. In the fall of her senior year, she was elected homecoming queen, but this honor was far less important than the one she received five months later. A special delivery letter from one of the prestigious military academies informed her that she had received a congressional appointment.

The news of Nancy's appointment spread throughout Newton. Her picture appeared on the front page of the local newspaper above the story giving all the details. In a community desperate for good news, Nancy's selection was cause for rejoicing.

However, about two weeks after receiving her good news, her life took a dramatic turn. On March 15, Janice Durnitz, an English teacher at Newton High School, entered the administrative office and requested to see the principal. Mr. Furtoski was in the cafeteria at the time having lunch with several teachers. Sensing the urgency of the situation, the receptionist went to the cafeteria to get him. On returning to his office, the principal greeted the teacher with his usual smile.

"Janice, what's the problem?" he asked.

"I've got bad news," she responded.

The smile left the administrator's face as he motioned for her to enter his office. Once inside, he quickly shut the door.

Janice had not even settled in a chair before she said, "Nancy Allison is in my honors English class and up until last week was doing quite well."

"Well, what's the problem?" inquired the principal.

"Students are expected to complete a critique of a contemporary novel. The assignment was given at the beginning of the semester. The deadline for submitting the critique was two days ago, and Nancy just gave me the assignment yesterday."

"This is why you made me interrupt my lunch?" Mr. Furtoski inquired.

"No. I read her paper last night, and that's when I discovered the real problem."

"Well, what exactly is it?"

"There is no doubt in my mind that Nancy plagiarized her report. I checked it carefully. She copied the review from a website," Mrs. Durnitz responded.

"You are absolutely sure about this?" asked the principal.

"It's no coincidence. Her paper contains verbatim passages from a book review that first appeared in a literary magazine about six months ago. It is now accessible through a website. I had read the review when it was first published and I recognized the language. In addition, the quality of writing was better than expected. I would say that 85 percent of Nancy's paper was copied from the book review. The school district has a zero-tolerance policy for cheating or plagiarizing in an honors class. Students guilty of this offense automatically receive a failing grade and must repeat the class."

"Have you confronted Nancy with this issue?" the principal asked.

"Yes. She admitted taking the material from the website. However, she contends that she was not aware that she was engaging in plagiarism. She contends that she read the book in question and agreed with the review she found on the Web. Therefore, she thought it was permissible to say the same things."

A pained look came over Mr. Furtoski's face and he stared out of his office window. He then turned and looked directly at Mrs. Durnitz.

"Well, what do you plan to do about this?" he asked.

"What do you mean? Our district policy gives us no choice. Nancy will fail the course," she answered.

"Janice, we have worked together for over 15 years. We have never had a student at Newton High School flunk a course because of plagiarism. Hell, half the people in this town don't even know what the word means. Isn't there some other solution? Can't we give her the benefit of the doubt? Maybe she is telling you the truth when she claims she didn't know she was breaking a rule. You know that if you give her an F, and especially an F for plagiarism, her appointment to the military academy may be rescinded. At the very least, she will have to go to summer school in order to graduate, and I'm not sure she can do that and report to the academy in late June. What if I talk to the superintendent and recommend an alternative penalty? For example, Nancy could be required to do a different assignment and receive a grade reduction."

"Look, Nick. I didn't develop this policy, but I admit that I agree with it. Plagiarism is cheating and an honors class is an honors class. What will we be saying to other students if we just slap Nancy's wrist? I feel badly too, but I can't let my emotions interfere with my duty. If enforcing the policy means she doesn't get into the military academy, so be it. She should have thought about potential consequences before she copied someone else's work." With those parting comments, the teacher turned and walked out of the principal's office.

Mr. Furtoski shut the door to his office and slumped in his chair. He sat quietly looking out his window and thinking. After about 15 minutes, he called the superintendent. As he waited for Mr. Sposis to come on the line, he was still unsure how to approach the matter. The easiest way out of this mess for him would be simply to support Mrs. Durnitz; he could use the same argument that a zero-tolerance policy gave him no choice in the matter. But he could not bring himself to do that for at least three reasons. First, he feared that failing her would cause serious political problems for the school. Second, he knew and liked the Allison family; he surmised that Nancy not being able to go to the military academy would devastate them. Last and more important, he thought that failing any student under these circumstances was excessive punishment. When the superintendent came on the line, Mr. Furtoski told him about the problem but did state his disposition on the matter.

Mr. Sposis responded, "This is just what I need, Nick! Do you know what will happen if Nancy Allison doesn't get to go to the academy? The mayor has been bragging about her appointment ever since it was first made public. The Allison family was just invited to city hall to take pictures with him last week. Nick, don't you think we need to find some alternative to having her fail this class?"

"Mrs. Durnitz can be real stubborn. I don't know about her personal relationship with Nancy, but I don't think there is anything personal affecting her decision. She made it clear to me that she plans to follow the policy and give Nancy an F. As you know, Janice is influential in the teachers' union, and if I remember correctly, the policy we're now discussing was endorsed by the union. My opinion is that Janice will not back away from this."

"Can't you come up with some alternative solution?" Mr. Sposis asked.

"One option would be to give Nancy the benefit of the doubt with regard to her alleged lack of knowledge about plagiarism. If she didn't understand the offense, a lesser punishment should be acceptable. This gives us a way around the policy. But when I suggested a lesser penalty to Janice, she balked."

The conversation between the two administrators continued for another 10 minutes. It concluded when Mr. Sposis told the principal that he would inform the school board about the matter when they met in two days. Mr. Furtoski immediately called Mrs. Durnitz and Nancy Allison and asked them to keep the matter confidential until the school board had been briefed. He promised to get back to them as soon as possible.

When Mr. Sposis informed the school board about the matter, the school board's attorney, June VanSilten, was present. She was bothered that the superintendent had not discussed the matter with her privately before presenting it to the board members. Even though she had not been briefed prior to the meeting, she was asked to advise the board. She offered three comments:

1. She believed that following the policy literally would induce serious conflict in the community and possibly in the school district. She did not specify whether the nature of this conflict would be legal or political.
2. She cautioned the board members not to discuss the matter with the media or any one else. If the policy was enforced and the student appealed, the due process procedure required board members to judge the merits of the appeal.
3. She recommended that no action be taken by the board or superintendent until the principal had formally submitted a recommendation on the matter.

The board agreed to follow her advice.

After the meeting, Superintendent Sposis called the principal and briefed him on the meeting. He emphasized that the board was expecting the principal to make a formal recommendation. Mr. Sposis added that the principal should not do this until Mrs. Durnitz submitted a written statement providing a rationale for enforcing the policy. The superintendent also explained that everyone needed to be careful about violating procedures, since Nancy's parents might decide to pursue legal action against them if they disagreed with the outcome.

The next day, the principal again met with Mrs. Durnitz and literally pleaded with her to give Nancy the benefit of the doubt in this matter. She refused. Moreover, she handed the principal a letter detailing her assessment of the situation and recommending that Nancy fail the class as per the board's policy. A copy of the letter was sent to the teachers' union president.

That afternoon, the union president telephoned the principal and informed him that he supported Mrs. Durnitz in this matter. He cited two reasons for his stance. First, the policy was adopted several years ago without resistance or hesitancy; the board either had to enforce the policy or rescind it. Second, he believed that judgments about cheating and plagiarism should be made by the teacher and not by the principal.

Once a copy of the letter from Mrs. Durnitz to the principal was given to the union president, the matter could no longer be held confidential. Mr. Furtoski first called Nancy's parents and told them about the situation. Mr. and Mrs. Allison had been personal friends of the principal for more than 20 years. They indicated that Nancy already had told them about the situation. The principal told them that he was doing what he could to ensure that the matter would be adjudicated quickly and fairly.

Mr. Furtoski then talked to two teachers he trusted implicitly. Both were coaches and both were active in the teachers' union. They told him that the union was not likely to back down on this matter, largely because they had endorsed the policy in the first place. Mr. Furtoski decided to forward the letter from Mrs. Durnitz to the superintendent. He attached his own letter that included the following statement:

> It is with deep regret that I must support the recommendation of Mrs. Durnitz that Nancy Allison be given a failing grade in honors English class. Mrs. Durnitz is convinced that the student knowingly engaged in plagiarism. Although Nancy Allison contends that she did not know she was committing this offense, I have no evidence to support the student's claim. The board's policy is explicit and does not allow for alternative penalties, even for first offenders.

The local newspaper learned about the incident the next day by virtue of an anonymous note sent to a reporter. When contacted by the media, the superintendent acknowledged that the problem had occurred and was being adjudicated. Reactions to the story in the community were mixed, largely along racial lines. In an interview with a reporter, Mr. and Mrs. Allison stated that they thought Nancy was not being treated fairly. She had always been a good student and she had never been in trouble before. They also stated that they believe their daughter when she says she didn't knowingly commit plagiarism. They noted that they already had retained an attorney and planned to contest a decision to give Nancy a failing grade.

The school district's due process policy allowed the parents to appeal the recommended action matter to the superintendent. A hearing was held in his conference room and was attended by Mr. and Mrs. Allison, Nancy, their attorney, Mrs. Durnitz, Mr. Furtoski, and the superintendent. Through their attorney, the Allison family argued that Nancy did not know she was committing plagiarism. Mrs. Durnitz argued that students are taught about plagiarism in freshman English, and Nancy should have known the nature of this offense. Mr. Furtoski testified that he had no knowledge to support Nancy's claim and he believed that Mrs. Durnitz was in the best position to judge whether the student had actually engaged in plagiarism. The superintendent denied the appeal.

At the next board meeting, Superintendent Sposis presented a recommendation to approve enforcement of the policy. He told the board members that he had weighed both sides of the issue during the appeal and felt compelled to support the principal and teacher in this matter. The board voted 3 to 2 to approve his recommendation. The two dissenting votes were cast by the board's two African American members.

Following the board meeting, a newspaper reporter again interviewed Mr. and Mrs. Allison, but this time their attorney was present. Mr. Allison said, "If this had been a white football player, do you think this would be happening? Isn't it strange that when they decide to make an example of someone, it just happens to be an African American female who is probably the best-known student in the school?"

The day after the board meeting, the Allison family attorney filed suit contesting the board's decision. Three weeks later, he contacted Ms. VanSilten and proposed a settlement. Fearing that the litigation would not be resolved before Nancy had to report to the academy, Mr. and Mrs. Allison offered a compromise. They would withdraw the lawsuit if Nancy were allowed to retake the English class with another teacher by arrangement. Phillip Jones, a member of the English department and an African American, had offered to direct the independent study that would permit Nancy to graduate with her class. Given the amount of time that would be needed to be devoted to the independent study, Nancy would withdraw from participating in spring sports.

Ms. VanSilten immediately urged the board members to accept the settlement. She cited three reasons for accepting the offer. First, she believed that proving that Nancy knowingly committed plagiarism would be difficult. The Allisons' attorney could have other students testify that they did not understand the concept of plagiarism. Second, the Allisons had secured the support of Mayor Diviak for their compromise. If the settlement offer were rejected, the school board and administration could be damaged politically. Third, the cost of litigation could be extensive and financial conditions in the school district were not favorable.

The superintendent and all five board members indicated that they could accept the settlement provided that Mr. Furtoski wrote a letter indicating that the compromise was acceptable to him. The board president personally called the principal and told him about the board's position.

"Nick, what do you think?" the board president asked. "We don't want to put you on the spot, but this proposed settlement is probably best for everyone."

The Challenge

Develop a rationale for either the principal's acceptance of the compromise or his rejection of the compromise.

Suggested Activities

1. Identify the possible alternatives that the principal may pursue in this matter. Evaluate the merits of each of them.

2. Discuss the potential merits and pitfalls of zero-tolerance policies. Also identify possible reasons why the teachers' union in this case supported such a policy for plagiarism in honors classes.

3. Discuss possible tensions between school board policies on academic issues and teacher professionalism.

4. Determine whether principals (or superintendents) in your state have the legal authority to change a grade assigned by a teacher. Also, discuss the merits of allowing these administrators to have this authority.

5. Ideally, administrators are expected to make rational and objective decisions. Identify factors that deter this outcome.

6. Complete the worksheet for Case 10.

Suggested Readings

Bartlett, L. (1987). Academic evaluation and student discipline don't mix: A critical review. *Journal of Law and Education, 16*(2), 155–165.

Browlee, G. (1987). Coping with plagiarism requires several strategies. *Journalism Educator, 41*(4), 25–29.

Corey, S. F., & Zeck, P. A. (2003). *Combating plagiarism.* Fastback #514. Bloomington, IN: Phi Delta Kappa Educational Foundation.

Daresh, J. C. (1997). Improving principal preparation: A review of common strategies. *NASSP Bulletin, 81*(585), 3–8.

Dowling-Sendor, B. (2001). What did he know, and when did he know it? *American School Board Journal, 188*(3), 14–15, 51.

Fennimore, B. S. (1997). When mediation and equity are at odds: Potential lessons in democracy. *Theory-into-Practice, 36*(1), 59–64.

Fris, J. (1992). Principals' encounters with conflict: Tactics they and others use. *Alberta Journal of Educational Research, 38*(1), 65–78.

Goldman, E. (1998). The significance of leadership style. *Educational Leadership, 55*(7), 20–22.

Henault, C. (2001). Zero tolerance in schools. *Journal of Law and Education, 30*(3), 547–553.

Hobbs, G. J. (1992). The legality of reducing student grades as a disciplinary measure. *The Clearing House, 65,* 284–285.

Holloway, J. H. (2002). The dilemma of zero tolerance. *Educational Leadership, 59*(4), 84–85.

Kaleva, E. A. (1998). *The trouble with academic discipline.* (ERIC Document Reproduction Service No. ED 426 464)

Saunders, E. J. (1993). Confronting academic dishonesty. *Journal of Social Work Education, 29*(2), 224–231.

Skiba, R., & Peterson, R. (1999). The dark side of zero tolerance: Can punishment lead to safe schools? *Phi Delta Kappan, 80*(5), 372–376, 381–382.

Verdugo, R. R. (2002). Race-ethnicity, social class, and zero-tolerance policies: The cultural and structural wars. *Education and Urban Society, 35*(1), 50–75.

References

Begley, P. T. (2000). Values and leadership: Theory development, new research, and an agenda for the future. *Alberta Journal of Educational Research, 46*(3), 233–249.

Hodgkinson, C. (1991). *Educational leadership: The moral art.* Albany: State University of New York Press.

Howlett, P. (1991). How you can stay on the straight and narrow. *Executive Educator, 13*(2), 19–21, 35.

Kowalski, T. J. (2003). *Contemporary school administration: An introduction* (2nd ed.). Boston: Allyn and Bacon.

Sergiovanni, T. J. (1992). *Moral leadership: Getting to the heart of school improvement.* San Francisco: Jossey-Bass.

Willower, D. J. (1994). Values, valuation and explanation in school organizations. *Journal of School Leadership, 4*(5), 466–483.

An Invisible Superintendent

Background Information

Research on administrative behavior reveals how superintendents and principals facilitate or hinder organizational goal attainment. In school districts, for example, superintendents often influence behavior norms and communicate what is to be accomplished. Both actions affect efforts to engage in school improvement.

Early studies of administrative behavior were based on an assumption that great leaders possessed unique personal qualities. These traits were first detailed in case biographies of great leaders and subsequently examined by researchers. Trait studies grew in popularity after World War II and their primary focus was to verify associations between effective administrative practice and selected psychological characteristics (e.g., personality type). By the 1960s, however, scholars recognized the importance of an administrator's approach to work (commonly referred to as leadership style) (Hanson, 2003).

Administrative style, including communication behavior, is produced by the intricate mix of five inputs (Kowalski, 2003):

1. *Personality,* which is the visible aspects of one's character (e.g., being introverted or extraverted)
2. *Personal values and beliefs,* which are philosophical dispositions developed outside of the professional knowledge base
3. *Socialization,* which is the conformity to the cultures of a profession and workplace (e.g., accepting certain values and beliefs as effective solutions to problems of practice)
4. *Context,* which includes the human and physical variables surrounding the administrator's work
5. *Professional knowledge,* which is theoretical knowledge acquired during formal preparation and craft knowledge (artistry) acquired during practice

The influence of each factor is not constant across administrators. The behavior of some principals, for instance, is shaped largely by personal values, an outcome that causes them to reject conflicting values in the professional knowledge base. As an example, a principal may reject teacher empowerment because he or she is convinced that most teachers are basically uninterested in work and will not perform at an adequate level unless they are closely supervised.

Administrators also have different perspectives about organizations. Some believe that schools and all other types of organizations share a common purpose—efficiency. This conviction prompts them to think that certain management practices are universally effective, including proper ways to communicate. Classical theory, a model that had a profound effect on American industry during and following the Industrial Revolution, identified one-way, top-down communication as the ideal. This perspective led top-level managers to devalue employee input; supervisors provided information to subordinates on an "as needed" basis (Kowalski, 2004). This norm was embraced by many superintendents who emulated successful business practices in the first half of the twentieth century. In districts and schools, however, such thinking can be counterproductive because theoretical and technical knowledge is dispersed among employees, including teachers. Often, administrators do not know more than employees about certain topics.

In this case, a newly employed superintendent in a relatively small school district spends considerable time away from his office. Employees, including central office administrators, have a difficult time arranging meetings with him. This behavior becomes problematic when one of the administrators pursues a grant requiring the superintendent's attention.

Key Areas for Reflection

1. Leadership behavior
2. Analysis of behavior in an organizational context
3. Communication processes
4. Conflict between personal and organizational interests
5. Delegating authority

The Case

Community

Placid Falls is a suburban community that began being developed in the early 1950s. Located approximately 35 miles from New York City, it is considered a community of choice by many upper-class families. House values range from approximately $450,000 to $1,200,000. The 2000 census set the population at 7,631 residents, and the average family income is over $280,000 per year. All of the land suitable for single-family dwelling in the community has been developed.

A five-member town council, mayor, and town manager govern the city of Placid Falls. The council members and mayor serve four-year terms. The city has never had a full-time mayor and currently the position is held by a retired physician. The town manager is appointed by the council and is responsible for managing day-to-day operations.

School District

The Placid Falls Public School District consists of four schools: two elementary schools (grades K–5), a middle school (grades 6–8), and a high school (grades 9–12). The district's enrollment has declined about 1 percent per year during the past decade; the current enrollment is approximately 1,800.

The community always has been proud of its local public schools, and many families elected to live in Placid Falls because of the perceived quality of these institutions. Approximately 90 percent of the high school graduates enroll in four-year institutions of higher learning within two years, with about one-third of them enrolling in highly selective, prestigious colleges and universities. Academic competition among students, especially at the high school, is intense. Precollegiate programs dominate the curriculum and only a few students elect to enroll in vocational courses offered by an area vocational school.

Per-pupil expenditures in the school system have been among the highest in the state. Nearly 15 percent of the teachers and 75 percent of the administrators have completed doctoral degrees. Teacher and administrator salaries, among the highest in the state, are a primary reason why the district receives literally dozens of applications for every vacancy.

Search for a New Superintendent

Three years ago when the Placid Falls school board searched for a new superintendent, they received 123 applications, most from highly qualified and experienced administrators. Dr. George Frieman, a well-known professor and placement consultant, was retained to assist the school board. His primary responsibility was to advertise the position and to conduct an initial screening of candidates. He was asked to recommend no fewer than 10 of the applicants to the board. The 10 he recommended included some of the best-known superintendents in the United States.

After studying the written application materials, the school board selected five candidates to be interviewed. One of them was Dr. Andrew Sagossi, then a superintendent of a large county school system in North Carolina. After the initial interviews, he was ranked as the board's top candidate. He and one other applicant were invited for a second interview, and then the board voted unanimously to offer the position to him. Dr. Sagossi told the board president that he would accept the position provided that his attorney and the board could agree on a contract. Having to negotiate a superintendent's contract with an agent might have disturbed many boards, but this was not true in Placid Falls. The board members actually were impressed that he had the foresight to use an attorney to handle such an important matter. Within a week, the parties agreed to a four-year contract with generous fringe benefits and an annual salary of $178,000.

Many of Dr. Sagossi's friends were surprised when they learned he was moving to Placid Falls, because they saw his decision as a strange career move. Prior to accepting this position, Dr. Sagossi had moved to progressively larger districts. His decision regarding Placid Falls was based largely on three factors:

1. *Compensation.* Although Placid Falls is a much smaller district than the one in North Carolina, the annual salary is about $30,000 more.
2. *Family.* Dr. Sagossi's mother resides about 30 miles from Placid Falls.
3. *Retirement program.* Dr. Sagossi needs five more years of service in New York to become eligible for maximum pension benefits in that state.

None of these factors, however, was mentioned to the school board members during the interviews. Instead, Dr. Sagossi cited the community's commitment to quality education as the primary reason for accepting the superintendency. In his second and final interview, he told the board members, "I have been superintendent in several large school systems. I can no longer equate success with the size of the organization I manage. The quality of the work experience is now much more important to me. In a community such as Placid Falls, the superintendent has more opportunities to work with community and state leaders to achieve educational excellence. Quite frankly, I don't want to spend the remainder of my career defending public schools. I'd rather be doing positive things in a community where good administrators, good teachers, and good schools are appreciated."

Assistant Superintendents

At the time of Dr. Sagossi's appointment, there were two assistant superintendents, Dr. Al Yanko and Dr. Joan Myers. Dr. Yanko was responsible for business management and facilities; Dr. Myers was responsible for curriculum. Dr. Yanko has been employed in the district for 21 years, the last 7 in his current position. Dr. Myers was employed just six months before Dr. Sagossi arrived.

Joan Myers was reared in an upper-middle-class family in New Jersey. Her father, now retired, was a dentist and her mother, also now retired, was a marketing executive for a large department store. Joan graduated from a prestigious liberal arts college. At the beginning of her sophomore year, she changed her major from pre-dentistry to social science education—a decision that disappointed her parents who had hoped that she would eventually assume her father's practice.

Joan finished her master's degree in school administration in Philadelphia while teaching high school. She then obtained a principal's license and accepted a position as an assistant principal in a large high school. Two years later, she resigned and became a doctoral fellow at a large state university majoring in school administration. One year after starting doctoral studies, she married Robert, a practicing attorney who taught part time at the university's law school. She completed a Doctor of Education degree 18 months later.

Shortly before Joan completed her doctorate, her husband accepted a partnership with a Manhattan law firm. The vacancy in Placid Falls caught her eye because the location was ideal and because she preferred to work in the area of curriculum and instruction. Although she had less administrative experience than the other candidates, she was invited to interview for the position largely because she could assume the position in the middle of the school year. The search committee included four principals and the superintendent. All of them were impressed with Joan's human relations skills and her intelligence. They concluded that she had tremendous potential and she was offered the position.

Although her title is "assistant superintendent," Dr. Myers is a staff administrator. That is, her work is primarily facilitative in nature; she does not have line authority for the principals. Rather, she collaborates with other administrators and teachers on curriculum projects, staff development, instructional technology, and performance evaluation.

Dr. Sagossi Arrives

During the first two to three weeks in Placid Falls, Dr. Sagossi held several administrative staff meetings and met with administrators individually. During these sessions, he outlined expectations and developed several general goals that he had for the school system. In general, he appeared to the administrative staff to be much like his predecessor—confident, articulate, and capable.

After those first weeks, however, the administrators had little contact with Dr. Sagossi. Even the central office secretaries commented that he spent very little time in his office. And when he was there, he either had appointments or worked with his personal secretary behind a closed door. This lack of visibility separated Dr. Sagossi from his predecessor. The former superintendent spent most of his time at the district's administrative offices and he frequently joined secretaries and other administrators for coffee.

Likewise, the district's four principals became curious about the new superintendent's work habits. Dr. Sagossi's predecessor typically met privately with them at least twice a month. Dr. Sagossi contacted the principals only when he felt it was necessary to do so, and almost always the conversations were conducted via telephone. When principals tried to contact the superintendent, his secretary usually referred them to Dr. Yanko. Dr. Sagossi had essentially relegated routine administrative responsibilities to him—a decision that Dr. Yanko liked. So when principals began asking questions about the superintendent, his assistant defended his behavior. Dr. Yanko told principals, "Dr. Sagossi is a community-oriented administrator. He is doing many positive things that do not directly involve schools, but these activities are important and pay dividends for the district in the long run."

Dr. Yanko's description of the new superintendent's work preferences was accurate. In just three months, Dr. Sagossi was highly involved in Placid Falls activities. He was appointed to the board of directors for a local bank and to the board of directors for the local United Way. In addition, he continued to serve as a member of the alumni council at his alma mater and he was the president-elect of a national suburban superintendents' association.

Problem

In December, Dr. Myers attended a national conference on gifted and talented education where she met Maggie Zerich, a program officer with a foundation. The foundation had funded programs for gifted and talented students in six school districts that involved providing mentors for selected middle grade students. Maggie told Joan that the foundation was seeking proposals to fund projects in at least three additional school districts.

Joan asked, "What can you tell me about this program?"

"The primary purpose is to examine the benefits of taking students in the seventh grade and linking them with mentors for two years," Maggie answered. "The mentors are usually local government officials, business leaders, or professional practitioners, such as physicians or lawyers. The students spend approximately three hours a week working with their mentors on approved projects. From a research perspective, we have two university professors studying whether these encounters have a positive effect on the student career choices.

Dr. Myers was highly interested in becoming part of the project. After learning about the Placid Falls School District, Maggie encouraged her to submit a proposal. Dr. Myers left the conference excited about the opportunity. She could hardly wait to tell Dr. Sagossi. Getting the grant would be a feather in her cap—proof to the new superintendent that she could make positive contributions. Her one concern was the time line. The proposal had to be received by the foundation within five weeks so that it could be reviewed for the upcoming funding cycle.

When Dr. Myers returned to Placid Falls, she immediately outlined what needed to be done. The list included the following tasks:

1. Talk to the middle school principal to ensure his support and cooperation.
2. Develop selection procedures for students and mentors.
3. Construct a list of prospective mentors.
4. Get Dr. Sagossi to agree to provide $45,000 in matching funds.

The first day back from the conference, December 7th, Dr. Myers walked across the hall to Dr. Sagossi's office in hopes of seeing him. Miss Halston, his secretary, told her that the superintendent was out of town at a conference and would not return until December 12th. Fearing that not seeing the superintendent until then could be problematic, she then went to see Dr. Yanko. She explained the proposal and asked if he could commit the required matching funds.

"Only the superintendent and the school board can make such a commitment," Dr. Yanko told her. "Besides, all proposals for outside funding must be approved by the school board before they are submitted to funding agencies. And as you know, nothing goes to the school board for consideration unless the superintendent has placed it on the agenda. When do you have to submit this?"

"I think the last date is January 12th," Dr. Myers replied.

"Well, you still have the January board meeting. Let's see, the first Wednesday in January is the 3rd. You'll be okay."

After the conversation, Dr. Myers went back to Miss Halston to make an appointment with the superintendent after he returned to the district. The secretary scheduled her for 10:00 A.M. on December 13th. She explained that December 12th would not be possible because the superintendent had a standard practice of not scheduling appointments on the day he returns after an absence of more than two days.

Dr. Myers continued working on the proposal. In a way, she thought the delay in seeing the superintendent could be beneficial because the proposal would be nearly completed by the time she met with him. This would allow him time to read the document.

Dr. Myers saw Dr. Sagossi briefly on Wednesday the 12th, the day he returned to Placid Falls. The two exchanged greetings in the hallway of the administrative office, but she did not mention the proposal. The following morning, they both attended an administrative staff meeting at 8:00 A.M. Such meetings were scheduled by the superintendent on an "as needed" basis. The meeting on the 13th was devoted to a series of state-level reports. The meeting ended at approximately 9:30 A.M. Promptly at 9:55, Joan arrived at Dr. Sagossi's office for her 10:00 A.M. appointment.

Miss Halston said, "I was just getting ready to call you, Dr. Myers. I'm afraid I have to reschedule. Dr. Sagossi just received a telephone call that his mother is quite ill. He intends to be back in the office on Monday and he recommended that you meet with him sometime that morning. Right now, his calendar is clear. I'll put you down for 9:00 A.M."

On Monday morning, Dr. Myers arrived for her appointment. This time, Miss Halston told her that the board president was with the superintendent and that she didn't know how long the meeting would take. Dr. Myers asked that she be contacted as soon as the board president left.

At about 10:30 A.M., Miss Halston called Dr. Myers and apologized on behalf of the superintendent. She told Dr. Myers that a problem had surfaced and that it would be necessary to reschedule the appointment for the next day. Dr. Myers looked at her calendar and told the secretary that she could not meet on Tuesday because she had to attend a meeting in Albany.

"How about Wednesday?" asked Dr. Myers. "Is he available on Wednesday?"

"No," the secretary answered. "He has to be at a university alumni board meeting. He will be back on Thursday."

At this point, Dr. Myers became frustrated and angry. She told Miss Halston, "Look, I need to see him about an important matter. This is not General Motors. I find it difficult to understand why I can't arrange to see the superintendent for just 30 minutes. There are thousands of dollars at stake, not to mention an excellent educational opportunity. I'm sure that if Dr. Sagossi knew why I wanted to see him, he would find the time."

"Dr. Myers," replied the secretary, "I'm just doing my job. Let me talk to Dr. Sagossi to see if he can see you before the end of the week."

Fifteen minutes later the secretary called back and informed Dr. Myers that she should talk to Dr. Yanko about the matter.

"Tell Dr. Sagossi that I have already done that and Al told me I had to talk to the superintendent," Joan impatiently responded. "Please tell the superintendent that I will send him something in writing and perhaps he can respond after he reads it."

After putting down the telephone, Dr. Myers realized that school would be dismissing for the holiday break in just four days. Further, she realized that the agenda for the January 3rd board meeting was probably being prepared. She went to the superintendent's office to see when board materials would be distributed for the January 3rd meeting. The secretary said that the packets, including the agenda, would be distributed, as always, one week before the meeting. Because Dr. Sagossi was going on vacation for 10 days commencing the 23rd of December, he intended to complete the board packets by the afternoon of Friday the 22nd. Once again, Dr. Myers pleaded her case, indicating that it was extremely important that she see the superintendent.

"Look, the only possible date left is Thursday, December 21st. What if something else comes up and he cancels the appointment again?" Dr. Myers asked.

The secretary looked at her and said slowly, "Dr. Sagossi is a busy person. You cannot expect that he will see you whenever you like. If you have deadlines on a grant proposal, you should have talked to him about it weeks ago."

Dejected, Dr. Myers walked back to her office.

The Challenge

Place yourself in Dr. Myers's position. What would you do at this point?

Suggested Activities

1. Discuss variables that may contribute to the superintendent's behavior in this case.

2. Share your experiences working in school districts with regard to communicating with the superintendent or with principals.

3. Share personal perceptions of the superintendent in this case.

4. Evaluate Dr. Myers's behavior in this case.

5. Discuss how organizational climate and size can affect communication in a school district.

6. Complete the worksheet for Case 11.

Suggested Readings

Brunner, C. C. (1997). Exercising power. *The School Administrator, 54*(6), 6–9.

Chalker, D., & Hurley, S. (1993). Beastly people. *Executive Educator, 15*(1), 24–26.

Comer, D. (1991). Organizational newcomers' acquisition of information from peers. *Management Communication Quarterly, 5*(1), 64–89.

Diggins, P. B. (1997). Reflections on leadership characteristics necessary to develop and sustain learning school communities. *School Leadership and Management, 17*(3), 413–425.

Duke, D. L. (1998). The normative context of organizational leadership. *Educational Administration Quarterly, 34*(2), 165–195.

Duttweiler, P. (1988). The dysfunctions of bureaucratic structure. *Educational Policy and Practice,* Issue 3.

Geddes, D. (1993). Empowerment through communication: Key people-to-people and organizational success. *People and Education, 1*(1), 76–104.

Goldman, E. (1998). The significance of leadership style. *Educational Leadership, 55*(7), 20–22.

Hoy, W., Newland, W., & Blaxovsky, R. (1977). Subordinate loyalty to superior, esprit, and aspects of bureaucratic structure. *Educational Administration Quarterly, 13*(1), 71–85.

Immegart, G. (1988). Leadership and leader behavior. In N. Boyan (Ed.), *Handbook of research on educational administration* (pp. 259–278). New York: Longman.

Kowalski, T. J. (1998). The role of communication in providing leadership for school restructuring. *Mid-Western Educational Researcher, 11*(1), 32–40.

Loose, W., & McManus, J. (1987). Corporate management techniques in the superintendent's office. *Thrust, 16*(7), 11–13.

Osterman, K. F. (1994). Communication skills: A key to collaboration and change. *Journal of School Leadership, 4*(4), 382–398.

Rusch, E. A. (1998). Leadership in evolving democratic school communities. *Journal of School Leadership, 8*(3), 214–250.

Shelton, M. M., & Powell, T. (1997). The ethics question. *American School Board Journal, 184*(12), 36–37.

Spaulding, A., & O'Hair, M. J. (2004). Public relations in a communication context (3rd ed.). In T. J. Kowalski (Ed.), *Public relations in schools* (pp. 96–124). Upper Saddle River, NJ: Merrill, Prentice Hall.

References

Hanson, E. M. (2003). *Educational administration and organizational behavior* (5th ed.). Boston: Allyn and Bacon.

Kowalski, T. J. (2003). *Contemporary school administration: An introduction* (2nd ed.). Boston: Allyn and Bacon.

Kowalski, T. J. (2004). School public relations: A new agenda. In T. J. Kowalski (Ed.), *Public relations in schools* (pp. 3–29). Upper Saddle River, NJ: Merrill, Prentice Hall.

Captain Punishment

Background Information

Role theory addresses variables that shape work behavior. These models provide conceptual frameworks that assist analysts to study job performance in relation to performance expectations (Gaynor, 1998). Such analysis often uncovers *role conflict*—disharmony between actual and ideal behavior. This common problem, experienced by most school principals, may be attributable to several factors. One of the most common is ambiguity, which results when the formal role is not clearly defined or when the administrator does not comprehend the expectations accurately (Hanson, 2003). Even when the formal role is clearly stated, differing expectations can be placed on a principal for philosophical reasons. Teachers, parents, superintendents, and school board members often have different and competing values and beliefs. These philosophical differences get expressed as role expectations. During a strike, for example, teachers may expect the principal to be sympathetic to their cause, whereas the school board and superintendent expect the principal to keep the school operational at all costs.

Not all role conflict involves other individuals and groups. An administrator may also experience intrapersonal conflict—tensions produced by ambivalence between two dispositions (Owens, 2001). Consider a principal who wants to be both stern and well liked. She takes a hard line on administering policy and rules with teachers, but then feels badly because doing so may have damaged personal relationships with teachers.

When confronted with role conflict, a principal may behave in several different ways. The administrator may

- Accept one expectation and reject the other(s)
- Simply withdraw from the situation (e.g., resign from the position)
- Attempt a reconciliation (i.e., ameliorating the differences between or among the expectations)
- Attempt to satisfy all expectations

- Seek protection from the formal organization (e.g., ask the superintendent to intervene by stressing the school district's role expectation)
- Ignore the conflict, hoping it will resolve itself

Contextual variables (i.e., conditions surrounding the work of an administrator) are instrumental in determining if any of these options are successful. Consequently, there is no "one best way" to deal with role conflict.

This case focuses on a popular middle school principal. Many parents believe that there is a nexus between his disciplinary actions and the school's positive image. Others, however, see him differently. They believe that corporal punishment is ineffective and cruel, and they argue that a principal should be guided by the profession's knowledge base and not personal convictions. The divergent expectations surface over an incident involving a student who disappears after being paddled by the principal.

Key Areas for Reflection

1. Role expectations
2. Role conflict
3. School and community cultures
4. Alternative approaches to discipline

The Case

Rogers Middle School is located in a major city in a southwestern state. The school was built nine years ago to accommodate population growth in low-cost housing areas. The attractive and well-maintained building is a source of pride for many local families. Although houses in the surrounding neighborhoods are less than 25 years old, they are inexpensive prefabricated structures and already many have fallen into poor condition.

Many Rogers Middle School students are bilingual. A statistical report prepared for district administration provided the following racial-ethnic profile:

- Hispanic American   41 percent
- African American   15 percent
- Caucasian   24 percent
- Native American   9 percent
- Asian American   9 percent
- Other   2 percent

The school's student and professional staff profiles are quite different; nearly 70 percent of the teachers, counselors, and administrators identify themselves as Caucasian.

Rogers Middle School contains grades 6 through 8 and accommodates a total enrollment of about 1,150. Data for the last three years indicate that it may be the most effective middle school in the district. When compared to the district's other 11 middle schools, Rogers had the highest scores on the state proficiency test, the lowest rate of expulsions and suspensions, and the highest participation rate in extracurricular activities. Accolades for these outcomes almost always are directed toward one person: Principal Pete Sanchez.

Ever since he was in the third grade, Pete Sanchez knew he wanted to be a teacher. One of nine children reared in a lower-middle-class family, he decided to pursue his dream by working in a local factory and driving 45 miles twice a week to take night classes at the nearest state university. After six years, he managed to complete three-fourths of the degree requirements. He had saved enough money to finish his last year as a full-time student.

Prior to becoming a full-time student, Pete had maintained an A– average. During that final year, he made all As. He was anxious to start teaching. He got married just before becoming a full-time student and soon his wife was pregnant. Pete accepted a position as a high school mathematics teacher. He also was assigned to be an assistant football coach and head track coach. He enrolled in graduate courses, primarily during the summers, and completed a master's degree in school administration. Although he really enjoyed teaching and coaching, he had decided that he wanted to be a principal.

Two years after completing graduate school, Pete was hired as an assistant high school principal in another school district. The principal with whom he worked characterized his job performance as being "excellent." Pete's primary assignments were student discipline and athletics.

State law did not prohibit corporal punishment and it was used in about 40 percent of the district's schools. As an assistant principal, Pete earned a reputation as a tough disciplinarian. He occasionally paddled male students and the principal condoned his actions. Students began to refer to him as "Captain Punishment."

After serving as assistant principal for just three years, Pete applied to be principal of the new middle school being built in the district. He was one of six candidates invited to interview for the position; all six were assistant principals in the district. During his interview with the selection committee, Pete emphasized that he was particularly qualified to work with students from low-income families. He believed that many of these students were highly capable but misdirected. He told the committee members that these students often were at risk of not completing high school because they lacked motivation and self-discipline.

One of committee members was the assistant superintendent for pupil services. She was an opponent of corporal punishment and was familiar with Mr. Sanchez's reputation. She asked him two questions related to this issue: Did he have any evidence that paddling was effective? Would he encourage his assistant principals to administer corporal punishment? He answered that his experiences as a teacher, coach, and assistant principal had convinced him that certain students responded positively to paddling. He shared an example of a football player he paddled on two occasions. He said the two became and remain close friends. The student eventually got a college athletic scholarship and is now an insurance salesman. He responded to the second question by saying that he never has encouraged others to paddle students. "No one told me how to discipline students when I became an assistant principal. And I don't intend to restrict my assistants when I become a principal. Each of us has to decide what is most effective. Most students I have paddled know that I am trying to help them." After interviewing the six candidates, the committee voted four to one to recommend Mr. Sanchez for the job.

Shortly after Rogers Middle School opened, Mr. Sanchez established a parent association. He actively recruited members and appointed many of them to school committees, including the Student Discipline Committee (SDC). The SDC was an advisory panel that consisted of seven parents, three teachers, and an assistant principal. The group reviews parent complaints, monitors policy and rules, and recommends improvements to the discipline program to the principal. On two occasions, the SDC received requests from a teacher to review the school's rule allowing corporal punishment. That rule basically indicates that an administrator or teacher may paddle a student provided that another teacher or administrator is present as a witness. The first request merely resulted in discussion; the second produced a motion from one of the teachers on the SDC to recommend that corporal punishment be prohibited at the school. Mr. Sanchez spoke against the motion, indicating that there had been no incidents when a student incurred physical injury, and he argued that this form of discipline was highly effective with certain students. The motion failed after only two teachers on the committee voted to support it.

During his tenure at Rogers Middle School, Mr. Sanchez has been the subject of numerous feature stories done by the city newspaper and local television stations. He usually was portrayed as a "no-nonsense" administrator who molded a highly successful school for students at risk. Two of the stories mentioned his nickname, Captain Punishment. The most recent media story, produced by a television station, focused entirely on corporal punishment and featured four parents and a teacher. Three of the four parents strongly approved of corporal punishment. One mother said, "Mr. Sanchez understands my children. He teaches them that they have to obey rules. Mr. Sanchez is like a father to my children and they have a lot of respect for him." One of the four parents and the teacher were opposed to the principal's methods. The teacher, Aaron Carson, was the person who had twice requested that the use of corporal punishment be reviewed by the SDC.

Mr. Carson moved to the Southwest because of chronic asthma. Previously, he had taught in a high school in suburban Washington, DC. He first challenged the use of corporal punishment about four years ago when he spoke against such action in a faculty meeting. His comments were basically ignored; only one other teacher spoke in support of his beliefs. Two years later, he raised the issue again in a faculty meeting. This time he was armed with articles from professional journals that he claimed supported his position. Again, his colleagues appeared to be indifferent. One teacher said, "If you have differences with Mr. Sanchez, you two ought to discuss them privately."

Mr. Carson and the principal did meet shortly after that meeting. The two had a candid exchange of ideas and both left clinging to their convictions. At that point, Mr. Carson made requests to SDC to review the matter. After failing to gain support, he basically dropped the matter—that is, until the Jimmy Longbow incident.

Every student at Rogers Middle School knew Jimmy Longbow. He was a good athlete with a knack for finding trouble. His father was deceased and he lived with his mother and two sisters. Jimmy's performance in the classroom did not match his performance on the athletic field. His favorite class was social studies and his favorite teacher was Mr. Carson.

Jimmy's least favorite class was English. The teacher, Mr. Draycroft, made students diagram sentences, study grammar, and read poetry—all things Jimmy found boring and irrelevant. One day, Mr. Draycroft was giving Jimmy a tongue-lashing before the entire class for not doing his homework. When the teacher finished, Jimmy looked directly at him and said, "This stuff we do in here is all crap. Why don't you teach us something else?"

The students could see the veins popping out the teacher's neck. Mr. Draycroft shook his finger at Jimmy and said, "Young man, we are going to the principal's office. I have had it with you. Maybe Mr. Sanchez knows what to do with you."

After escorting Jimmy to the office, the teacher told the principal what had happened. Jimmy and Mr. Sanchez were not strangers. According to the school grapevine, Jimmy had tasted the sting of the principal's paddle at least twice before.

"Jimmy," Mr. Sanchez began, "when are you going to learn? You can't talk to your teachers in this manner. You have to learn there are consequences for improper behavior. You're not in elementary school any longer. Yet, you make me treat you like a second-grader."

The principal then directed the student to empty his back pockets, to bend over, and to hold his ankles. Mr. Draycroft stood off to the side with his arms folded; he seemed pleased that the principal was being forceful. But this time, Jimmy refused to comply with the principal's order.

"You're not going to hit me with that paddle again," he said. "You can take your school and shove it."

Jimmy then ran from the school building. The principal immediately called Jimmy's mother and told her what had happened. She was a waitress in a restaurant near the school. She left work immediately to search for her son, but the effort proved fruitless. Jimmy did not come home that night, or the next, or the next.

Various accounts of the incident spread quickly through the school. Aaron Carson was furious and blamed the principal for what had happened. The next morning, he met with Mr. Sanchez before school started. Unlike previous encounters between the two, this one was not civil. The two exchanged some harsh words and their meeting lasted less than five minutes. Later that day, Mr. Carson telephoned Dr. Penelope Mackee, the assistant superintendent for secondary education and Mr. Sanchez's immediate supervisor. He again blamed the principal for the student's disappearance and demanded that some action be taken. She responded by expressing sorrow about the incident and pointing out that the principal had not violated policy.

Concluding that the assistant superintendent and other school officials would protect Pete Sanchez at any cost, Aaron Carson presented his concern to the media. He did so by writing the following letter to the city's major newspaper:

> The public needs to know the story of Jimmy Longbow, a young Native American student at Rogers Middle School who is now a runaway. Jimmy is no angel, but neither is he some type of second-class citizen who should be whipped every time he does something improper. Corporal punishment is a practice that has been discontinued in most American public schools, but it is alive and well at Rogers Middle School. Jimmy Longbow is now somewhere on the streets because his teachers and his principal thought that brutality was more effective than counseling and constructive behavior modification. Parents of Rogers Middle School students and citizens of this community, wake up! Wake up before it is too late. Let your school board members know what you think about corporal punishment. Let's put a stop to this. Hopefully, Jimmy Longbow will come home, reenter school, and prove that he can be successful. Let's do something before there are more tragic stories.
> Sincerely,
> Aaron Carson,
> Social studies teacher, Rogers Middle School

After the letter was published, over 300 citizens called the superintendent or school board members to support Mr. Carson's views. The letter also prompted the education editor to do a three-part report on the Jimmy Longbow incident and on the use of corporal punishment. Those articles sparked support for Mr. Sanchez. Numerous letters praising him were written to the editor and a paid ad signed by more than 400 supporters appeared in the paper.

The lingering controversy began to disturb school board members. They directed the superintendent, Fred Lopson, to give them a full report on the matter. The superintendent informed Mr. Sanchez that the board was becoming increasingly interested in the matter—information he subsequently shared with some of his key supporters. Before the board received the superintendent's report, a petition was drafted and being circulated in the neighborhoods served by Rogers Middle School. It read as follows:

> We the undersigned fully support the leadership of Principal Pete Sanchez. He has made Rogers Middle School the most successful school in this district. Obviously, the incident involving Jimmy Longbow is disturbing. We hope that the student is found and returned to his mother quickly. However, we disagree with those are blaming Mr. Sanchez for this situation. We urge the school board to join us in supporting a great

principal. Rogers Middle School teachers who discredit our principal should be reprimanded and moved to other schools.

In one week, nearly 700 names appeared on the petition. Organizers mailed copies to each board member and to Dr. Lopson.

A large group of Mr. Sanchez's supporters attended the next school board meeting knowing that Dr. Lopson would be presenting his report on the Jimmy Longbow incident. In his verbal summary of the document, the superintendent pointed out that existing school district policy did not prohibit the use of corporal punishment. Moreover, he believed that most parents supported the principal and his discipline procedures. Other pertinent comments included:

- The SDC has discussed the issue of corporal punishment on two occasions and both times the committee members elected not to make changes.
- As evidenced by the petitions sent to the school board, Mr. Sanchez enjoys strong support from parents.
- Teachers at the school are divided over the principal's use of corporal punishment. Even so, only two or three teachers believe that the principal is responsible for what has happened to Jimmy Longbow.

After the superintendent finished summarizing his report, George Manulita, the only Native American board member, asked to be recognized.

"I think we are all aware of Mr. Sanchez's successes," he said. "In my opinion, his success and popularity are not the issues. The real issue is this: What are we are going to do about allowing corporal punishment in our schools? The current incident at Rogers Middle School is unfortunate; we all can agree on that. Hopefully, he will be found and he will return to school. Our action now should consider the future. I want to know, Dr. Lopson, what you recommend with regard to policies governing corporal punishment. Do you think we should continue to permit such activity? Should we pass new policy to prohibit it?"

Mr. Manulita's questions were answered with shouts of "no" from the principal's supporters in the audience.

Darren Marshall, another board member, spoke next.

"Remember that we're talking about one of our best schools. Do we want to get in the way of a highly successful principal? Mr. Sanchez has done a great job. Quite frankly, I feel comfortable with the current policy. Mr. Sanchez is a professional. He should know when to use corporal punishment. Maybe we should be focusing on teachers who are destroying a fine principal's reputation."

This time the principal's supporter stood and applauded. Then they began to chant, "Mr. Sanchez, Mr. Sanchez."

The Challenge

Evaluate Mr. Sanchez's actions. Identify positive and negative behaviors.

Suggested Activities

1. Discuss the legal status of administering corporal punishment and determine whether class members support the existing laws.

2. Formulate recommendations for resolving this conflict.

3. Identify political issues that may influence the superintendent's recommendation and the school board's decision.

4. Discuss whether the evidence in the case supports the claim that Rogers is an outstanding middle school.

5. Complete the worksheet for Case 12.

Suggested Readings

Barbour, N. (1991). Ban the hickory stick. *Childhood Education, 68*(2), 69–70.

Campbell-Evans, G. (1990). Nature and influence of values in principal decision making. *Alberta Journal of Educational Research, 37*(2), 167–178.

Carey, M. (1986). School discipline: Better to be loved or feared? *Momentum, 17*(2), 20–21.

Curwin, R., & Mendler, A. (1988). *Discipline with dignity.* Arlington, VA: Association for Supervision and Curriculum Development.

Dowling-Sendor, B. (2001). A shock to the conscience: The due process clause and corporal punishment. *American School Board Journal, 188*(4), 62–63, 78.

Erickson, H. (1988). The boy who couldn't be disciplined. *Principal, 67*(5), 36–37.

Glickman, C. (1991). Pretending not to know what we know. *Educational Leadership, 48*(8), 4–10.

Grasmick, H. (1992). Support for corporal punishment in the schools: A comparison of the effects of socioeconomic status and religion. *Social Science Quarterly, 73*(1), 177–187.

Griffin, M. M., Robinson, D. H., & Carpenter, H. M. (2000). Changing teacher education students' attitudes toward using corporal punishment in the classroom. *Research in the Schools, 7*(1), 27–30.

Gusky, D. (1992). Spare the child. *Teacher Magazine, 3*(5), 16–19.

Harding, D. (2000). A model of respect. *Principal Leadership, 1*(1), 10–15.

Henley, M. (1997). Why punishment doesn't work. *Principal, 77*(2), 45–46.

Hinchey, P. (2003). Corporal punishment legalities, realities, and implications. *The Clearing House, 76*(3), 127–131.

Hyman, I. A. (1997). *The case against spanking: How to discipline your child without hitting.* San Francisco: Jossey-Bass.

Hyman, I. A., & Snook, P. A. (2000). Dangerous schools and what you can do about them. *Phi Delta Kappan, 81*(7), 488–498, 500–501.

Hyman, I. A., Stefkovich, J. A., & Taich, S. (2002). Paddling and pro-paddling polemics: Refuting nineteenth century pedagogy. *Journal of Law & Education, 31*(1), 74–84.

Mukuria, G. (2002). Disciplinary challenges: How do principals address this dilemma? *Urban Education, 37*(3), 432–452.

Nolte, M. (1985). Before you take a paddling in court, read this corporal punishment advice. *American School Board Journal, 173*(7), 27, 35.

Pearce, A. (1992). Investigating allegations of inappropriate physical punishment of students by school employees. *School Law Bulletin, 23*(2), 15–21.

Rose, T. (1984). Current uses of corporal punishment in American public schools. *Journal of Educational Psychology, 76*(3), 427–441.

Roy, L. (2001). Corporal punishment in American public schools and the rights of the child. *Journal of Law and Education, 30*(3), 554–563.

Straus, M. A. (2001). New evidence for the benefits of never spanking. *Society, 38*(6), 52–60.

Taylor, K. R. (2002). Is your discipline conscience-shocking or constitutional? *The Education Digest, 68*(3), 28–33.

Zirkel, P., & Gluckman, I. (1988). A legal brief: Constitutionalizing corporal punishment. *NASSP Bulletin, 72*(506), 105–109.

References

Gaynor, A. K. (1998). *Analyzing problems in schools and school systems: A theoretical approach.* Mahwah, NJ: Erlbaum.

Hanson, E. M. (2003). *Educational administration and organizational behavior* (5th ed.). Boston: Allyn and Bacon.

Owens, R. (2001). *Organizational behavior in education* (7th ed.). Boston: Allyn and Bacon.

An Ambitious Assistant Principal

Background Information

Research on administrator career patterns has focused on regularities as practitioners ascend from lower-level to higher-level positions. Such studies reveal that the assistant principalship has been the main entry position to school administration, especially in secondary schools (Miklos, 1988). Consequently, many practitioners remained in the position for only a few years. Today, however, conditions are different. Fewer administrators appear to be willing to relocate or change employers for promotions and more assistant principals appear content to remain in the job. Studies of assistant principal job satisfaction indicate that the job is fulfilling for a relatively high percentage of the office holders (e.g., Chen, Blendinger, & McGrath, 2000; Sutter, 1996). Awareness of these career pattern changes has affected employer expectations; some principals seek assistant principals who are willing to make long-term commitments.

Career decisions often spark legal and ethical questions for school administrators and their employers. Consider these queries: Are administrators legally and ethically bound to fulfill the terms of an employment contract before accepting another position? Should an administrator be honest with a prospective employer about career intentions?

School reform is a major factor causing concern about the turnover of building-level administrators. As the locus of improvement has shifted to the district and school levels, leadership stability has become a greater concern. When a school's administrative offices have revolving doors, the critical tasks of developing a shared vision and an effective plan for reaching it become less probable (Kowalski, 2003). In addition, upwardly mobile assistant principals have been criticized for misleading their employers about the number of years they are willing to commit to this position. Upwardly mobile assistant principals often counter by pointing out that employers provide few incentives to remain in the position. Job security is modest at best and the potential for salary advancements are usually limited.

This case involves an ambitious young man who accepts an assistant principal position in a small rural secondary school. When pursuing the job, he indicates that he intends to remain in this position for at least five years. In truth, he plans to obtain a principalship as soon as possible.

Key Areas for Reflection

1. Administrator career patterns
2. Ethical and legal dimensions of career decisions
3. The assistant principalship
4. Principal and assistant principal relationships

The Case

Community

Bentonville is located in northern Iowa. It is a friendly town of about 2,500 residents, many of whom have never lived anywhere else. Downtown is just a few blocks of old stores that include a bank, a Sears outlet store, a restaurant, a grocery store, two taverns, two churches, and a farm equipment business. Residents drive about 17 miles to the county seat to do most of their shopping.

People who live in Bentonville know each other. The town picnics, one in early June and one in late August, are the social highlights of the year. The town's largest business is a corn processing plant and about 150 local residents are employed by it.

Bentonville Junior/Senior High School

Bentonville Community School District serves two adjoining townships that include the town of Bentonville. The district has only two schools: Bentonville Junior/Senior High School and Bentonville Elementary School. The junior/senior high school includes grades 7 to 12 and enrolls approximately 450 pupils. The principal, Oscar McCammick, has been an administrator in the school for 16 years—the first 6 years as the assistant principal. The school is housed in an attractive building located one mile from Bentonville in a rural setting.

Hiring a New Assistant Principal

When Mr. McCammick was promoted to be principal, he convinced the superintendent and school board to hire a close friend and coach at the school to be his successor. George Stileke remained in the position for 10 years and then retired and moved to Florida. Initially, the superintendent, Becky Potter, and the principal agreed that it would be best to find a person in the school district to replace him. An internal job search, however, produced no applicants. Mr. McCammick then unsuccessfully tried to persuade three teachers to pursue the job. In mid-June, Superintendent Potter announced that the search was being extended and opened to external candidates. By the cutoff date of July 15, only six applications were received. Two of them were from persons residing outside of Iowa, one of whom was the only candidate with administrative experience. The principal made telephone calls inquiring about five of the six candidates; the sixth candidate was eliminated during the initial screening because he did not have a degree in school administration. Reference checks eliminated three more of the candidates, leaving the principal with only two remaining options.

Norman Emons was 51 years old and a teacher at a middle school in Des Moines. He recently completed principal certification. During his interview, he told the superintendent and principal that he wanted to end his career as an administrator. He indicated that he did not complete the education requirements for a principal's license earlier in his career because he worked as a painter during the summers. When the last of his three children graduated from college, he quit painting and pursued a second master's degree in school administration.

Raymond Tyler was 29 years old and a teacher in Davenport where he has been employed for six years. Given the small applicant pool, Mr. Tyler seemed too good to be true. He was well groomed, self-confident, energetic, and his principal in Davenport described him as the "best young teacher he had ever supervised." Raymond had attended high school in a Chicago suburb and attended both undergraduate and graduate school in Iowa. Based on initial impressions, he clearly was the top candidate.

During his interview, Mr. Tyler was asked how long he would stay at Bentonville Junior/Senior High School if he were hired. He responded that he wanted to work under a highly experienced principal such as Mr. McCammick for at least five years. He added that his career goal was to become a principal before he was 40 years old. Superintendent Potter noted that he was single and had never lived in a rural community. She asked him to express his feeling about doing so. He assured her that he had no reservations, provided he could find a place to live.

In weighing the merits of the two finalists, the superintendent and principal agreed that Mr. Tyler was the more promising individual. Yet, they agreed that he would likely not remain in the position for more than five years. Mr. McCammick would retire in about nine years, and it would be beneficial to have an assistant who will move into the principal's office at that time. Mr. Emons was evaluated as "acceptable" but "unexciting." The job was given to Mr. Tyler.

First Year

Ray Tyler started his new job on August 10. He was able to rent an apartment in a house owned by two retired teachers in Bentonville. During the first two months, he was consumed by the job. He often had weekend responsibilities, such as Friday night football games and school social events. Mr. McCammick initially was very pleased with his work. Ray related well to the students, he was intelligent and learned how to do things very quickly, and he was accepted by the teachers and parents. The principal even commented to the superintendent that he no longer had apprehensions about him.

In early November, Ray moved to the county seat. He explained that he preferred to live in an apartment complex rather than to rent an apartment in a private residence. The principal was not pleased. Administrators customarily lived in the school district, and although there was no requirement to do so, he felt that most board members and parents would not react positively to his decision.

Ray became friends with two coaches at the school. They were approximately the same age, and the three had attended two college football games together that fall. His relationship with the remaining employees was congenial but professional. By the second semester, Ray had made several comments to the coaches indicating that he was not pleased working in a rural school. He told them that he would probably stay in Bentonville for two years and then try to find a better job in a larger school.

In early April, Ray had his evaluation conference with Mr. McCammick. The principal was generally pleased with his performance but still unhappy that he was not residing in the school district. He rated the assistant principal's overall performance as "average to above average" and noted that the assistant principal needed to exhibit more maturity when dealing with students. Ray was not happy with the evaluation. As a teacher, he consistently received "excellent" ratings and he felt the principal was being unfair. When he shared is disappointment with the evaluation, Mr. McCammick responded, "This is a pretty good evaluation for a first-year assistant principal. And you are being recommended for re-employment with a salary increase." Ray signed the evaluation form as required by district policy but he still thought the principal had not evaluated him objectively.

Conflict Emerges

As school was drawing to a close in late May, one of the coaches who spent time with Ray mentioned to the principal that it would be a shame if Ray left. "Do you know if he is planning to leave?" the principal asked.

"No. But he is a terrific guy and some superintendent or principal may try to persuade him to change jobs."

A week later, Mr. McCammick received a telephone call from Dr. Jean Carmen, a principal in a suburban Chicago school district. She was inquiring about Mr. Tyler. Dr. Carmen said that Ray had just interviewed with her for an assistant principal's job. Mr. McCammick was stunned.

"He has applied for a job with you for next year?" he asked.

"That's correct."

"Did he tell you that he has been in Bentonville for less than a year?"

"He did."

"Well, aren't you concerned that he is looking for a new job so quickly?"

There was a pause and then Dr. Carmen said, "Frankly, I'm not concerned. Our school has 2,100 students, four assistant principals, and the salary is about 35 percent higher than his current salary. Mr. Tyler also indicated that he had been accepted to a doctoral program in this area and wished to begin his studies on a part-time basis in the fall. What I would appreciate is some feedback about his performance over the past year. I talked to his former principal in Davenport, and he described Mr. Tyler as a super candidate. My impressions of him after the interview are very positive as well."

"When I hired Ray last summer, he told the superintendent and me that he promised to stay in this job for at least five years. Apparently, he lied to us. I'm really upset about this. I don't look forward to having another assistant principal search. At this point, I don't think I could give you an objective assessment of his performance."

Dr. Carmen thanked Mr. McCammick for talking with her and she ended the conversation. Mr. McCammick immediately called Superintendent Potter and expressed his anger.

"Is there some way we can make him stay here? Legally, I mean. Doesn't he have some obligation to remain here as he promised?" he asked the superintendent.

"Even if there were a legal constraint, would you want to keep him under the circumstances?"

Mr. McCammick said he would talk to Ray and discuss the matter with the superintendent in greater detail after that conversation.

As soon as he hung up the telephone, Mr. McCammick stormed into Ray's office. In an angry tone he told him about the telephone call from Dr. Carmen. He then said, "You made a promise when you took this job. You said you would stay here at least five years. Now, you're trying to leave after just one year. How could you be so dishonest?"

"I never promised I would stay here for five years. I said I wanted to work under a highly experienced principal for five years. This opportunity just happened to come up. I'm planning on getting engaged and my fiancée is a teacher in a neighboring district. Also, I have been accepted to a doctoral program at a university that is only 20 minutes from the district. I didn't plan this. If the job is not offered to me, I'll stay here and work as hard as I did this year."

Mr. McCammick did not like Ray's answers. "If you don't withdraw your candidacy for this job, you'll never get a good evaluation from me. Integrity is very important and I will have to tell prospective employers that you deceived us. My hope is that you will come to your senses. You have a bright future here. You must give me an answer by tomorrow."

The principal then left Ray's office and slammed the door.

The Challenge

Place yourself in Ray's position. What would you do?

Suggested Activities_____

1. Discuss the legal dimensions of an administrator's employment contract, especially with respect to the rights of both the employer and employee.

2. Identify possible factors that are contributing to the assistant principal's job dissatisfaction.

3. Divide into two groups and debate the advantages and disadvantages of employers demanding that assistant principals remain in that job for a specified period of time.

4. Assume you were principal of Bentonville Junior/Senior High School. Develop the ideal and required qualifications for your assistant principal.

5. Complete the worksheet for Case 13.

Suggested Readings_____

Calabrese, R. L., & Tucker-Ladd, P. R. (1991). The principal and the assistant principal: A mentoring relationship. *NASSP Bulletin, 75*, 67–74.

Glanz, J. (1994). Dilemmas of assistant principals in their supervisory role: Reflections of an assistant principal. *Journal of School Leadership, 4*(5), 577–590.

Goodson, C. P. (2000). Assisting the assistant principal. *Principal, 79*(4), 56–57.

Hart, A. (1991). Leader succession and socialization: A synthesis. *Review of Educational Research, 61*, 451–474.

Hartzell, G. N. (1993). When you're not at the top. *High School Magazine, 1*(2), 16–19.

Hibert, K. M. (2000). Mentoring leadership. *Phi Delta Kappan, 82*(1), 16–18.

Murray, K. T., & Murray, B. A. (1999). The administrative contract: Implications for reform. *NASSP Bulletin, 83*(606), 33–38.

Sutter, M. R. (1996). What do we know about the job and career satisfaction of secondary school assistant principals? *NASSP Bulletin, 80*(579), 108–111.

Tooms, A. (2003). The rookie's playbook: Insights and dirt for new principals. *Phi Delta Kappan, 84*(7), 530–533.

Winter, P. A., & Partenheimer, P. R. (2002). *Applicant attraction to assistant principal jobs: An experimental assessment.* (ERIC Document Reproduction Service No. ED 471 558)

References _____

Chen, K., Blendinger, J., & McGrath, V. (2000, November). *Job satisfaction among high school assistant principals.* Paper presented at the Annual Meeting of the Mid-South Educational Research Association, Bowling Green, Kentucky.

Kowalski, T. J. (2003). *Contemporary school administration: An introduction* (2nd ed.). Boston: Allyn and Bacon.

Miklos, E. (1988). Administrator selection, career patterns, succession, and socialization. In N. Boyan (Ed.), *Handbook of research on educational administration* (pp. 53–76). New York: Longman.

Sutter, M. R. (1996). What do we know about the job and career satisfaction of secondary school assistant principals? *NASSP Bulletin, 80*(579), 108–111.

A One-Trick Principal

Background Information

In the present age of school reform, the ideal role of school principal entails both leadership and management functions. As a leader, a principal is expected to engage in visioning, planning, and facilitative activities that enable the school to adjust continuously to changing needs and interests. As a manager, the principal ensures that human and material resources are protected and used efficiently (Kowalski, 2003). Historically, principals devoted most of their time and energy to managerial responsibilities; decisions about the school's primary foci and organization were made either at the state or district level. Today, however, the locus of school improvement is at the school level. This transition, rooted in the belief that reform is most likely to succeed if it occurs closest to the students affected, has created new role expectations for principals.

Leadership and management are broad functions requiring a broad base of knowledge and skills. The following three-skill taxonomy has often been used to discuss relevant expertise:

1. *Technical skills.* This category includes knowledge related to certain procedures and methods essential to administering schools; application examples include managing fiscal resources and operating a school-based food service program.
2. *Human relations skills.* This category focuses on knowledge of human behavior, motivation, attitudes, communication, and other facets of organizational life; application examples include school-community relations, conflict resolution, and communication.
3. *Conceptual skills.* This category includes analytical and problem-solving skills that are primarily associated with leadership responsibilities; application examples include visioning and planning (Yukl, 2002).

The application of knowledge and skills is affected by context. Factors such as school climate, prevailing problems, community culture, and people are contextual variables that often determine whether an administrator's actions are successful or unsuccessful. Conditions surrounding a decision are a major reason why a principal's behavior is highly successful in one setting but terribly ineffective in another setting (Gaynor, 1998).

All administrators experience some level of role conflict (Hanson, 2003). Such tensions can occur for a variety of reasons and the following three are common:

1. Principals often discover that expectations expressed by supervisors and school employees are not congruous. As an example, the superintendent may expect a principal to be an efficient manager; the teachers expect the principal to be an instructional leader.
2. Principals often find that their own needs compete with job expectations. As an example, a principal may have a high need to be liked and accepted by others; the position, however, requires him or her to be stern, objective, and task oriented.
3. Individuals and groups outside of the formal organization (i.e., the school district) often have expectations of a principal that differ from those expressed inside the organization. For example, parents may expect a principal to be warm and compassionate; the superintendent and school board expect the principal to enforce policy and rules without emotion.

In this case, an experienced principal assumes a new position and devotes much of his time and energy to community relations. His behavior is rewarded by the superintendent and the associate superintendent but attacked by the senior assistant principal. The assistant believes that she is doing most of the principal's work, primarily because he is narcissist who takes advantage of subordinates. She also is convinced that her peers, two male assistant principals, have not been treated in the same manner.

Key Areas for Reflection

1. Principal responsibilities in a large high school
2. Community and school district cultures as determinants of ideal and real roles
3. Role conflict
4. Male and female administrator relationships
5. School public relations

The Case

Wellington

One of Peter Farley's earliest memories of Wellington involved a demolition project in the downtown area, a scene he observed on his first trip to this city. He was there to interview for the job of high school principal. As he drove his new Buick down Main Street searching for the administrative office, he saw two large stores, each more than 100 years old, being flattened by a swinging steel ball.

Wellington, an industrial community that fell on hard times in the past 20 years, is one of the larger cities in this New England state. Recently, however, Wellington's fortunes have been changing. An upward economic trend started about the time that Dan Shea was elected mayor. An energetic and popular attorney who previously served two terms in the state legislature, Mayor Shea promised during his campaign that he would work to bring new businesses to the city. Since his successful election just 18 months ago, two technology-based corporations have moved to the city.

After becoming mayor, Mr. Shea also got involved directly with the public schools. One of his law partners, John O'Dell, was on the school board. Working through O'Dell, the mayor played an influential role in hiring a new superintendent and now he was injecting himself into the search for a new high school principal. He convinced the board members and superintendent to seek an experienced administrator with good communication and human relations skills.

Search for a New Principal

The composition of the school board in Wellington has changed substantially as a result of the last two elections. The same political groups that had supported Mayor Shea played a pivotal role in school board elections. Largely because of their efforts, four new individuals were elected to the board in the last few years. These new board members worked closely with Mayor Shea in selecting Dr. Collin Durbin as superintendent. Superintendent Durbin became a political ally of the mayor and both had made improving the city's image a top priority.

About 15 months after arriving in Wellington, Superintendent Durbin requested and received a resignation from the high school principal, Joseph Wycuff. Wellington High School enrolls about 2,300 students and in addition to the principal, the administrative staff consists of three assistant principals, an athletic director, and a director of counseling services. Department chairs are not considered administrative staff under the master contract with the Wellington Teachers' Association. Mr. Wycuff was an efficient manager who was well liked by the teachers. He spent much of his time doing what he had done as an assistant principal—handling student discipline and scheduling. He rarely left the school and this was one factor that contributed to the negative performance evaluation he received from Superintendent Durbin.

After conferring with the mayor, the superintendent recommended to the board that a national search be conducted for a new principal. An impressive brochure listing the following qualifications was sent to universities, professional associations, and search consultants:

- Because the principal of Wellington High School represents the district and school to multiple publics, candidates for the position must possess outstanding public relations and communication skills.
- Candidates must be able to relate effectively to diverse community groups.
- Candidates must be committed to working closely with local governmental agencies.
- Candidates must take an active role in community activities.
- Candidates must be committed to school improvement.

Although other qualifications were mentioned, the brochure unambiguously transmitted a message that the principal was expected to be highly involved with the community. Based on his experiences in the state legislature, Mayor Shea believed that in the case of schools, image was everything. Therefore, rebuilding the city required administrators who could change public opinion, and especially opinions about the district's flagship—Wellington High School.

When first contacted by the search consultant about the vacancy at Wellington High School, Peter Farley was ambivalent. He had never been to Wellington, but he was aware of the city's past economic problems. The consultant, however, persuaded him to apply for the position. Peter subsequently was invited to interview for the position, and although he accepted the invitation, he had doubts about the position.

The search committee for the position consisted of the superintendent, the associate superintendent (Susan Mays), a school board member (Mr. O'Dell), and a teacher from the school (Constance Goldman, chair of the English Department). The committee members were selected by the superintendent because he was confident that each person shared his convictions about the type of principal who should be hired. The committee interviewed six candidates and they invited two of them, including Mr. Farley, to return for a second interview.

Many of Peter Farley's apprehensions were resolved after his initial encounter with the search committee. He was impressed with them and he felt that their interests matched his strengths. He had been a high school principal in a suburban community in a neighboring state for six years. The school had an excellent reputation and better than average resources. Peter delegated managerial responsibilities to his assistants, allowing him to be away from the school a majority of the time. He successfully garnered economic and political support from the business community—an accomplishment that did not go unnoticed by the Wellington search committee.

When he came to Wellington for the second interview, Peter was accompanied by his wife, Margo. The first evening, they had dinner with Mayor Shea and his wife, which was an unexpected but welcome feature of the second interview.

The next morning, Mrs. Farley was taken on a community tour by a realtor and Mr. Farley met the high school faculty at a reception. Later in the morning, he met with the school's administrative staff and counselors. The interview concluded with a working lunch hosted by the selection committee. By 2:00 P.M., the Farleys were driving back home.

The search committee discussed the two finalists the next day. John O'Dell indicated that Mayor Shea thought that Peter was definitely the best person for the job. The members of the search committee quickly agreed, but they feared that he might not accept the position. They decided to make him an offer he could not refuse. One week later, Mr. Farley accepted the offer.

New Principal Arrives

When Mr. Farley arrived in his new office on July 1, his first order of business was a meeting with the assistant principals. Teresa Howard, the most senior of the three, had applied for the principalship but was not invited for an interview. She has worked at the school for 23 years, the last 11 as an assistant principal. She was a staunch supporter of the previous principal—a negative factor in the eyes of Dr. Durbin. Mike Petrov has been an assistant principal at the school for six years; he was chair of the school's Physical Education and Health Department before that. The third assistant principal, Ron Kazka, has only two years of administrative experience.

During the first meeting, Mr. Farley primarily listened as the assistant principals shared their perceptions of the school, the district, and community politics. He quickly surmised that Mrs. Howard was the dominant assistant principal. Whenever he asked a controversial question, for example, the two men looked at her, hoping she would answer.

During the first two weeks, the four administrators met six times, some of the meetings lasting more than four hours. At their seventh meeting, Mr. Farley announced some decisions that had been made after consulting with Superintendent Durbin. First, Mrs. Howard's title would be changed to associate principal, pending approval of the superintendent's recommendation to the school board. The new title meant that she was now second in command; she would be in charge of the school when the principal was not present. Second, he wanted the administrators to know that he would be devoting a great deal of his time to community relations. Third, he wanted them, under the direction of Mrs. Howard, to determine how administrative responsibilities would be divided.

Principal Succeeds?

Both the mayor and superintendent made sure that Mr. Farley got community exposure. They arranged for him to speak to the service clubs and the Chamber of Commerce. He received positive treatment by the local media, especially after successfully negotiating three separate partnerships involving the high school and local business. One of these partnerships, for example, provided 20 new computers for the school over a two-year period.

The other high school administrators, teachers, and staff quickly discovered that Mr. Farley was not like Mr. Wycuff. In fact, the principal and his predecessor were nearly direct opposites. Whereas Mr. Wycuff rarely left the school during the day, Mr. Farley was rarely there. Mr. Wycuff was well liked by the teachers and spent a great deal of time interacting with them; the teachers barely knew Mr. Farley. When asked what the new principal was like, one teacher told a neighbor, "How would I know? I get my information from the newspaper just as you do."

During the first two years in Wellington, Principal Farley launched a vigorous public relations campaign to improve the school's image. He personally took charge of the school newsletter, which now was being published six times a year instead of just twice. Twice a month, he invited a group of 20 parents to meet with him for coffee. He also managed to get continuous and positive media coverage by working closely with the superintendent, mayor, and the district's public relations director. Before the end of his second year as principal, he was named the outstanding educator of the year by the Wellington Chamber of Commerce and the school won the outstanding public relations award from the state's high school principals' association. Both Mayor Shea and Superintendent Durbin were confident they had selected the right person for the job.

Conflict Emerges

Every Monday morning, the principal and associate principal met for about two hours so that the principal could be briefed on current issues and problems. At first, Mrs. Howard thought the meetings were advantageous because they were an opportunity to receive feedback on her performance. However, she was growing increasingly concerned about the principal's lack of involvement in the day-to-day operation of the school. She repeatedly suggested that he needed to spend more time at school, especially building rapport with teachers and with managing resources. He basically ignored the suggestions. Finally, out of frustration, she told him, "My advice is that you need to spend more time here at school. The employees refer to you as the 'phantom principal.' The other assistant principals also think you should be working more closely with them."

"Look, Teresa, the proof is in the outcomes. Things are going well. I believe we are all doing what we do best. You have excellent rapport with the teachers and you know how to manage the school. Why change just because we should do things the way the textbooks say we should do it?"

The first year, Mr. Farley evaluated Mrs. Howard's performance as being excellent and recommended her for the maximum merit increase. The second year, he planned to do the same. When they met for the evaluation conference, he was stunned when she referred to her evaluation as meaningless. She then told the principal that she was considering resigning.

"Why?" he asked. "Are you ill? What's the problem?"

"No. My health is fine. Answering your question may take quite some time, and you're usually in a hurry to end meetings," she responded.

"I will listen and I will take as much time as you need. I'll cancel appointments if necessary. There is no one more valuable on the administrative staff than you."

She had to meet with the department chairs in 45 minutes, so she requested that they meet for lunch the next day to discuss the matter. He agreed to do so. He offered to take her to one of Wellington's finest restaurants but she said she preferred to meet in his office.

When they met the next day, Principal Farley started the conversation by reiterating his positive feelings about his associate. He then asked her to explain why she was thinking about resigning.

"I really don't know where to begin. But here goes. Staff members at the school are concerned—no, let me rephrase that. I am concerned that you don't get involved in critical administrative functions. I have to give you detailed briefings so you have some idea of what is occurring. Some employees believe that you don't know how to manage a big high school. Some even refer to you as a "one-trick pony"—a principal who only knows how to deal with community relations. Personally, I don't believe that their assessment is accurate, but they make these judgments when they see you delegating all the difficult work to me."

Principal Farley was a bit stunned by her words. He reflected for a moment and then asked, "This concern about me is being expressed by most of the administrators, teachers, and staff?"

"Yes, I believe it is. The other assistant principals and I are not used to having a principal who is away from the campus 60 or 70 percent of the time. We all speculate about what you're doing when you're gone. People form their own conclusions."

"What else are they, or you, concerned about?" he asked.

"I feel I'm running this school and you're getting all the credit. Last week at the annual Chamber of Commerce meeting, Mayor Shea gave you a plaque recognizing you as educator of the year. You never once acknowledged how much help you received from me or the two assistant principals. Then there's the matter of salary. I'm making $22,000 less than you, and I'm the one managing the school. If the tables were turned, would you consider this arrangement fair?"

"Teresa, the superintendent and school board want me to improve the school's image. Their intentions were not secret. When I first arrived, I told you what I would be doing. I never misled you, and I certainly have not abused you."

"I work darn hard, Peter, and you know it. I get here early and leave late every day. I have no idea how many hours you work. Some of the secretaries and most of the teachers don't even know you well. You rarely visit with them; and when you do, it is usually an incidental encounter.

At that point Mrs. Howard lost her composure. Mr. Farley sat quietly until she was able to continue speaking.

"I'll be blunt. I don't think a male associate would be treated the way I have been treated. You probably know that I applied to be the principal, but the superintendent did not even extend the courtesy of inviting me to interview for the position. Yet, I am deemed competent to run the school. If you want me to continue as associate principal, two things must happen. First, I want a major salary increase—at least $10,000. Second, I want you to promise that you'll spend more time at school. You let me know your answer by the end of the week." Mrs. Howard then got up and left the office before the principal could respond.

Principal Farley was stunned. He tried imagining himself in her position. Would he have reacted in the same way? Until yesterday, he had never questioned whether he had been an effective principal. He worried about the staff perceptions and about how they would react if Mrs. Howard resigned. Yet, he was convinced that Superintendent Durbin would never agree to support her demands.

The Challenge

Assume you are Principal Farley. What decision would you make?

Suggested Activities

1. Discuss whether gender is a legitimate issue in this case.

2. Identify communication problems that have contributed to the conflict between Principal Farley and Associate Principal Howard.

3. Discuss the behavior of principals with whom you have been associated to determine whether their behavior was similar or dissimilar to Principal Farley's behavior.

4. Develop a characterization of an ideal high school principal with respect to how he or she would allocate his or her time.

5. Evaluate the principal in this case and decide whether you would like to work with him.

6. Complete the worksheet for Case 14.

Suggested Readings

Armistead, L. (2000). Public relations: Harness your school's power. *High School Magazine, 7*(6), 24–27.

Black, B. (2002). An insider's view. *American School Board Journal, 189*(2), 37–38.

Carr, A. A. (1997). Leadership and community participation: Four case studies. *Journal of Curriculum and Supervision, 12*(2), 152–168.

Copland, M. A. (2001). The myth of the superprincipal. *Phi Delta Kappan, 82*(7), 528–533.

Glanz, J. (1994). Dilemmas of assistant principals in their supervisory role: Reflections of an assistant principal. *Journal of School Leadership, 4*(5), 577–590.

Hale, R. P. (1994). Aspirations and frustrations of female secondary administrators. *Professional Educator, 16*(2), 45–50.

Hassenpflug, A. (1996). The selection of female secondary school assistant principals and transformational leadership. *Research in the Schools, 3*(1), 51–59.

Hibert, K. M. (2000). Mentoring leadership. *Phi Delta Kappan, 82*(1), 16–18.

Hines, R. W. (1993). Principal starts with PR. *Principal, 72*(3), 45–46.

Marshall, C. (1992). School administrators' values: A focus on atypicals. *Educational Administration Quarterly, 28*(3), 368–386.

Mertz, N. T., & McNeely, S. R. (1999). *Through the looking glass: An up front and personal look at the world of the assistant principal.* (ERIC Document Reproduction Service No. ED 435 124)

Reis, S. B., Young, I. P., & Jury, J. C. (1999). Female administrators: A crack in the glass ceiling. *Journal of Personnel Evaluation in Education, 13*(1), 71–82.

Ripley, D. (1997). Current tensions in the principalship: Finding an appropriate balance. *NASSP Bulletin, 81*(589), 55–65.

Sutter, M. R. (1996). What do we know about the job and career satisfaction of secondary school assistant principals? *NASSP Bulletin, 80*(579), 108–111.

References _____

Gaynor, A. K. (1998). *Analyzing problems in schools and school systems: A theoretical approach.* Mahwah, NJ: L. Erlbaum.

Hanson, E. M. (2003). *Educational administration and organizational behavior* (5th ed.). Boston: Allyn and Bacon.

Kowalski, T. J. (2003). *Contemporary school administration: An introduction* (2nd ed.). Boston: Allyn and Bacon.

Yukl, G. (2002). *Leadership in organizations* (5th ed.). Upper Saddle River, NJ: Prentice-Hall.

A Maverick Board Member

Background Information

Relationships between superintendents and school board members often affect operations in the entire school system. In public education, various groups inside and outside the formal school district can exercise power—a reality that makes teamwork between the superintendent and school board very important (Carr, 2003). Superintendents build and maintain positive rapport with board members by being honest, providing knowledge and assistance, using two-way communication, building mutual respect, cooperating, and earning trust (Kowalski, 1999). Although the superintendent has the primary responsibility to build these relationships, they are a two-way street. Both parties must be committed to maintaining them.

From the superintendent's perspective, two board-member behaviors that are likely to prevent a positive working relationship are using the office to pursue personal interests and intruding into the domain of school administration (Amundson, 2000). Both are exhibited by a school board member in this case. He attempts to use his office to seek revenge on a football coach and to seek favor for a family member. Although the board president recognizes the unethical behavior, he believes it is best to ignore it. When the superintendent is unwilling to do so, the board president asks him if he would be willing to issue a reprimand to the offending board member, provided that the action is approved by a majority of the board. The question places the superintendent in a difficult situation in which he must weigh his responsibility to be an ethical leader and the need to maintain a positive relationship with all board members.

Key Areas for Reflection

1. Superintendent and school board relationships
2. Ethical behavior of school board members
3. Conflict resolution
4. Scope of superintendent responsibilities

The Case

School District and School Board

The Richmond County School District covers 420 square miles of predominantly rural land. There are 7,800 pupils enrolled in 2 high schools, 5 middle schools, and 10 elementary schools. The area has been experiencing modest growth in the past decade largely because of the county's proximity to the state capital, which is only 35 miles away. Land costs and taxes in Richmond County have made it an attractive site for small manufacturing companies. Nearly 500 new homes have been built in the school district during the last decade, most in a rural subdivision. The county seat, Collins, has a stable population of about 20,000.

The seven school board members are elected from designated geographic areas to ensure balanced representation across the 12 townships. Twenty-five years ago, six of the seven were farmers, but since then, the board has become more diverse. The current members include:

> John Mosure (president), a farmer
> Iris Dembica, a housewife
> Elizabeth Highland, a real estate broker
> Elmer Hodson, a farmer
> Norman Salliter, an accountant and state employee
> Martin Schultz, an attorney
> Alicia Waddell, a pharmacist

Mr. Hodson has been on the board for 10 years, longer than any other member. Mr. Mosure and Ms. Highland are next in seniority, each having been on the board for 6 years. The remaining four board members took office 2 years ago.

In the past two years, split votes have been common, yet the board is not factionalized. Elmer Hodson, however, has voted more often than the others not to support the superintendent's recommendations. He has always perceived himself as a political delegate representing two rural townships in the school district. Consequently, he has consistently protected the political interests of the townships' residents in matters such as taxes and school boundaries. In fact, he has opposed every recommendation to increase taxes since he has been on the school board. Nevertheless, his personal relationships with the other board members and superintendent have not been adversarial.

Superintendent

Matthew Karman has been superintendent of the district for three years. Previously, he was superintendent of a smaller district in the same state. His predecessor had been dismissed largely because of poor rapport with five of the board members, three of whom are no longer on the school board. Knowing the history of board-superintendent relationships in the district, Mr. Karman has worked very hard to avoid common pitfalls, and as a result, the last performance evaluation he received from the board rated his relationships with them as "excellent." Mr. Karman's success is related to the following activities:

- He has lunch with the school board president twice each month.
- He invites the school board members to two social events at his house each year.
- He has lunch with each board member several times a year.
- He makes himself accessible to board members; for example, telephone calls from board members receive top priority.
- Prior to board meetings, he personally delivers materials to each member, either at their homes or places of business.

After receiving his second annual performance evaluation, the board voted unanimously to renew his contract for another three years. This surprised some observers for two reasons: He still had another year remaining on his initial contract and four of the board members had worked with him for less than one year. Two of the new board members commented to the local newspaper reporter that Superintendent Karman had done an excellent job of keeping them informed and of helping them learn their responsibilities.

Problem

Superintendent Karman was driving down a lonely country road as the winds swirled across barren cornfields partially covered by snow. He was delivering school board packets for an upcoming meeting. The packets included the superintendent's recommendations for action items and background information pertinent to his disposition. Although it was only mid-November, the chilling temperatures made it feel more like January. The fields were dotted with cornstalks cut about two inches above the ground; they looked like wooden spikes someone had arranged to discourage trespassers.

When the superintendent pulled into the driveway beside a large three-story farmhouse, a German Shepherd barking alongside his car greeted him. The dog's barking summoned John Mosure from his barn where he was repairing a tractor. The board president's bib-overalls and hands were stained with grease and oil.

"Greetings, John. I have your board packet," Mr. Karman said.

"Come in to the house and we'll have a cup of coffee," John said as he tried to wipe his hands with a rag from his back pocket.

Although John Mosure has been on the board for six years, this was his first year as president. The two men had become good friends, and they worked well together. Their wives also had become friends, and about every two months, the four of them had dinner together.

"John, I hope you've got some time today. I want to discuss a sticky issue with you, and it may take a little while."

The board member responded, "Well, we'll find time. I'm not sure I'm going to be able to fix that tractor anyway. Something is wrong with the transmission and I probably will have to take it to the dealer to get it repaired."

The two sat back enjoying the warmth of the kitchen and their coffee as Mr. Karman began describing the problem.

"Two days ago, one of our high school principals, Bob Dailey at North Richmond High, received a telephone call from a friend who is the assistant commissioner of the state high school athletic association. Bob's friend asked him if he knew Elmer Hodson."

There was a moment of silence and John said, "Oh, no!"

Although the superintendent and other board members maintained congenial relationships with Elmer, they all considered him to be a troublemaker. Many observers thought that John Mosure and Elmer Hodson would be political allies because they both farmers, but more often then not, they disagreed over critical issues. As an example, the two board members have taken opposite positions on all three building-related referenda in the past six years. John is about 20 years younger than Elmer and has three children who attend school in the district.

The superintendent continued with his story. "So, Bob tells his friend that he knows Elmer and explains that he is a school board member. Bob's friend then says that Elmer is sitting in his outer office wanting to file a complaint against coach Yates, the football coach at North Richmond High."

"A complaint about what?" asked the board president.

"Well, Bob's friend didn't know at the time because he had not talked to Elmer yet. His secretary had told him the reason why Elmer wanted to see him. Bob's friend then said he would talk to Elmer and then call Bob again. About an hour later, Bob received the second call. He learned that Elmer was claiming that the coach and school had violated the state athletic association rules by allowing the starting quarterback to remain in school even though his parents no longer resided in the district. In fact, the student in question, Jeb Boswell, is living with Coach Yates. Elmer is insisting that the athletic association take action against North Richmond High School, Coach Yates, and the principal. At the very least, Elmer also wants the student to be declared ineligible."

"Is there any merit to Elmer's charges?" John Mosure asked.

"First," the superintendent answered, "the student is living with the Yates family. Jeb's parents moved to Colorado last June. Jeb and Coach Yates are pretty close, so Jeb asked his parents if he could finish his senior year at Richmond North and live with Coach Yates. He convinced them that paying Coach Yates $200 a month was a good investment since he was likely to get athletic scholarship offers from colleges. The parents agreed and Jeb has been living with the Yates family since last June."

"Is such an arrangement permissible under the rules of the state athletic association?"

"Apparently so," the superintendent answered. "Coach Yates had asked the athletic director at North Richmond to seek a ruling from officials at the athletic association. The athletic director received a letter from the state commissioner stating that Jeb could finish his senior year at North Richmond without jeopardizing his eligibility, provided that Jeb's parents and the school principal agreed to the arrangement. Principal Dailey and the parents assured Coach Yates that they had no objections to the boy staying here and continuing to play football."

"So from a legal perspective, Elmer really doesn't have a valid complaint?"

"John, there is more to the story. Here we are, one week before the state football tournament. North Richmond has a 9 and 1 record and is one of the favorites to win the championship in their division. Jeb Boswell, the student in question, is the star of the team—he may even end up being all-state. You know who his backup is?"

The board president said he had no idea. "You have to remember, Matt, I don't live in the North Richmond area. I'm a South Richmond booster [the other high school in the district]."

"The second string quarterback is a senior named Ron Hodson."

The two looked at each other and John smiled. The superintendent continued, "You got it, John. The second string quarterback is none other than Elmer Hodson's grandson. Get the picture? Elmer's got an axe to grind because he feels this other kid has prevented his grandson from being the starting quarterback. Now that the team has been successful and will be in the state championship playoffs, Elmer wants his grandson to move into the spotlight. Principal Dailey told me that the grandson is probably innocent in this matter. He's a good kid and the principal thinks he would be embarrassed if he knew what his grandfather was doing."

"You know, I just remembered something," commented John. "Do you recall last summer when we were approving contracts for driver education teachers? Elmer opposed the recommendation to extend a contract to Coach Yates even though he has taught driver education during the summer for at least the last 12 years. Elmer claimed that he had received complaints indicating that Coach Yates was not a good instructor. Do you think that matter is connected to all of this?"

"Who knows? With Elmer, it's hard to tell. He votes against a lot of things. Going to the athletic association without informing the board or the administration, however, is an ethical issue. As a board member, he should have voiced his concerns to either you or me before filing a complaint to the state athletic association. Had he talked to us first, he would have found out that his charge has no merit. Taking this matter to the athletic association is an administrative matter. In addition to being unethical, he has probably made all of us look like a bunch of second-rate politicians."

"What did the fellow from the athletic association do about Elmer?"

"Elmer identified himself as a school board member and demanded to know what would be done to adjudicate the matter. Bob's friend at the athletic association explained that there was no violation and he even showed him a copy of the letter the commissioner had written to North Richmond's athletic director last May indicating that the arrangement was acceptable. Elmer then stormed out of office, suggesting that the school board should have been informed on this matter."

"Matt, let me make a suggestion. Let's forget about this. Elmer is Elmer. He'll always be a pain in the neck. Why voters keep electing him is beyond me. Sometimes I think they enjoy watching him stir up trouble."

The superintendent had a different opinion. "At the very least, we need to inform the other board members. I believe that Elmer should be reprimanded or censured. What he did was clearly unethical. Maybe it's time to say 'enough.'"

The board president got up to refill the coffee cups. He then returned to his chair. "I don't know. I'm not sure a reprimand will do any good. Elmer's pretty stubborn. We might just give him more publicity, and you know how he loves to get his name in the paper. Matt, how about if you talk to him? You're more experienced in dealing with conflict. Maybe the best way to handle this is to have you give him the reprimand. We should get the support of the other board members, though, and then you can tell him you are speaking for all of us. Don't you think this would be the best way to handle this?"

The Challenge

Place yourself in the Superintendent Karman's situation. What would you do?

Suggested Activities

1. Obtain a copy of the code of ethics for school board members in your state. Determine if the code includes material pertinent to this case.

2. Discuss the legal authority of school board members attempting to act independently.

3. Discuss the ideal roles of school board members and superintendents. Determine how these role compliment each other.

4. Complete the worksheet for Case 15.

Suggested Readings

Banach, W. (1984). Communications and internal relations are problems for board members. *Journal of Educational Public Relations, 7*(3), 8–9.

Bolman, L., & Deal, T. (1992). Images of leadership. *American School Board Journal, 179*(4), 36–39.

Bryant, M., & Grady, M. (1990). Where boards cross the line. *American School Board Journal, 177*(10), 20–21.

Castallo, R. (1992). Clear signals. *American School Board Journal, 179*(2), 32–34.

Duffy, F. M. (2002). Courage, passion, and vision: Leading systemic school improvement. *International Journal of Educational Reform, 11*(1), 63–76.

Hamilton, D. (1987). Healing power: How your board can overcome the heartbreak of disharmony. *American School Board Journal, 174*(9), 36–37.

Harrison, P. (2002). Can this marriage be saved? *American School Board Journal, 189*(6), 36–37.

Hayden, J. (1987). Superintendent-board conflict: Working it out. *Education Digest, 52*(8), 11–13.

Herman, J. (1991). Coping with conflict. *American School Board Journal, 178*(8), 39–41.

Irvine, J. (1998). Welcome to the board. *American School Board Journal, 185*(7), 38–40.

Kowalski, T. J. (1999). *The school superintendent: Theory, practice, and cases.* Upper Saddle River, NJ: Merrill, Prentice Hall (see Chapter 5).

Marlowe, J. (1997). Good board, bad board. *American School Board Journal, 184*(6), 22–24.

Myer, R. (1983). How to handle a board member who wants to play his own game. *American School Board Journal, 170*(11), 27–29.

Natale, J. (1990). School board ethics: On thin ice? *American School Board Journal, 177*(10), 16–19.

Ondrovich, P. (1997). Hold them, fold them, or walk away: Twelve cardinal rules for dealing with school board conflict. *The School Administrator, 5*(2), 12-15.

Rickabaugh, J. R., & Kremer, M. L. (1997). Six habits to make you a hit with your school board. *The School Administrator, 54*(6), 30–32.

References

Amundson, K. J. (2000). What I wish I'd known . . . *American School Board Journal, 187*(1), 32–33, 36.

Carr, N. (2003). Leadership: The toughest job in America. *Education vital signs: A supplement to the American School Board Journal, 14,* 15, 18–20.

Kowalski, T. J. (1999). *The school superintendent: Theory, practice, and cases.* Upper Saddle River, NJ: Merrill, Prentice Hall.

Excessive Punishment
or Just Politics?

Background Information

In the 1990s, school violence became a national concern resulting in political pressure for superintendents and school boards to adopt "get tough" policies. Often, such policies were adopted with little forethought about possible legal entanglements and about the possible negative effects for students and society (Holloway, 2002). In this case, several African American males are initially expelled for two years for engaging in violent acts at a school football game. The black community in the school district reacts negatively, claiming the punishment is excessive and biased. After being expelled, the teenagers are charged with criminal offenses. A national civil rights leader gets involved and tensions worsen in a city that has had a history of racial strife.

Philosophy and community cultures are two variables influencing the substance and process of student discipline in public schools. Decisions related to regulating pupil conduct, even violent behavior, may spark intense political conflict because not all members of the school's communities share the same values and beliefs. Some parents, for example, believe that discipline's primary purpose is to protect the school and broader community. Other parents, however, believe the purpose of discipline is to correct the behavior of the student being punished. Similar disagreements exist among professional personnel who influence school policy. Some teachers and administrators, for instance, favor zero-tolerance policies for threats or acts of violence. By comparison, many mental health experts argue that punishment should be individualized and based on an objective analysis of motives of extenuating circumstances (Rasicot, 1999). Clearly, then, the challenge facing administrators and school board members formulating discipline policy and rules is to balance school safety and student rights (Essex, 2000).

Key Areas for Reflection

1. Race relations
2. Race and student discipline
3. The appropriateness of zero-tolerance policies
4. Violence in schools
5. Managing political conflict
6. Using conflict to produce positive change

The Case

Centralville

Centralville is an industrial community with a population of approximately 76,000. The primary industry is a chemical plant owned by a large national corporation. There are two other large employers: a stamping plant that makes truck fenders and a candy company. Approximately 13 percent of the city's residents are African American and approximately 2 percent are Hispanic American. In the past two decades, the population of Centralville has declined by about 8,000. Much of this decline occurred during the 1980s when auto-related industries cut back production and employment levels. Recent attempts by the Chamber of Commerce to attract new businesses have had little success.

The city has a history of segregation in housing patterns. Virtually all of the African American population resides in two areas just south and west of the center of the city; virtually all Hispanic Americans live in an area just east of the center of the city. A newspaper in the state capital recently referred to Centralville as a "blue-collar, union town." There have been relatively few new single-family dwellings built in the past 25 years. Much of the new housing activity in the area is occurring in two small towns north of the city.

Recently, the mayor and other public officials have made an effort to improve race relations. Several months ago, a local African American leader interviewed on a local radio program said that conditions in Centralville had improved. "Things aren't as bad as they were 25 years ago. Racism was very obvious back then. Now, we are trying to deal with the lingering effects of institutional racism." Just two weeks after his interview, however, a white policeman shot and killed an African American male who had shot at him. The tragedy rekindled pessimism in the African American neighborhoods.

School District

The Centralville School District has a total enrollment of approximately 10,000. The peak enrollment, 12,300 students, occurred in 1985. The district operates 12 elementary schools (grades K–5), four middle schools (grades 6–8), and two high schools (grades 9–12).

Prior to 1979, the district had only one high school. When the second high school opened, the name of the original school remained Centralville High School. This building is located near the business district of the city. The newer school, Centralville North High School, is located in the city's most affluent residential area.

Although only 13 percent of Centralville's 80,000 residents are black, 44 percent of the district's enrollment is black because many whites send their children to private schools. Data for the two schools are as follows:

Centralville North High School
- Enrollment   1,850
- African American Enrollment   18 percent
- Hispanic American Enrollment   1 percent

Centralville High School
- Enrollment   2,375
- African American Enrollment   46 percent
- Hispanic American Enrollment   2 percent

There are seven members on the district's school board; four are elected from specific areas of the city and three are elected at-large. Currently, two of the board members are African American. The superintendent, Dr. Thomas Yundt, and the principals of both high schools are white males. Dr. Yundt has been in his present position for three years, having moved to Centralville after serving as superintendent in a smaller school district. One of the three assistant superintendents reporting to Dr. Yundt, Dr. Robin Daniels, is an African American.

Incident

Although the two high schools belong to different athletic conferences, they play each other in all sports. The football game between the two schools occurred during the third week of September on a Friday evening. Midway through the second quarter, a brawl broke out in the bleachers, causing the game to be stopped. A group of black students appeared to engage in a fistfight and then the turmoil spread indiscriminately through the crowd. School officials, including the principals of both schools, and several law-enforcement officers attempted to intervene. One of the students involved allegedly grabbed the principal from Centralville High School by the shirt and hit him in the chest with his fist. Although there were no hospital reports of injuries, there were conflicting stories as to whether people had been hurt.

The Centralville School District had adopted a zero-tolerance policy with regard to violence at school or school events 18 months prior to the incident at the football game. The two principals identified nine black teenagers who they believed were part of the group initiating the fighting. The principals recommended a two-year expulsion for the seven who were students in the school at the time. The recommendation was based on provisions in the board's zero-tolerance policy. Separate due process hearings were set for the students. Only one student attended his hearing. He and his parent requested that he be allowed to withdraw from school to avoid being expelled—an act that would protect his permanent record. The hearing officer recommended that the request should be honored, but argued that expulsion recommendations for the six students who did not appear at their hearings should be upheld. Dr. Yundt concurred with all of the hearing officer's recommendations and so informed the school board. He pointed out the period of the expulsion, two years, was based on the egregious nature of the offense. However, the students could seek reinstatement after only one year if they produced evidence of positive behavior, such as staying out of trouble, pursuing tutoring and counseling, or performing community service. The board voted six to one to approve the superintendent's recommendation; one of the black board members voted against the recommendation.

Fallout

During the weeks that followed the board's approval of the expulsions, police were careful not to label the brawl as "gang related." Nevertheless, rumors flowed through the community that the fight was the continuation of an altercation that occurred between two groups of teenagers several days earlier. Eventually, criminal charges were filed against the nine black teenagers. Four were charged as adults with felony mob action and one of them, an 18-year-old, was also accused of aggravated battery and resisting a peace officer. The remaining five were charged in juvenile petitions.

Many in the black community believed that the punishment given to the seven students by the school board was excessive. When the criminal charges were filed weeks later, the disapproval changed to anger. At that point, a national civil rights figure, Reverend Arnold James, became involved. He spoke at a rally held in Centralville to protest the treatment of the students and to start a defense fund for the teenagers. Rev. James made the following points in his speech to the angry crowd:

- He condemned the action of the school board and superintendent, arguing that they had rushed to judgment and overreacted.
- He insisted that the key issue in this matter was fairness rather than race. He argued that black students had been disproportionately the subjects of harsh discipline; he cited a statistic indicating that of the six students expelled the previous year, five were black. He also noted that the board had expelled a white student who had committed what he considered to be a much more serious offense (sending a bomb threat note) for only one year.
- He contended that the punishment given to the students was excessive for a fistfight in which no weapons were involved.

- He condemned the filing of criminal charges, insisting that the school board was working in tandem with law enforcement. He noted that by making the students criminals, the board was, in essence, justifying the unusually long expulsions.

Within days of Rev. James's appearance in Centralville, the controversy was covered by the national media. Both the governor and state school superintendent were drawn into the issue, and even local elected officials weighed in on the issue. Unrest in the African American community was getting progressively tense, and Superintendent Yundt decided to close the schools for three days, fearing an outbreak of additional violence.

In the midst of growing national interest, the board president issued a statement in which she noted, "I really resent the fact that we have outsiders telling us how to run our schools." The governor was able to get both sides to attend a daylong meeting that resulted in the school board agreeing to reduce the punishment to an expulsion for the remainder of the school year. In addition, the expelled students would be allowed to attend the district's alternative high school program. Rev. James called the board's concession inadequate, and the governor indicated that he merely tried to bring the two sides together. Both the governor and the state school superintendent maintained the position that the matter should be resolved locally.

Key figures on both sides were inundated with requests for media interviews. Leaders in the local black community met with reporters and restated many of the claims that Rev. James made in his initial speech in Centralville. School officials who previously refused to disclose any information about the students now made selected data available to the media and public. For example, Dr. Yundt appeared on a national news show and revealed that three of the students were third-year freshmen and that collectively the seven students had missed 350 days of school the previous year. In addition, school officials made available an amateur videotape of the incident. The camera captured the last third of the brawl and shows spectators scurrying to get away from a group of teenagers throwing punches and tossing each other down the cement bleacher steps.

In the aftermath of the board's concession and the viewing of the videotape, conservative media commentators and politicians started criticizing Rev. James for misstating the facts and for intensifying the conflict surrounding this situation. They refuted his contention that no one was hurt, and they argued that criminal activity was indeed an issue. They pointed to the video as clear evidence that Rev. James either erred in reporting the facts of this case or purposely misled the public.

Continuing Controversy

Despite the school board's decision to reduce the expulsion period, tensions did not subside. Rev. James and his supporters filed a 13-page civil rights complaint in U.S. District Court, alleging that the school board had violated the students' constitutional rights in the following ways:

- Failing to have an explicit zero-tolerance policy in writing
- Labeling the conduct as "gang related" without evidence
- Failing to notify the students about alternative education options
- Punishing the the students too harshly for a fistfight void of weapons

At the same time that anger lingered in the black community, many white residents criticized the school board and superintendent for having reduced the expulsion periods.

Reverend James repeatedly warned community officials and the media that the matter was not resolved just because the punishment was reduced. In addition, he now accused school officials of having violated privacy laws by disclosing information about the case to the news media. He vowed to continue his activities in Centralville until the teenagers were cleared of criminal charges. He announced that he would lead a march through the city the following week. Clearly, the matter was not resolved, and the superintendent, school board, and other school officials continued to be criticized by leaders in the black community.

The Challenge

Assume you are the superintendent. Would you have handled this situation differently? If so, what would you have done differently?

Suggested Activities_____

1. Discuss the relevance of the community's history to this case.

2. Debate whether zero-tolerance policies are appropriate for either threatened or actual acts of violence.

3. In the aftermath of this incident, identify actions you would recommend with regard to increasing security at school-sponsored events.

4. Discuss possible objectives of student expulsion. Identify the least and most important objective.

5. Complete the worksheet for Case 16.

Suggested Readings_____

Baker, J. A. (1998). Are we missing the forest for the trees? Considering the social context of school violence. *Journal of School Psychology, 36*(1), 29–44.

Bock, S. J., Savner, J. L., & Tapscott, K. E. (1998). Suspension and expulsion: Effective management of students? *Intervention in School and Clinic, 34*(1), 50–52.

Casella, R. (2003). Zero tolerance policy in schools: Reationale, consequences, and alternatives. *Teachers College Record, 105*(5), 872–892.

Clark, C. (1998). The violence that creates school dropouts. *Multicultural Education, 6*(1), 19–22.

Costenbader, V., & Markson, S. (1998). School suspension: A study with secondary school students. *Journal of School Psychology, 36*(1), 59–82.

Edmonson, H. M., & Bullock, L. M. (1998). Youth with aggressive and violent behaviors: Pieces of a puzzle. *Preventing School Failure, 42*(3), 135–141.

Gable, R. A., Quinn, M. M., & Rutherford, R. B. (1998). Addressing problem behaviors in schools: Use of functional assessments and behavior intervention plans. *Preventing School Failure, 42*(3), 106–119.

Gordon, J. A. (1998). Caring through control. *Journal for a Just and Caring Education, 4*(4), 18–40.

Haynes, R. M., & Chalker, D. M. (1999). A nation of violence. *American School Board Journal, 186*(3), 22–25.

Holloway, J. H. (2001). The dilemma of zero tolerance. *Educational Leadership, 59*(4), 84–85.

Hyman, I. A., & Perone, D. C. (1998). The other side of school violence: Educator policies and practices that may contribute to student misbehavior. *Journal of School Psychology, 36*(1), 7–27.

McEvoy, A., Erickson, E., & Randolph, N. (1997). Why the brutality? *Student Intervention Report, 10*(4).

Morrison, G. M., & D'Incau, B. (1997). The web of zero-tolerance: Characteristics of students who are recommended for expulsion from school. *Education and Treatment of Children, 20*(3), 316–335.

Roper, D. A. (1998). Facing anger in our schools. *Educational Forum, 62*(4), 363–368.

St. George, D. M., & Thomas, S. B. (1997). Perceived risk of fighting and actual fighting behavior among middle school students. *Journal of School Health, 67*(5), 178–181.

Stefkovich, J. A., & Guba, G. J. (1998). School violence, school reform, and the Fourth Amendment in public schools. *International Journal of Educational Reform, 7*(3), 217–225.

Toby, J. (1998). Getting serious about school discipline. *Public Interest*, (133), 68–83.

Zirkel, P. A., & Gluckman, I. B. (1997). Due process in student suspensions and expulsions. *Principal, 76*(4), 62–63.

References

Essex, N. L. (2000). Zero tolerance approach to school violence: Is it going too far? *American Secondary Education, 29*(2), 37–40.

Holloway, J. H. (2002). The dilemma of zero tolerance. *Educational Leadership, 59*(4), 84–85.

Rasicot, J. (1999). The threat of harm. *American School Board Journal, 186*(3), 14–18.

The Passive Principal

Background Information

After 1980, policymakers attempted to improve schools first by making students do more of what they were already doing and second by raising standards for preparing and licensing administrators. Although these actions had some positive effects, they failed to produce the desired levels of school improvement. Since approximately 1990, the strategy of intensification mandates has been replaced by efforts to restructure schools. The current approach is nested in two beliefs:

1. Reform is more effective when it is pursued at the district and individual school levels. Both state deregulation and district decentralization are manifestations of this prevailing improvement strategy.
2. Unless the basic structure of schools, including organizational culture, is adjusted to address the real needs of students, the outcomes of reform will be limited (Kowalski, 2003).

School-based management (SBM) is arguably the most recognizable product of contemporary school reform strategies.

The decentralization of authority and decision making in public education stems from several beliefs, including the following:

- Teachers become more effective when treated as true professionals.
- Instructional decisions are improved when teachers are empowered to tailor their classroom activities to the real needs of their students.
- School productivity improves when principals and teachers are not manacled by a seemingly endless list of policies and rules.
- Democratic decision making and community involvement in governance have a positive influence on school productivity.

Flexibility and adaptability are primary decentralization objectives; that is, allowing individual schools to reshape themselves based on the clientele they serve.

Decentralization, however, has often elevated state accountability standards. As an example, some states have given local districts greater leeway to determine curriculum, but at the same time, they require students to take state proficiency examinations intended to measure learning outcomes.

The principal is often the person most affected by decentralization (Brown, 1990). This is true for at least three reasons:

1. Principals assume greater leadership responsibility (i.e., determining what should be done) without a corresponding decrease in managerial responsibilities (i.e., being responsible for how things are done).
2. Engaging in shared decision making is often threatening to a principal if he or she remains personally accountable for group decisions.
3. Participatory decision making typically increases the frequency and severity of conflict, and principals must manage and resolve these tensions.

A summary of research on SBM does little to alleviate administrative apprehensions. Findings often indicate that this decentralization approach increases political activity, is time consuming, is not always supported by teachers, and is not always adequately funded (Brown, 2001). Yet, most scholars recognize the potentialities of SBM and continue to advocate its use.

This case is about an experienced principal who volunteers to participate in a first phase of implementing SBM. In creating a school council, he decides to permit council members to be elected by the groups they represent (teachers, parents, and staff), and although he, too, is a council member, he assumes a passive role. Teachers representing two factions of the school's faculty are elected to the council and they vie for power. The principal's laissez-faire attitude in the context of this conflict angers the council chair, who is a parent and the president of the school's parent-teacher association (PTA).

Key Areas for Reflection

1. Problems associated with decentralized governance of schools
2. Social conflict among individuals and groups in schools
3. Dynamics of group decision making
4. Leadership style and participatory decision making
5. Leadership role in conflict resolution

The Case

Community and School District

Sunland is a prosperous city in a southern state. With a population of approximately 75,000, it has grown nearly 25 percent in the last 20 years. New industries and businesses continue to locate in or near the city, and population projections indicate that there will be 100,000 by the year 2012. Sunland also is the county seat for LaSalle County.

Serving the entire county, including the city of Sunland, the LaSalle County School District has 3 high schools, 6 middle schools, and 19 elementary schools. Although population is increasing across the county, the growth has been the greatest and most rapid in Sunland. As a result, a new middle school and three new elementary schools have been built in the city in the past decade.

Superintendent and SBM

Three years ago, the school board employed Dr. Ursula Jones as superintendent. The 42-year-old administrator had been associate superintendent for instruction in a large-city school system in an adjoining state. Prior to coming to LaSalle County, Dr. Jones had established a reputation as a change agent. When the newspaper announced her employment, her former superintendent was quoted as saying, "LaSalle County is getting a top-notch superintendent. Dr. Jones is one of the most creative and bold administrators I have known."

During her first year as superintendent, Dr. Jones developed a decentralization plan for the district. It called for the adoption of school-based management. The initial phase involved implementation in one to three elementary schools. Selection of the schools was based on interviews of principals who had expressed an interest in becoming part of the first phase. Six principals were interviewed and the superintendent then selected three of them.

Financial support was provided for the three participating schools. This included funding for the principals to attend a two-week seminar during the summer to help them implement the process and a $20,000 allocation for staff development. The only restriction placed on the staff development funds was that the money had to be used for SBM-related activities. In addition, the principals were given budgetary control over two critical areas: supplies/equipment and staff travel.

Elm Street Elementary School and the Principal

Elm Street Elementary is one of the district's newest buildings. It opened just four years ago to accommodate the growing population of students in Sunland. The school has three sections per grade level in kindergarten through fifth grade, but there are plans to add a fourth section at each grade level if the enrollment projections prove to be accurate. When the school was opened, teachers from across the district had an opportunity to apply for a transfer to the new building; consequently, about 70 percent of the faculty were teachers who were already employed in the district.

Albert Batz had been the principal of a small elementary school in LaSalle County when he was selected as Elm Street's first principal. An outgoing, friendly individual, he relates well to students, staff, and parents. Prior to becoming an administrator, he had taught fifth grade for 12 years.

As principal of Elm Street, Mr. Batz spends virtually all of his time wandering around the building. He enjoys interacting with teachers, students, and other school personnel. It is not uncommon for him to walk into a classroom and join whatever activities are taking place. He usually makes two or three trips a day to the teachers' lounge, and one of his favorite mid-morning hideaways is the kitchen. Teachers often comment that they don't know if he is more interested in getting the latest gossip from the cooks or in sampling that day's dessert.

The teachers view Albert as a unique principal. He would rather be seen as just another teacher than as a manager. When he came to Elm Street, he brought his secretary, Mrs. Lumans, with him. The two work well together because she is willing to and capable of handling many of the routine management tasks that consume an elementary school principal's day.

Implementing SBM

When Dr. Jones announced that three elementary schools would be selected for the first phase of SBM implementation, Albert Batz was the first to contact her and express interest. He was committed to shared decision making, and, unlike some of his peers, maintaining power over teachers was not an issue. Before contacting the superintendent, however, Albert had asked for and received overwhelming support from the school's employees to do so.

In addition to being in philosophical agreement with the superintendent's plan, Albert had another motive for wanting to participate in SBM. When he came to Elm Street School, he encountered what was for him a novel problem. Two faculty factions had emerged. One consisted of four teachers who previously had taught at Harrison Elementary School, an older school in Sunland. The spokesperson for this group was Jenny Bales. The other consisted of three teachers who previously taught at Weakland Township Elementary School, one of the district's rural schools. The designated leader of this group was Leonard Teel. Although neither faction was very large, the two groups constantly vied for political support from the remaining faculty members.

Albert concluded that Mrs. Bales and Mr. Teel had similar traits and needs. In their previous schools, each had been the "alpha" teacher—that is, the teacher in the school who had the greatest power to influence others. Now, each was attempting to establish the same stature at Elm Street Elementary School. For the most part, the 15 teachers who were not aligned with either faction remained neutral.

When Elm Street was selected for the SBM project, Mr. Batz had to establish a governance committee. The size and composition of the committee was not specified by the superintendent. He chose to have an 11-member committee consisting of 6 teachers, 3 parents, 1 other school employee, and the principal. Rather than appointing the members, he asked the faculty, the PTA, and the school's nonteaching staff to select their representatives.

The faculty decided to hold an election to select its representatives. Any faculty member could file as a candidate. All seven members of the two factions announced their candidacy. Two other faculty members did likewise. Thus, nine teachers competed for the six council positions. Each teacher could vote for up to six candidates. Amy Raddison and Tim Paxton, who were not aligned with either faction, received the most votes. The other four successful candidates were Jenny Bales, Arlene McFadden (aligned with Mrs. Bales), Leonard Teel, and Lucille Isacson (aligned with Mr. Teel). Both Miss Raddison and Mr. Paxton were relatively young and inexperienced teachers.

Mr. Batz had hoped that being on the school council would satisfy the egos of both Mrs. Bales and Mr. Teel. He even thought that the two might find ways to reconcile their differences by interacting more frequently. After just four or five months, however, he realized that his hopes would not likely be realized. The adversarial relationship between the two teachers and their factions actually became more intense. The council simply provided a formal arena for their battles. As an example, an agenda item for the December meeting was approval to send a team of five teachers to a mid-January conference on SBM. Among the five teachers who were to attend the meeting in California were Mr. Teel and another teacher politically aligned with him. Mrs. Bales spoke against approving the request.

"Just because we have a budget for staff development doesn't mean that we should send people to California to learn about SBM."

Leonard Teel shot back immediately, "This conference focuses on model SBM programs. Teachers from all over the United States will be there. We can learn a great deal by participating. It's not my decision to have the conference in California. Why do you care where it is held?"

Mrs. Bales answered. "There are plenty of good programs closer to home. And for that reason, I urge everyone to vote against this request."

Barbara Whitlow, president of the PTA, had been elected as a parent representative to the council and subsequently as the council chair. Having to preside over yet another fight between Mrs. Bales and Mr. Teel, she turned to Mr. Batz and asked him if he recommended approval of the travel request.

He answered, "You know that I don't like to take sides. As principal, I need to be neutral. I have to work closely with all teachers. There is merit to both positions. Is it a good conference? Probably. Are there good conferences and workshops closer to home? Probably."

The principal's role on the council had been questioned on a number of occasions by Mrs. Whitlow. She had asked Mr. Batz several times to explain how his role as principal interfaced with his role as council member. His consistent response was that he was just like all the other council members and should be treated as such. Mrs. Whitlow considered his answer to be evasive, and in front of the other council members, she told him so. When the council was first formed, she had assumed that the principal would be the chair. When he declined to serve in this capacity, the other members did not object to his decision.

Both Mrs. Bales and Mr. Teel had consistently supported Mr. Batz's decision not to assume leadership of the council. Mrs. Whitlow concluded that the two actually preferred the principal's passive role.

After Mr. Batz evaded the question of whether he recommended approval of the conference request, Mrs. Bales made a formal motion to deny approval. His motion was seconded by Mrs. McFadden, the council member politically aligned with her. Mr. Teel requested that the vote on the motion be taken by secret ballot. The council was increasingly taking secret votes, and Mrs. Whitlow saw this process as counterproductive to building team spirit. The two other parents on the council were becoming increasingly disgruntled as well because most meetings were immersed in conflict.

The motion made by Mrs. Bales was defeated by a one-vote margin. One of the parents then made a motion to approve the travel request and it passed. The dispute, however, had an obvious negative affect on the climate in the room.

The next day, Mrs. Whitlow visited with Mr. Batz. She wanted to know why he refused to assume any form of leadership on the council.

"I just don't understand how you can sit back and allow Mrs. Bales and Mr. Teel to constantly be at each other. Don't you understand the destructive nature of their behavior?" she asked.

"Barbara, I still hope that those two will reconcile their differences and learn to cooperate. And even if I intervene, they will interpret my intervention as taking sides."

Mrs. Whitlow was frustrated with Mr. Batz and told him that unless he became a more active council member, she would resign. "You know, Albert, I have plenty to do besides spending 10 to 12 hours a week here at the school. I'm more than willing to volunteer my time; however, only if we start making progress. And right now, that is not happening. All the council members have done is sit and listen to those two argue. If this is SBM, I say we get rid of it. As principal, you have a responsibility to do something about this negative behavior."

Mr. Batz pleaded with Mrs. Whitlow to be patient. He told her that her continued leadership was essential to the council. Yet, he again sidestepped making a commitment to change his behavior. He told Mrs. Whitlow that he would think about being more vocal at the meetings.

Two days after visiting the principal, Mrs. Whitlow wrote a letter to Mr. Batz resigning from the council. Copies were sent to the superintendent, Dr. Jones, and each member of the LaSalle County school board. In her letter, she suggested that the whole idea of SBM ought to be examined more closely before it was adopted in all schools. She wrote:

> If schools are given leeway and added resources, we need to be certain that proper leadership is in place. Simply sharing power and authority does not ensure that our children will receive a better education. I am resigning from the Elm Street Elementary School Council because I'm frustrated—frustrated that I was unable to accomplish more as council chair and frustrated that the ambiguities concerning the principal's role on the council have not been resolved.

After reading the letter, Mr. Batz put it in his top desk drawer and thought about how the superintendent, school board, and Elm Street faculty would react.

After about a minute, he left his office, walking toward the school cafeteria. A smile came over his face as he got close enough to smell the freshly baked cookies.

The Challenge

Analyze the behavior of the principal in this case. Do you agree with Mrs. Whitlow that the principal has to take a more active role in the council? Why or why not?

Suggested Activities

1. Evaluate the process used by the superintendent to implement SBM in this school district. Identify other alternatives that could have been used to implement the program.

2. Discuss actions you would take to resolve the conflict between the two teacher factions if you were the principal of Elm Street Elementary School.

3. Discuss possible reasons why Mrs. Bales and Mr. Teel support the principal's behavior as a council member.

4. Identify knowledge and skills a principal should possess if the school to which he or she is assigned is engaged in SBM.

5. Complete the worksheet for Case 17.

Suggested Readings

Bergman, A. (1992). Lessons for principals from school-based management. *Educational Leadership, 50*(1), 48–51.

Conway, J. (1984). The myth, mystery, and mastery of participative decision making in education. *Educational Administration Quarterly, 21*(1), 11–40.

Delaney, J. G. (1997). Principal leadership: A primary factor in school-based management and school improvement. *NASSP Bulletin, 81*(586), 107–111.

Epp, J. R., & MacNeil, C. (1997). Perceptions of shared governance in an elementary school. *Canadian Journal of Education, 22*(3), 254–267.

Ferris, J. (1992). School-based decision making: A principal-agent perspective. *Educational Evaluation and Policy Analysis, 14*(4), 333–346.

Fraze, L., & Melton, G. (1992). Manager or participatory leader. *NASSP Bulletin, 76*(540), 17–24.

Golarz, R. (1992). School-based management pitfalls: How to avoid some and deal with others. *School Community Journal, 2*(1), 38–52.

Henkin, A. B., Cistone, P. J., & Dee, J. R. (2000). Conflict management strategies of principals in school-based managed schools. *Journal of Educational Administration, 38*(2), 142–158.

Hoyle, J. (1991). The principal and the pear tree. *Journal of School Leadership, 1*(2), 106–118.

Kowalski, T., Reitzug, U., McDaniel, P., & Otto, D. (1992). Perceptions of desired skills for effective principals. *Journal of School Leadership, 2*(3), 299–309.

Lange, J. (1993). School-based, shared decision making: A resource for restructuring. *NASSP Bulletin, 76*(549), 98–107.

Laud, L. E. (1998). Changing the way we communicate. *Educational Leadership, 55*(7), 23–25.

Leithwood, K., & Menzies, T. (1998). A review of research concerning the implementation of school-based management. *School Effectiveness and School Improvement, 9*(3), 233–285.

Michel, G. (1991). The principal's skills in school-based management. *Illinois Schools Journal, 71*(1), 33–38.

Midgley, C., & Wood, S. (1993). Beyond school-based management: Empowering teachers to reform schools. *Phi Delta Kappan, 75*(3), 245–252.

Miles, W. (1982). The school-site politics of education: A review of the literature. *Planning and Changing, 12*(4), 200–218.

Smylie, M. (1992). Teacher participation in school decision making: Assessing willingness to participate. *Educational Evaluation and Policy Analysis, 14*(1), 53–67.

Turk, R. L. (2002). What principals should know about building and maintaining teams. *NASSP Bulletin, 87*, 15–23.

Watkins, P. (1990). Agenda, power and text: The formulation of policy in school councils. *Journal of Education Policy, 5*(4), 315–331.

References

Brown, D. J. (1990). *Decentralization and school-based management*. London: Falmer.

Brown, F. (2001). School-based management: Is it still central to the school reform movement? *School Business Affairs, 67*(4), 5–6, 8–9.

Kowalski, T. J. (2003). *Contemporary school administration: An introduction*. Boston: Allyn and Bacon.

CASE 18

A Disillusioned Assistant Principal

Background Information

The behavior in schools is determined by a combination of personal, professional, and contextual variables. One of the most influential factors is socialization. This process begins during professional preparation. At this phase, professors usually expose students to values and beliefs commonly accepted by the profession and expressed in the formal knowledge base. Examples include advocating that educators place students above all else and promoting the idea that professionals have a commitment to be lifelong learners. Socialization continues when individuals begin their student teaching and subsequently practice as licensed teachers. However, the intensity and direction of the process are now influenced primarily by the prevailing culture of the workplace (Aiken, 2002). The same process of enculturation is repeated when a teacher becomes an administrator.

School culture represents the shared values and beliefs of those who work in the school. Over time, these values and beliefs represent accepted behavioral norms, especially in relation to how teachers and administrators should solve problems and make decisions (Hanson, 2003). A school's culture may be weak or strong; strong cultures are those in which educators share the same values and beliefs. A culture also may be negative or positive; positive cultures are those in which the shared values and beliefs are congruous with the professional knowledge base (Kowalski, 2003).

Adaptations to socialization vary. Most educators elect to adapt to the dominant values of the workplace, even when those values are incompatible with either professional norms or personal convictions. Some, however, resist. As an example, a principal may cling to a conviction that corporal punishment is effective even though an opposite belief is expressed in the professional literature and workplace. Within a relatively short period of time, typically one or two years, it becomes apparent if an administrator accepts or rejects the underlying beliefs of the workplace culture. Those who are successfully socialized typically do well; those who are not typically face unpleasant choices. That is, they may be dismissed, resign, or become mired in personal conflict. In the latter circumstance, they remain in the position but constantly struggle to reconcile their convictions (usually a combination of personal and professional beliefs) and the dominant values of the school's culture (Kowalski, 2003).

This case is about a young female teacher who becomes an assistant principal. During her first year, she realizes that her perception of administration differs from the principal's perception. She must decide if she can tolerate this conflict, if she is able to change her values and beliefs, or if she should pursue a new position.

Key Areas for Reflection

1. School culture
2. Socialization in organizations
3. Entry into school administration
4. Applications of the professional knowledge base
5. Ethical behavior
6. Determinants of administrative behavior

The Case

Amber Jackson sat in her office at Polk Middle School trying to finish work assigned by the principal. It was nearly 9:00 in the evening, and the three night custodians were the only other people in the building. She was tired and frustrated, making it difficult for her to focus. She kept glancing at the clock, realizing that she was not going to get much sleep that evening.

Amber had started teaching English and physical education at the middle school level at age 22. Two years later, she started coaching volleyball and enrolled as a part-time student in a master's degree program in English. Although teaching, coaching, and being a graduate student was taxing, she enjoyed all three of these roles.

After completing two graduate English classes, Amber inquired about changing her major to educational administration. She was told that she would have to apply to be admitted to the new program, and if accepted, her two English classes could be applied toward the professionalization of her teaching license. After changing majors, Dr. Tom Westerbrook, an assistant professor, was assigned to be her adviser. He was 40 years old, and previously he had been a principal in a suburban school district near San Diego. Amber enrolled in two of his classes: community relations and the principalship. Professor Westerbrook became both an adviser and a mentor for Amber. He considered her to be the best student he had encountered in the master's program. As she was nearing the end of her master's program, he told her, "Amber, you have a very promising career awaiting you in school administration. You are intelligent and your work ethic is great. I think you should start applying for assistant principal jobs. And once you find the right job, you should apply to be admitted to our doctoral program."

Amber had been teaching for five years and she recently became engaged to an Air Force captain whom she had known since undergraduate school. Although Professor Westerbrook's advice was flattering, and although the prospect of becoming an assistant principal was exciting, she had doubts about making the career move. She wondered whether five years of teaching was sufficient; she wondered whether getting married and becoming an assistant principal at the same time was a good idea.

Amber informed Professor Westerbrook that she was going to wait at least one year before applying for administrative positions. "I'm getting married in November, and my fiancé is an Air Force pilot currently stationed in Texas. His tour of duty will be over in about eight months, and then he plans to seek employment as a pilot. Therefore, I'm not sure where I'll be living a year from now. Once we get settled and he has a job, I'll apply for an administrative position."

Over the course of the following school year, Amber got married as planned and her husband became employed as a co-pilot for an air freight company based in Chicago. Once they relocated, Amber applied for both teaching and administrative positions in the Chicago area. By late June, she had two job offers: one for a teaching position in an affluent suburban district and the other for a middle school assistant principalship in a "blue-collar" suburban district. She elected to accept the latter.

Polk Middle School was constructed in the early 1960s when the population immediately south of Chicago was growing rapidly. The school had just over 800 students enrolled in grades 7 and 8. The school district's racial ethnic composition was nearly identical to school's composition.

White	72 percent (most of eastern European extraction)
African American	13 percent
Hispanic American	13 percent
Other	2 percent

Emil Denko has been principal at Polk for 14 years. He attended school in the district and most of his relatives still resided in the local community. The school's other assistant principal was Ernest Tarver, an African American. Both Mr. Denko and Mr. Tarver have announced plans to retire within three years.

Amber discovered that Polk and the California middle school where she previously taught were quite dissimilar. She had expected Polk to have more discipline and academic problems, and this proved to be true. She did not anticipate, however, that relationships among teachers and administrators would be substantially different. Confrontations between Polk teachers and administrators were common and the conflict was almost always resolved in one of two ways: either a settlement was negotiated between the principal and the teachers or the matter was adjudicated under the grievance procedures in the teachers' union master contract.

Despite their frequent disagreements with faculty, Mr. Denko and Mr. Carver seemed to have positive personal relationships with most teachers. Amber surmised that the parties had agreed to distinguish between political and personal relationships.

Amber also did not expect the teachers in the school to have such low expectations of their students. She felt that many teachers accepted the fact that 20 to 30 percent of the students were doomed to fail, largely because of their ability or because of their family conditions. She found the negative attitudes to be depressing.

After just three months at Polk, Amber was becoming dissatisfied with her job. She knew that discipline and management tasks were commonly assigned to assistant principals, but she never imagined that her entire job would be consumed by these activities. By the middle of the school year, she was considering submitting her resignation.

Amber telephoned her mentor, Dr. Westerbrook, and told him about her dissatisfaction. He told her, "It's difficult for me to give you advice because I don't know what Polk is really like. But before you do anything, you should talk to the principal. Be candid with him about your concerns. Maybe you would be better off in another school. But I don't think you should quit in the middle of the year. Doing so would make it difficult for you to get another administrative job."

Heeding Dr. Westerbrook's advice, Amber met with Mr. Denko and shared her concerns. She was specific about two of them.

"I don't understand why teachers have such a low opinion of students at this school. Have they created a self-fulfilling prophecy? Are they giving up on the students who most need their help? We talked about setting student expectations in several of my graduate classes, and I believe that setting high expectations affects students positively. One of my professors said that it was especially important for administrators to believe that students could succeed."

Mr. Denko was having difficulty listening to Amber because he was still trying to get past his surprise that she was dissatisfied with her job.

"How could you be dissatisfied? Here you are, not even 30 years old. You're already an administrator and you're making nearly twice as much as most teachers your age. And I think you're doing a pretty good job. Are you sure there isn't something outside of work bothering you?"

"Yes, I'm sure," Amber replied. "I just feel increasingly uncomfortable about the atmosphere in this school. Everyone seems negative about students. Many of the teachers appear to dislike their work, and they don't take much pride in being Polk employees. I'm not used to such attitudes."

"Well, maybe you never have seen the other side of the tracks before. It's easy to be critical and to prescribe solutions when you haven't worked in this type of community. But being here, working with all these problems day after day gives others a different perspective. Did you ever consider the possibility that the teachers are just being honest? Or did you consider that maybe they really are dedicated but they have to let off steam every so often?" he asked rhetorically. "The figures show that about 30 percent of these kids won't graduate from high school—at least not before they become adults. Many of them are from homes where education is not valued. I know. I have lived here all my life. Sure, we all like to dream that every student will go to college and become wealthy. The truth is that most of them will not be able to do this. I, too, had idealistic professors who talked about every student being potentially gifted and every student succeeding in school. And this was 25 years ago. The problem then and now is that many of these professors had no idea of what it is like to teach in a school like Polk."

At that point, Amber shifted the discussion to another concern. "Emil, I'm also bothered by the fact that I have little or no opportunity to work with teachers on instructional matters. I don't mind handling discipline problems, and I don't mind doing things like supervising students getting on and off buses. I expected that I would have some of these responsibilities—I just didn't expect them to be my entire job. One reason why I wanted to be an administrator was to work closely with teachers. When I started teaching, I had an excellent principal who showed interest in my professional growth. She was a terrific role model. And when I was working on my master's degree, my classes focused much more on instructional leadership than they did on supervising the lunch room or writing a discipline report. I just want to know if I will be involved in other types of administrative duties."

"Sure, you will," Mr. Denko answered. "For example, we have to do evaluations in March and you'll be helping us. You'll be assigned to evaluate about 10 teachers. That means you will have to observe each of them at least twice. But you need to understand, managing the school is our top priority. Teachers do not expect us to hold their hands. If they want help, they ask. And that rarely happens. The union discourages them from becoming dependent on us."

"Why?"

"Because that's the way unions operate. If teachers believe principals can solve their problems, they don't need a union. The doubts you're having about your work are not unusual. When teachers move from the classroom to administration, they have grand ideas about saving poor teachers and helping troubled students. But they quickly learn that these are unreachable dreams. You learn that in the real world, your job is to keep the school operating efficiently and safely. The taxpayers expect safe school environments so serious students can learn. That's the way it was when I started teaching in this community and that's the way it is today. You're at a point where you miss being with the students. There's a sense of freedom and power associated with having your own classroom and being able to shut the door to the rest of the school. In a couple of months, things will look different. Trust me. You have a real bright future here. In three years, you could be principal."

Hours after her meeting with the principal, Amber sat at her desk trying to finish the student discipline report. But her thoughts kept drifting back to Mr. Denko's comments. If anything, she was more dissatisfied than ever. The suggestion that she might become principal in a few years did nothing to boost her morale.

At 10:15 that evening, Amber finally finished the report and left school. As she drove home, she again compared Polk to the middle school where she previously taught English and coached volleyball. When she got home, she telephoned Dr. Westerbrook and told him that she had followed his advice about meeting with the principal. She then conveyed the principal's comments. "This does sound pretty negative," he told her. "Even so, I think it would be a mistake to resign immediately. At least wait until the end of the school year. Then apply for other jobs or consider entering a doctoral program."

The Challenge

Imagine that you find yourself in Amber's position. What would you do?

Suggested Activities

1. Discuss the meaning of school culture in relation to norms and administrative behavior.

2. Develop examples of the following: a weak negative school culture; a weak positive school culture; a strong negative culture; a strong positive culture. Determine which of the culture types is least and most preferred.

3. Identify the nexus between school culture and socialization. Also describe how the focus of socialization often changes when an educator begins practicing in schools.

4. One could argue that the central figure in this case (Amber) should have made a greater effort to examine school culture before becoming an assistant principal. Identify questions that an applicant could ask during interviews to determine if certain values and beliefs are dominant in the school.

5. Evaluate the principal in this case and decide whether you would like to work with him.

6. Complete the worksheet for Case 18.

Suggested Readings

Cantwell, Z. M. (1993). School-based leadership and the professional socialization of the assistant principal. *Urban Education, 28*(1), 49–68.

Derpak, D., & Yarema, J. (2002). Climate control. *Principal Leadership, 3*(4), 42–45.

Glanz, J. (1994). Dilemmas of assistant principals in the supervisory role: Reflections of an assistant principal. *Journal of School Leadership, 4*(5), 577–590.

Golanda, E. L. (1991). Preparing tomorrow's educational leaders: An inquiry regarding the wisdom of utilizing the position of assistant principal as an internship or apprenticeship to prepare future principals. *Journal of School Leadership, 1*(3), 266–283.

Goldring, L. (2002). The power of school culture. *Leadership, 32*(2), 32–35.

Hanna, J. W. (1998). School climate: Changing fear to fun. *Contemporary Education, 69*(2), 83–85.

Hartzell, G. N. (1993). When you're not at the top. *High School Magazine, 1*(2), 16–19.

Keedy, J. L., & Simpson, D. S. (2001). Principal priorities, school norms, and teacher influence: A study of sociocultural leadership in the high school. *Journal of Educational Administration and Foundations, 16*(1), 10–41.

Koru, J. M. (1993). The assistant principal: Crisis manager, custodian, or visionary? *NASSP Bulletin, 77*(556), 67–71.

Marshall, C. (1991). *The assistant principal: Leadership choices and challenges*. (ERIC Document Reproduction Service No. ED 342 086)

Michel, G. J. (1996). *Socialization and career orientation of the assistant principal*. (ERIC Document Reproduction Service No. ED 395 381)

Peterson, K. D. (2002). Positive or negative. *Journal of Staff Development, 23*(3), 10–15.

Picucci, A. C., Brownson, A., & Kahlert, R. (2002). Shaping school culture. *Principal Leadership (Middle School Ed.), 3*(4), 38–41.

Scoggins, A. J., & Bishop, H. L. (1993*). A review of literature regarding roles and responsibilities of assistant principals*. (ERIC Document Reproduction Service No. ED 371 436)

Toth, C., & Siemaszko, E. (1996). Restructuring the assistant principalship: A practitioner's guide. *NASSP Bulletin, 80*(578), 87–98.

References

Aiken, J. A. (2002). The socialization of new principals: Another perspective on principal retention. *Education Leadership Review, 3*(1), 32–40.

Hanson, E. M. (2003). *Educational administration and organizational behavior* (5th ed.). Boston: Allyn and Bacon.

Kowalski, T. J. (2003). *Contemporary school administration: An introduction* (2nd ed.). Boston: Allyn and Bacon.

Dissention over the Vocational School

Background Information

In many states, taxpayers have resisted consolidation because they did not want to lose control of their community-based public schools. Small districts and schools, however, faced the problem of providing adequate programming, especially in areas such as special education and vocational education. One solution to this problem has been the creation of joint service agencies. Existing in most states, these entities have the primary purposes of providing better and more efficient services through district and school collaboration. Notable examples include low-incidence special education programs and vocational education.

Vocational schools are found across the county; however, the governance and funding of these institutions are not uniform from state to state. Some vocational high schools are part of a statewide network (e.g., Delaware), some only serve students in a single district, but most are operated by a joint service agency—basically confederations that are independent or quasi-independent cooperatives structured under state laws (Kowalski, 1999). Even among confederation-operated schools, differences are found in the following areas:

1. *Funding.* In some states, the confederations are allowed to levy taxes independently; in other states, revenues are generated by charging member districts fees.
2. *Organization.* Some vocational schools are independent of area high schools, only enroll full-time students, and grant their own diplomas; others are legally attached to one or more regular high schools, enroll only part-time students, and do not grant diplomas (diplomas are granted by the student's home high school).
3. *Scope of programming.* Some vocational schools offer only vocational programs and courses; others offer a broader curriculum (e.g., offering both vocational programs and remedial programs in the basic subjects).

As the school reform movement gained energy during the 1980s, a number of questions were raised about the need for and value of vocational high schools. Ernest Boyer (1983) charged that vocational education did not provide students with a sufficiently broad education and did not prepare them adequately for careers. John Goodlad (1984) pointed out that the purposes of these schools were no longer valid in an information-based society. Others (e.g., Oakes, 1985) claimed that vocational schools essentially perpetuated student tracking, a concept that separates students into groups so that they can receive a curriculum deemed to be based on their ability and interests. Critics of tracking claim that the practice has been especially detrimental for minority and low-income students.

Proponents of vocational education typically have responded to these criticisms by claiming three benefits:

1. Many students who attend vocational schools would otherwise not complete high school.
2. The academic skills of vocational school students do not deteriorate; their scores on standardized academic tests are no different from students in traditional schools who are at the same ability level.
3. Area employers are strongly supportive of vocational schools and view them to be successful. Demands for skilled workers are increasing, not decreasing.

Despite these counterarguments, the future of vocational education remains uncertain in some states. Although intense criticisms over the past two decades have not eliminated area vocational high schools, they certainly succeeded in casting a cloud over them. To this day, policymakers and educators disagree over their need and value.

This case is about conflict among superintendents and principals who are members of a confederation operating an area vocational school. The conflict intensifies to the point that the future of the confederation, and the vocational high school it operates, are placed in doubt.

Key Areas for Reflection

1. Collaboration among school districts
2. Ethical, moral, and legal obligations
3. Vocational education
4. Reform in high schools

The Case

Medford Area Vocational High School (MAVHS) has a proud history. Established in southern Indiana in the early 1960s, it often has been cited as a model school. Located in a serene rural setting, the school serves nearly 600 students coming from

15 school districts and 19 high schools across 6 counties; all students attend the vocational school on a half-time basis. The school's governing board consists of the superintendents from each of the participating districts, and the 19 high school principals are members of the school's curriculum advisory council.

Prior to the early 1990s, virtually no dissatisfaction had been voiced about MAVHS. In its first 30 years of operation, the school had only two principals; the third and current principal, Roscoe Emmons, was not employed until 1995. He is a former vocational agriculture teacher and high school assistant principal. After assuming the principalship, he discovered several problems that he pointed out to the superintendents:

1. Enrollment has been declining steadily at a rate of about 1 percent per year for the previous six years.
2. The facility, constructed in 1963, has not been renovated or improved, and some areas are now in poor condition.
3. Much of the equipment is outdated and needed to be replaced.
4. The curriculum has not changed very much since the school first opened.
5. Some high school principals report parental resistance to enrolling their children in MAVHS either because the school has acquired a reputation for serving low-achieving students or because of the perception that many of the school's students are discipline problems.

Mr. Emmons recommended that the board retain a consultant to examine these problems. Only two of the superintendents were supportive; the others basically commented that the problems were exaggerated.

Five years later, nothing had been done to address the problems identified by Principal Emmons. The enrollment dipped below 600 for the first time since 1965, several critical letters about the school were printed in local newspapers, and needed programs could not be added to the curriculum, either because of physical environment restrictions or because of a lack of technology. Moreover, tensions between the principals on the curriculum advisory board and MAVHS staff members were intensifying. Conflict emerged in two areas: student discipline and the location of selected vocational programs. The first issue centered on disputes over how students should be disciplined for infractions that occurred at the vocational school. Since the students were still enrolled in their home high schools, the principals of those high schools felt they had to agree to any disciplinary action recommended by MAVHS staff. Historically, punishment administered by the vocational school administrators was honored by the home school administrators. Now, several new principals were taking exception to this arrangement. The second issue was more complex. Some high schools in the confederation had lost considerable enrollment and their principals were seeking to satellite some of the vocational school's programs in their schools. Doing so would provide revenue to the depressed districts, because their high schools would receive a fee for housing the programs. Two other high schools had grown substantially in the past decade and their principals were seeking to duplicate programs now offered by the vocational school. As an example, one principal wanted to start a construction trades class at his school because he now had sufficient enrollment to operate the program independently.

At the beginning of the 2002 school year, Principal Emmons announced that he would be retiring in two years and shared his concerns about MAVHS's future. Efforts to recruit students had slowed but not eliminated enrollment declines; the building was deteriorating rapidly; curriculum revisions were badly needed; and the school's image was increasingly being tarnished by its critics. Principal Emmons made a commitment to press these issues with the governing board.

The governing board had experienced considerable change since 1995; nearly half (seven) of the members changed between 1995 and 2002. Mr. Emmons was hopeful that the new superintendents would be more interested in dealing with the vocational school's problems. Additionally, he felt that the tensions between the home school principals and the vocational school staff had to be resolved.

In 2002, the chair of the governing board was Madeline Watkins, superintendent of the second smallest district in the confederation. She was a staunch supporter of MAVHS and of Principal Emmons. Uncertain as to how the board members would react when the principal raised these issues, she made the effort to speak to other 14 superintendents separately. She received mixed reactions. Five of her colleagues appeared supportive; three clearly were still opposed to dealing with these issues; the remainder said they were open-minded.

At the November meeting, Principal Emmons made a detailed report on the vocational school and its lingering problems. He again recommended that the board commission an external consultant to study the problems, including tensions with the home school principals. After a lengthy discussion, a motion to approve the superintendent's recommendation passed by a vote of 8 to 3, with 4 members abstaining.

A professor from one of the state universities was retained to study the issues outlined by the principal. Over the next six months, the consultant interviewed over 160 people, including parents, students, staff, home school administrators, board members, and advisory council members. In addition, data were collected from over 30 local employers regarding their satisfaction with MAVHS graduates and their future employment needs.

The consultant presented his findings and conclusions to the governing board in late June of 2003. A summary of his report follows:

- The vocational school's curriculum should be revamped. A greater emphasis needs to be placed on technology-based courses and programs. Several programs should be deleted because of low enrollment, low demand for graduates, or both.
- After the curriculum is revised, the facility should be completely renovated and new spaces created to accommodate the new technology-based courses/programs.
- The vocational school staff should develop and execute a public relations plan to increase communication with external publics and to enhance the school's image.

- Discipline problems should be adjudicated via collaboration between administrators from the home high schools and the vocational school.
- Member high schools should not be allowed to develop duplicate programs and programs now housed at the vocational school should not be relocated to home high schools. Making such decisions on the basis of evolving needs in member districts would set a negative precedent and jeopardize the welfare of the confederation.
- A long-term equipment replacement plan needs to be developed and coordinated with program changes and facility improvements.

All 15 superintendents and Mr. Emmons were present but there was virtually no discussion after the consultant finished his presentation. Several questions were asked, but no superintendent commented as to whether he or she agreed with the findings and recommendations. Superintendent Watkins thanked the consultant and the meeting ended.

Mr. Emmons met with the vocational school staff later that day. Although school was not in session because of the summer break, nearly all of the staff attended the meeting. The principal said he was pleased with all of the consultant's recommendations except for the one addressing student discipline. He urged his staff to support all of the recommendations, however, since accepting the recommendation on discipline would be an indicator of good faith.

Principal Emmons and Superintendent Watkins were anxious to reconvene the governing board so that they could determine reactions to the consultant's report. The next scheduled meeting was in late August, and they tried to get the superintendents to meet in July. Six of them said they were unavailable and objected to the meeting being held without them being present. Given this feedback, Superintendent Watkins again called each of her colleagues to see if they would share their response to the report. Again, the superintendents were divided. The most controversial issue was the renovation of the facility. Under state law, all of the member districts had to share in the cost based on the percentage of district enrollment to the total enrollment in the consortium. Six superintendents declared that they would openly oppose spending money on the facility. They argued that the future of vocational education was in question, and until that matter was resolved, they were not going to recommend to their school boards that they support the construction costs. Four superintendents said they would support all of the consultant's recommendations. The remaining five superintendents said they were undecided; they wanted to hear the reactions of other superintendents and of their own board members.

When Principal Emmons was told how the superintendents reacted to the report, he was disappointed. He had developed some political insights about the behavior of the board members, and he surmised that when they convened in August, the dissenters would control the outcome. This was because at least three of the undecided superintendents typically followed the lead of several superintendents who were part of the dissenter group. Thus, he concluded that simply waiting until the August meeting and hoping that his prediction about the outcome would be wrong was a risky alternative.

Principal Emmons desperately wanted to develop a positive agenda for MAVHS before he retired in approximately 13 months. But this goal now looked like it was out of reach. Even worse, it appeared that he would be forced to leave his successor with more and deeper problems than those he had inherited nearly a decade ago. Roscoe Emmons has never been inclined to solve problems politically, but this situation was causing him to consider such options. Should he try to win over the superintendents by meeting with them one on one? He had never tried to influence their votes in the past. Should he mobilize the school's supporters, such as local employers and members of the trades advisory councils, and direct them to take political action? He was confident that many of these individuals would become vocal if they thought the future of the school was in jeopardy. Should he take his case directly to the media? In the past, he had avoided reporters and preferred that MAVHS maintain a low profile. Or should he try to compromise with the dissenters? Perhaps they would be willing to support some of the recommendations, and salvaging these points might be better than losing on all points.

The Challenge

Assume that Principal Emmons is a friend and colleague. What advice would you give him regarding this situation?

Suggested Activities

1. Evaluate the political alternatives mentioned at the end of the case. Determine how you would treat each one if you were principal.

2. Determine what you would like to accomplish in dealing with this matter if you were one of the superintendents on the governing board.

3. Discuss the status of vocational schools in your state and determine if the future of these schools is in question.

4. Evaluate the consultant's recommendation that the home school and vocational school administrators should collaborate on discipline issues.

5. Discuss issues that have led critics to call for the demise of vocational schools and determine whether you agree or disagree with the critics.

6. Complete the worksheet for Case 19.

Suggested Readings

Bamford, P. J. (1995). Success by design: The restructuring of a Vo-Tech center. *Tech Directions, 54*(7), 15–17.

Dembicki, M. (2000). He's got the hook. *Techniques: Connecting Education and Careers, 75*(3), 28–31.

Harkins, A. M. (2002). The futures of career and technical education in a continuous innovation society. *Journal of Vocational Education Research, 27*(1), 35–64.

Jenkins, J. M. (2000). Looking backward: Educational reform in the twentieth century. *International Journal of Educational Reform, 9*(1), 74–78.

Lynch, R. L. (2000). High school career and technical education for the first decade of the 21st century. *Journal of Vocational Education Research, 25*(2), 155–198.

MacIver, M. A., & Legters, N. (2001). Partnerships for career-centered high school reform in an urban school system. *Journal of Vocational Education Research, 26*(3), 412–446.

Reese, S. (2001). High school career tech at the crossroads. *Techniques: Connecting Education and Careers, 76*(7), 33–35.

Ries, E. (1999). Packed by popular demand. *Techniques: Making Education and Career Connections, 74*(3), 22–25.

Rossetti, R. (1991). *Factors that influence students not to enroll at the Vanguard Joint Vocational School. Factors that influence students not to enroll at the Lawrence County Joint Vocational School.* (ERIC Document Reproduction Service No. ED 334 357)

Shumer, R. (2001). A new, old vision of learning, working, and living: Vocational education in the 21st century. *Journal of Vocational Education Research, 26*(3), 447–461.

Seccurro, W. B., & Thomas, D. W. (1998). School improvement through Tech Prep: How one vocational school changed its program and image. *Tech Directions, 57*(8), 22–23.

References

Boyer, E. L. (1983). *High school.* New York: Harper.

Goodlad, J. I. (1984). *A place called school.* New York: McGraw-Hill.

Kowalski, T. J. (1999). *The school superintendent: Theory, practice, and cases.* Upper Saddle River, NJ: Merrill, Prentice Hall.

Oakes, J. (1985). *Keeping track: How schools structure inequality.* New Haven, CT: Yale University.

In-School Suspension:
An Effective Idea?

Background Information

Substance abuse policies and rules present a major challenge to school administrators for two reasons. First, they have been a source of controversy for some time because members of the school community often disagree about the causes of these problems and how they should be handled. As an example, some principals treat illegal drug use as a criminal matter and they advocate harsh penalties and zero-tolerance policies. Others treat substance abuse as a disability and they advocate counseling or other therapeutic measures that allow a student to remain in school. Regardless of beliefs, however, all administrators recognize that illegal drugs are disruptive and dangerous in schools. Second, policy and rules related to the possession, use, or sale of illegal drugs are often tested in the courts. For example, zero-tolerance policies established by school boards have been the subject of litigation in recent years (Henault, 2001; Zirkel, 1999).

Suspension is commonly used as a disciplinary measure in high school. This form of punishment may occur outside or inside the school. In-school suspensions isolate students from the main population while requiring those being disciplined to remain in school. Such programs are often designed to be punitive but some are structured to provide either academic or behavioral remediation (Sheets, 1996). Critics of in-school suspension programs argue that the behavior of some students placed in the program is sufficient to exclude from the school's general population.

This case is about an inexperienced principal who establishes an in-school suspension program in a high school that has been experiencing high rates of expulsions and dropouts. Some parents object to this form of punishment, especially for students committing violent acts or caught using drugs. Criticisms are magnified when two students in the in-school suspension program are arrested for selling cocaine in the school's parking lot. The conflict causes the principal to question whether she wants to continue in her present role.

Key Areas for Reflection

1. Readiness for the principalship
2. Job satisfaction
3. Control of pupil conduct
4. Job-related stress
5. Principal and staff relationships
6. Political dimensions of controversial decisions

The Case

"Are you serious?" Lowell Tatum asked his wife as they were having dinner at their favorite San Francisco restaurant. "Now let me get this straight. You want to leave your job as coordinator of English Education to become a high school principal? You ought to think about this. You know what high school students are like and you should know that a principalship would be a much more taxing position."

Patricia Tatum has met challenges successfully throughout her life. Born in Los Angeles in a low-income family, she is the oldest of six children. Neither of her parents graduated from high school, but they provided a warm, caring family environment. They also set high expectations for their children, especially with respect to education.

All through school, Patricia was a good student and leader. Her interests were diversified. She was an athlete (track), a cheerleader, and president of the student council. When she graduated from high school, she ranked sixth in a class of 389. She received an academic scholarship to attend a private university, which was only 20 miles from her home. Even though she maintained two part-time jobs, she finished her degree in four years and graduated cum laude.

One of Pat's part-time jobs during college was as a teacher's aide in a parochial elementary school. It was there that she first thought about becoming a teacher and abandoning her original goal of going to law school. As she started her last semester of undergraduate work, she agonized about her future. Becoming a teacher would require more academic study because she had not been pursuing a teacher's license in conjunction with her English major. In addition, she already had been accepted by two reputable law schools. Just three weeks before graduating, she decided that she really wanted to be a teacher.

After graduating, Pat was employed as a copy editor with a small publishing firm and enrolled in evening courses to pursue a master's program in English Education. While in graduate school, she met Lowell Tatum, a graduate student completing a master's in business administration. Lowell worked as a stockbroker in Los Angeles. After they finished graduate school, they got married. Lowell received a promotion and was transferred to San Francisco. Pat applied for teaching positions in the Bay area and accepted a job teaching in a public suburban high school.

Four years later Pat and Lowell had their first child. Pat resigned from her teaching position and she had a second child two years later. During the six years she was away from teaching, Pat enrolled in several classes at a local university. Encouraged by one of her professors, she entered the university's doctoral program in educational administration. Three years later, she completed her degree and decided to return to work. She initially applied for assistant principal positions, two of which were in the school district where she formerly had been a teacher. Several weeks after filing application, that district's personnel director contacted her, not about the assistant principal positions but rather about a vacancy for an English Education coordinator. Pat knew about the job but had not applied because of her lack of administrative experience. Subject area coordinators in this district were staff administrators; they focused on curriculum and instructional programs and facilitated teacher needs. She immediately expressed interest in the position. After an interview with several assistant superintendents, she was selected for the job.

Initially, Dr. Tatum enjoyed being a coordinator. Toward the end of her first year in that position, however, she raised the possibility of being a principal with her immediate supervisor, Dr. Ernesto Javier, the associate superintendent for instruction.

"I don't want you to think I'm unhappy, because I'm not," she told him. "It's just that I miss being with students. I can't explain it. What I would really like is to be a building-level administrator. That's what I intended to do when I finished my doctorate, but when the opportunity to be a coordinator came along, I couldn't say no."

Dr. Javier was an experienced administrator, having been a principal for 14 years before becoming an assistant superintendent. He looked at Dr. Tatum and said, "I don't think we will have any assistant principal positions open for next year. As you know, we just filled two positions last summer. I will help you find a job in another district if that is what you really want. Personally, I want you stay on my staff. You're doing really well as a coordinator—I have heard many positive comments from teachers and principals about your work."

Dr. Tatum had mixed feelings when she left Dr. Javier's office. She was pleased with the evaluation of her work but disappointed that there were no assistant principal vacancies. She did not tell her husband about the conversation with Dr. Javier and decided to wait until the school term finished in about three weeks before deciding whether to apply for a new job in another district.

Two weeks after meeting with Dr. Javier, he called her and requested that she see him as soon as possible. He said he wanted to discuss a possible job opportunity with her. They met in his office that afternoon.

"Pat, Mr. Malovidge at Western Valley High School just submitted his resignation. He is moving to Seattle to take another position," Dr. Javier told her. "I talked to the superintendent this morning, and we have decided that you would make an excellent interim principal. I shared your interest in a building-level position with him, and this arrangement should be mutually beneficial. Our intention is to conduct a search for a permanent principal for the following school year."

Dr. Tatum was surprised.

"Why me?" she asked. "Don't the assistant principals at Western Valley want the job?"

"That's the problem. Two of the three assistants very much want the job. Picking one over the other could create tension. Each has a group of supporters on the faculty. But that is not the only reason that we think you are the right person for the job. We are looking for fresh ideas."

Dr. Tatum requested several days to consider the job offer. Dr. Javier told her she had 48 hours.

"Before I leave, would you explain the implications of this being an interim position?" she requested.

"Certainly. If you do well and want to remain in the job, you would have an excellent chance of being named the permanent principal. We will conduct a search around December or January, and at that time, you will have to decide if you want to be an applicant. At least you will find out if you like working at the building level more than you like working in the central office."

The prospect of his wife becoming a high school principal was disconcerting to Lowell Tatum. Although he supported her career interests, he worried about the time demands and stress that were associated with being a high school principal. How would this job affect the time she spent with him and the children? Would she have to work on weekends? He quickly discovered, however, that Pat had already decided to take the job.

Western Valley High School has about 2,300 students in grades 9 through 12. The school's student population is diverse, both economically and racially. Most students come from middle-class homes and about 55 percent of the graduates enroll in four-year institutions of higher education.

Dr. Tatum had been to Western Valley High School about a dozen times in the previous year in her coordinator capacity and had become acquainted with all the English teachers and the three assistant principals. Joe Howey and Bill Fine are the two assistant principals who wanted to be the interim principal. When the announcement was made that Patricia Tatum would become the interim principal, both of them were surprised. Each had substantially more experience than she. The third assistant principal, Sally Farmer, was approximately Dr. Tatum's age, and she had only one year of administrative experience. Unlike her two colleagues, she was relieved by the announcement; she feared that appointing either Mr. Howey or Mr. Fine would divide the faculty and parents.

In her first meetings with the assistant principals after starting her new job at Western Valley, Dr. Tatum outlined her expectations for the next year. She stressed that they would work as a team and then asked them to recommend how administrative responsibilities would be divided. Collectively, they decided that Dr. Tatum and Ms. Farmer would have primary responsibility for the instructional programs. Mr. Howey would be responsible for most management functions, such as food services, scheduling, budgets, and the like. Mr. Fine agreed to supervise extracurricular programs, including athletics. Student discipline, the assignment none of them wanted, would be shared by all four administrators.

After school started, Dr. Tatum realized that it was difficult for her to spend most of her time working with instructional programs. No matter how meticulously she planned, her intentions were thwarted by unanticipated day-to-day problems. And although the four administrators were sharing discipline responsibilities, almost all of the more serious cases were referred to her office. This was especially true of substance abuse cases.

The former principal had taken a hard line toward illegal drugs; generally, students caught possessing, using, or selling drugs were expelled. Western Valley had the highest expulsion rate among the district's four high schools. The assistant principals supported this zero-tolerance position. Dr. Tatum, however, was less inclined to support such an inflexible rule. She preferred to judge cases on their merits. As an example, she believed that a first offense for possessing marijuana should not be treated the same as either a second offense or a first offense involving selling drugs. However, her attempt to revise the school's rule on drugs met with resistance from the three assistant principals. Not dissuaded, Dr. Tatum immediately appointed a committee consisting of two parents, one a social worker and the other a psychologist, Mr. Fine, and four teachers to study the matter. The committee was asked to make recommendation prior to school opening in late August.

The committee examined the rules used by the district's other schools and by schools in neighboring districts. The members also heard testimony from several experts, including narcotics officers. Based on a 4 to 3 vote, the committee recommended the following:

- First-time offenders for possession or use of an illegal drug would be placed in an in-school suspension. The length of suspension would depend on the nature of the drug and the student's overall discipline record.
- Second-time offenders for possession or use would either receive an out-of-school suspension or be expelled.
- All students found guilty of selling illegal drugs will be expelled.

Mr. Fine overtly opposed the recommendations and he warned Dr. Tatum that she would be making a big mistake if she abandoned the current zero-tolerance rule.

Dr. Tatum discussed the recommendations with Dr. Javier before making a decision. She wanted to make sure that the recommendations did not conflict with district policy. Dr. Javier told her that the district's policy allowed principals to establish their own penalties for first-time offenders; individuals caught possessing, using, or selling drugs or alcohol a second time had to be expelled. Thus, the committee's recommendation on second-time offenders could not be adopted.

Dr. Javier then asked, "Are you sure you want to do this while you are an interim principal? The safe alternative would be to wait. If you are selected as the permanent principal, you would be in a better political position to handle this matter."

Dr. Tatum spent much of the following week weighing the committee's recommendation regarding an in-school suspension program. School was opening in about two weeks and she could wait no longer. She asked Dr. Javier to seek approval from the superintendent and school board. Approval was granted at the September school board meeting and the program was established on October 1.

In February, Dr. Tatum was named the school's regular principal. Despite initial concerns, the in-school suspension program did not cause problems the first year. A total of 14 students were placed in the program; only 2 of them were first-time drug possession offenders. The school's expulsion rate dropped about 15 percent.

During the first few weeks of the next school year, the number of drug-related discipline cases increased substantially. By late October, seven students had received in-school suspensions as first-time drug offenders. Dr. Tatum started receiving complaints from faculty and parents who believed that the in-school suspension program had created a "relaxed attitude" about drugs at the school. One parent wrote the following letter to the principal.

> Dear Dr. Tatum:
>
> It has come to my attention that students who are caught using drugs are being allowed to stay in school. As a parent, I think this sends the wrong message. My wife and I tell our children that using illegal drugs is a serious offense. I'm not sure that your approach to dealing with the problem reinforces what we tell them. I urge you to discontinue the in-school suspension program.

Bill Fine did not hide his sentiments. He told several disgruntled teachers and parents that he had always opposed the in-school suspension program. Joe Howey and Sally Farmer began distancing themselves from the program. As an example, they stressed that they had not been members of the committee that recommended it be established. Dr. Tatum, however, remained convinced that the benefits outweighed the costs.

In early November, two students in the in-school suspension program for marijuana possession were arrested for selling cocaine to undercover police in the school's parking lot. The arrests made the evening news, and for the next few days, it received considerable media coverage. A television reporter interviewed several disgruntled parents who blamed the principal for creating loopholes in the zero-tolerance policy. Even several teachers commented publicly that the in-school suspension program was a bad idea.

One of the local television stations aired a 10-minute report on drugs at Western Valley High School. The commentator began by saying:

> In-school suspension at Western Valley: a solution or a problem? Parents and teachers at Western Valley are up in arms over an in-school suspension program for first-time drug and alcohol offenders. Parents and faculty who favored a zero-tolerance policy that was in place under the previous principal have criticized the current principal, Dr. Patricia Tatum. They believe that the in-school suspension program she created has contributed to a rise in drug use at the school. Their concerns were

heightened by the recent arrests of two students in this program. They were initially caught smoking marijuana in a school restroom and were placed in the in-school suspension program for three months. Only five weeks later they were caught selling cocaine to undercover police in the school's parking lot. School district officials said they are reconsidering the future of the in-school suspension program.

Two days after the arrests, Dr. Tatum met with the district's superintendent, Dr. Nicolas Constantine, at his request. He had several questions. The first was whether students in the in-school suspension program had received counseling. She answered that they were required to see a school counselor at least one hour each week. The counselor could recommend placement in a drug education program as a condition for being readmitted to the school's regular program. Neither of the students who had been arrested had been referred for such a program.

Dr. Constantine also discussed alternatives for students who were expelled. The district operated both an alternative high school and an adult evening school. Students expelled from a high school were eligible for either of these programs.

"Why do you think in-school suspension is better than having these students at an alternative school?" he asked.

"Our records show that expelled students don't enroll at the alternative school. This option was examined in detail by the committee that recommended the in-school suspension program," Dr. Tatum explained.

As the meeting ended, Dr. Constantine said that the in-school suspension program could continue, but he told the principal that closer supervision and mandatory drug education had to be provided.

After leaving the superintendent's office, Dr. Tatum went to see Dr. Javier.

"Listen, Pat, controversy is part of a principal's life," he told her. "This isn't the first time students got busted for selling drugs in the parking lot, and it certainly won't be the last. The issue is in-school suspension for first-time drug offenders. My advice is to keep the program but go back to the zero-tolerance policy for drugs. You're taking too much heat over this."

Two days later, Dr. Tatum received an anonymous letter accusing her of being incompetent. The author contended that the superintendent was protecting her simply because she is an African American female. The letter was written on Western Valley High School stationery.

For the first time, Dr. Tatum began thinking that her husband may have been correct about her decision to be a high school principal. She called Dr. Javier and shared her self-doubts.

"Pat, I am partly to blame because I talked you into taking this job. If you leave the principalship just because of the in-school suspension issue, you would be making a mistake. The job is much more than drugs and discipline. Think about the many ways you have had a positive effect on students and faculty. However, if you decide you want out of this job, I'll approve a transfer back to my division. I'll be supportive no matter what you decide to do."

The Challenge

Place yourself in Dr. Tatum's position. What would you do?

Suggested Activities

1. Discuss the advantages and disadvantages of in-school suspension programs.

2. Develop a list of qualifications that you believe are essential for becoming a high school principal. Compare your list of qualifications to the licensing requirements in your state.

3. Compare policies and rules in school districts represented in your class for dealing with the possession, use, or sale of illegal drugs. Determine which policies and rules are most and least effective.

4. Assume that the principal in this case was a white male. Determine what if any issues would be different.

5. Complete the worksheet for Case 20.

Suggested Readings

Eckman, E. W. (2002). Women high school principals: Perspectives on role conflict, role commitment, and job satisfaction. *Journal of School Leadership, 12*(1), 57–77.

Holtkamp, L. A. (2002). Crossing borders: An analysis of the characteristics and attributes of female public school principals. *Advancing Women in Leadership Journal, 10*(1), 2–6.

Johnston, J. (1989). High school completion of in-school suspension students. *NASSP Bulletin, 73*(521), 89–95.

Lohrmann, D., & Fors, S. (1988). Can school-based educational programs really be expected to solve the adolescent drug abuse problem? *Journal of Drug Education, 16*(4), 327–339.

Sheets, J. (1996). Designing an effective in-school suspension program to change student behavior. *NASSP Bulletin, 80*(579), 86–90.

Skiba, R., & Peterson, R. (1999). The dark side of zero tolerance: Can punishment lead to safe schools? *Phi Delta Kappan, 80*(5), 372–376, 381–382.

Sullivan, J. (1989). Elements of a successful in-school suspension program. *NASSP Bulletin, 73*(516), 32–38.

Watson, D., & Bright, A. (1988). So you caught them using drugs: Now what? *Thrust, 17*(3), 34–36.

Whitfield, D., & Bulach, C. (1996). A study of the effectiveness of in-school suspension. (ERIC Document Reproduction Service No. ED 396 372)

Zirkel, P. A. (1996). Discipline and the law. *Executive Educator, 18*(7), 21–23.

Zorn, R. (1988). New alternatives to student suspensions for substance abuse. *American Secondary Education, 17*(2), 30–32.

References

Henault, C. (2001). Zero tolerance in schools. *Journal of Law and Education, 30*(3) 547–553.

Sheets, J. (1996). Designing an effective in-school suspension program to change student behavior. *NASSP Bulletin, 80*(579), 86–90.

Zirkel, P. A. (1999). Zero tolerance expulsions. *NASSP Bulletin, 83*(605), 101–105.

Let's Not Rap

Background Information

Diversity creates new challenges for many administrators. In the past, most administrators have been employed in rural and small districts with basically homogeneous populations. Although a majority of administrators continue to work outside of urban districts, the environmental context of their work has changed. Even many small farming communities now have minority populations. Diversity has been recognized as a cogent reform issue. For example, those who have studied highly diverse urban districts (e.g., Miron, St. John, & Davidson, 1998) often conclude that resolving racial conflict is essential to implementing school improvement initiatives effectively.

Multiculturalism has become a major political topic both within and outside of public education. Factions in many communities take opposite positions on issues such as bilingual education and the study of diverse culture. Even affluent suburban communities have not escaped this type of controversy. As an example, the courts already have intervened in some situations where school boards and employees have clashed over the advocacy of multiculturalism (Zirkel, 2001).

The social and cultural contexts found in many school district challenge administrators in several ways. This case describes a situation in which two community groups take opposite sides over the scheduling of a school convocation. A "rap" group's offer to present a program that encourages students not to use illegal drugs has been accepted by the school's administration. When the convocation's program is announced publicly, Jewish families in the community demand that it be cancelled. Their objections stem from a belief that several of the performers are anti-Semites. Members of the school's African American community respond aggressively, demanding that the convocation not be cancelled.

As you read this case, pay particular attention to how both economic and ethnic diversity become intertwined. Decisions made by public officials are not always determined by majority opinions. Administrators also have a responsibility to protect the rights of minorities and to make moral and ethical decisions.

Key Areas for Reflection

1. Multicultural school environments
2. School and community relationships
3. Diversity and its effects on education
4. Factors influencing administrative decisions
5. Resolving conflict
6. Free speech and public schools

The Case

Principal

Barb Doran is principal of Roosevelt High School, a highly respected institution located in a suburb of a major city in a mid-Atlantic state. She has been in this position for less than two years, but she has already established a reputation as an effective administrator.

After teaching English for 12 years, Ms. Doran has had three progressively challenging administrative positions. The first was as assistant principal of a 350-student middle school; the second was as principal of a 500-student rural high school; and the third was as principal of Roosevelt—a school that is over five times as large as the one in which she previously worked.

Bad News

Barb Doran had just returned from a conference in Orlando, Florida. She was driving from the airport to her office at approximately 7:30 in the evening. The car's radio was tuned to a station that aired a local talk program. After listening to just two callers state their views, Barb knew that tonight's topic was Roosevelt High School. As the show's host accepted another call, Barb increased the volume.

"I think the principal should have the courage to cancel this convocation. What good does it do to expose students to anti-drug messages if the people delivering the messages express hatred toward others? There are other more acceptable ways to teach students not to use drugs than having the message delivered by negative role models."

The next caller took an opposite position, "We all know about racial tensions at Roosevelt High. African American students don't get treated equally or fairly at that school. Let me give you an example. Someone told me that a white kid who got caught smoking in the restroom got only one hour of detention. The very next day a black kid got caught smoking, and he got a three-day suspension. Now, you have to admit that the Roosevelt administrators are not being even-handed. Given the track record of the principal and her staff, I bet she cancels the convocation. She's going to back down from the Jewish community. But she better be careful because the African American community is not going to just sit back and take it."

Without responding to the caller, the show's host prepared for a commercial break, "For those of you who just tuned in, tonight's topic deals with yet another controversy at Roosevelt High. Should the school allow a "rap" group to deliver an anti-drug program? Some parents argue that several of the group's members have a track record as anti-Semites. These parents are demanding that the principal cancel the convocation. Others obviously disagree. Like our last caller, they argue that canceling the program will be another slap in the face to the African American community. What do you think? Here is your chance to join the debate. Give us a call at 555–1500. I'll be back in a moment to take more calls."

Barb Doran stared at the road ahead as she continued toward her office. She asked herself how all of this could have happened during the few days she was out of town. She knew about the convocation but she was not aware that it has sparked a firestorm. She whispered to herself, "Why me, Lord?"

School

Roosevelt enrolls about 2,750 pupils. Most come from middle-class families; however, students from families at all levels of the economic continuum are represented. The student population is mixed racially, ethnically, and religiously. Nearly 40 percent of the student body is classified as minorities (31 percent African American, 4 percent Asian American, and 3 percent Hispanic American). About 10 percent of the students identify their religion as Judaism, and another 5 percent indicate that they are Muslims.

Over the years, the school has won numerous athletic and academic awards. It is considered to be one of the finest schools in the state, and political and educational leaders have frequently cited it as a model multicultural environment. About 60 percent of the graduates enroll in four-year institutions of higher education.

PARA

In a recent interview conducted by a newspaper reporter, Principal Doran said that her greatest concern about Roosevelt High was the criticism that African American students were not being treated fairly. A group of about 25 parents formed an organization last year called PARA (Parents Advocating Racial Awareness). At a press conference announcing the group's formation, leaders said that their purpose was to ensure fair and equal treatment of all Roosevelt students. They argued that the following problems existed at the school:

- The curriculum did not offer African American students ample opportunity to study their cultural heritage.
- Teachers and administrators often disciplined African American students more harshly than others.
- School officials had done little to ensure that the African American community would have a representative voice in critical decisions affecting the school and its students.

Sensitive to these criticisms, Principal Doran asked permission to attend PARA meetings. Her request was approved and she attended when her schedule permitted her to do so. She also appointed a PARA member to the principal's advisory council, which consisted of six teachers, six parents, and six students (currently, one-third of whom were African American).

Nature of the Problem

Several weeks before the conflict about the convocation became public, Reggie Colter, a senior student, had an appointment with the principal to suggest a possible convocation. Reggie, the only African American member on Roosevelt's Student Council, often was the spokesperson for school's black students. His father, an attorney, is a PARA member.

During their meeting, Reggie told the principal, "I have a great opportunity for our school, and I wanted to see how you felt about it. My cousin is a sound technician for a music group called The Inner City. They're on a concert tour and scheduled to appear here in the near future. One of the things they do while on tour is to present several free shows at area high schools. They do this as a public service. The purpose is to discourage students from using drugs. My cousin said he could probably get them to do a program at Roosevelt. Could this be arranged?"

"Well, I don't know, Reggie. I've never heard of this group. What type of show do they do?" Ms. Doran asked.

"They are a 'rap' group. During these school programs, they do some of their popular songs and talk about how drugs can really mess up students. The group's members grew up living with these problems, and they have the ability to reach students. My cousin said that there won't be any foul language or dirty dancing."

Reggie then showed her the group's promotional brochure.

"And the best thing, Ms. Doran, is that this program would be free. Their concert tickets cost $30 or more. My cousin needs to know as soon as possible if we are interested."

Ms. Doran was interested in the idea, partly because she thought that PARA and other elements of the African American community would respond positively to it. She told Reggie to see Wallace Slater, one of the assistant principals, about making arrangements for the convocation. Mr. Slater was in charge of extracurricular activities and the school's only African American administrator.

Mr. Slater asked Reggie to provide him with a list of schools where the group had performed. Within a week, Reggie produced a list of 13 high schools, all located in other states. Mr. Slater contacted administrators at two of them, both inner-city schools with predominately African American students. The feedback from both schools about the rap group was positive. Having the benefit of this input, Mr. Slater told Reggie to have the group's representative call him so they could establish a date and time for the convocation. Mr. Slater then wrote the following note to Ms. Doran.

Barb,

I talked to Reggie this morning about the proposed convocation. I checked this group out with two principals who had the program presented in their schools. They didn't have any problems. They said students reacted positively. Unless I hear otherwise, I will move forward to schedule the group. As soon as a date is set, I'll let you know.

Wallace

About two weeks later, the principal was sent another note indicating that a date and time for the convocation had been determined.

Shortly after Ms. Doran left to attend the conference in Orlando, concerns about the impending appearance of The Inner City at Roosevelt High started to surface. The convocation was announced in the student paper. Some leaders in the Jewish community became outraged when they read about it. About three months earlier, a national tabloid published a story indicating that The Inner City had been accused of anti-Semitism. The charges were made after the group recorded a record containing lyrics that blamed Jews for oppressing inner-city blacks. The tabloid story contained several derogatory quotes from two of the group's members.

After the convocation was announced in the student paper, copies of the tabloid article were distributed through a local synagogue. Almost overnight, a major controversy erupted. Leaders of the Jewish community held a press conference demanding that the convocation be cancelled; PARA officials responded by holding their own news conference announcing that they would protest if the convocation were cancelled.

Wallace Slater and the two other assistant principals met after hearing about the press conferences. They decided to wait until Barb Doran returned from the conference to make a final decision on the convocation. They thought waiting a few days to make a decision would not matter. They also discussed whether they should contact the principal about the matter, but they decided they did not want to ruin her trip.

Reaching a Decision

As Ms. Doran drove into the school's parking lot, she was still listening to callers voice opposing views on the impending convocation. When she walked into her office, she immediately saw a stack of mail sitting on her desk. At the top was a folder containing information about the rap group controversy. A copy of an article from yesterday's newspaper was one of the items in it.

Another Controversy "Rocks" Roosevelt High

Some parents of Roosevelt High School students are objecting to a convocation that is to be presented by a music group called "The Inner City." The parents contend that at least two members of the group have made anti-Semitic statements to the press and that lyrics in some of their songs are distasteful and not in the best interests of racial harmony. Principal Barb Doran has not been available for comment. Assistant principal Wallace Slater said the purpose of the convocation was to have the group deliver an anti-drug message. He said their appearance had nothing to do with either politics or race, and he went on to note that appearances at other high schools had not resulted in problems. He said school officials are examining the matter and will make a decision about the convocation shortly. Superintendent Paul Tolliver said he would talk to Principal Doran when she returns to her office tomorrow.

Also in the folder were over two dozen phone messages pertaining to the convocation. Ms. Doran telephoned Dr. Tolliver at his home.

"Barb, I'm glad you're back," he told the principal after answering the phone. "I suppose by now you know what is going on. What do you know about this rap group?"

"I did not know about the anti-Semitism charges until tonight. I learned about it listening to the radio while driving from the airport. Before I left for Florida, Wallace Slater checked out the group, and all of the feedback he got was positive. We didn't see any reason not to schedule the event. If we had said no, PARA would have been all over us about denying an African American group the opportunity to perform before our students."

"I tried to reach you in Orlando this afternoon, but you had already checked out of the hotel. Listen, we have to make a decision—and the sooner, the better. The Jewish community is really upset and PARA is promising boycotts and protests if the program is cancelled. How do we end up with these seemingly no-win situations?"

"Dr. Tolliver, I accept responsibility for this. I gave Wallace approval to book the group. I have been trying to work with PARA, and maybe I was too anxious to score some positive points. I should have been more cautious. I will meet with my administrative staff first thing tomorrow morning, and I'll have a recommendation to you by 10:00 A.M."

"Barb, let's say this situation were reversed. If a Jewish group that had been accused of putting out an anti–African American message, would we bring them into the school—even if they were delivering an anti-drug message?"

"Are you saying, Dr. Tolliver," asked Ms. Doran, "that I should cancel the program?"

"No, I'm not telling you what to do. I'm just trying to point out that both sides have valid arguments. I don't interfere in the way you operate the school unless my involvement is essential. I have confidence that you and your staff will do whatever is best."

Ms. Doran sat at her desk and thought about options to resolve the controversy. How would she react as an African American parent or student? How would she react as a Jewish parent or student? She believed that schools should provide a forum for exchanging ideas, provided that those ideas did not violate community standards. But what standards would apply to this situation? With all of these thoughts running through her mind, she called the three assistant principals and asked them to meet with her at 6:30 the next morning.

During the meeting with the assistant principals, Ms. Doran indicated that a decision had to be made in the next hour. Mr. Slater spoke first, suggesting that the convocation not be cancelled. He thought that canceling it based on accusations would set a bad precedent. He recommended that a debate between the group members and leaders of the Jewish community should be part of the convocation.

"Why not discuss the controversy openly and candidly before the students? Shouldn't they hear both sides? Of course, we don't know if the parties would agree to the discussion." he told the other administrators.

The other two assistant principals voiced disagreement. They thought a debate could lead to even more tensions. One of them suggested that the convocation be cancelled. "The best way to resolve this is just to back away from it. Within two weeks, every thing will be back to normal."

The other assistant principal proposed having two simultaneous convocations—one presented by the rap group and the other presented by a panel of community leaders and students on the topic of multiculturism. "We would allow students to select which one they would attend."

As the discussion continued, Principal Doran concluded that they would not reach consensus. An hour had passed and they had to conclude the meeting because students were arriving at the school. Ms. Doran looked at the clock on the wall in her office. In less than two hours, she had to call Dr. Tolliver. Should she reconvene the meeting with her assistants once school started? Should she make the decision alone? Should she ask the superintendent to make the decision for her?

The Challenge

Assume you are the principal. What would you do?

Suggested Activities

1. Develop a list of possible decisions that could be made regarding the convocation and evaluate the merits of each.

2. Discuss why multiculturalism has become a controversial topic in this country.

3. Identify moral and ethical issues that could affect a decision in this case.

4. Contrast ethical and political considerations that are relevant to making a decision about the convocation.

5. Complete the case worksheet.

Suggested Readings

Banister, J., & Maher, M. (1998). Recentering multiculturalism: Moving toward community. *Urban Education, 33*(2), 182–217.

Harrington-Lueker, D. (1993). Practicing tolerance. *Executive Educator, 15*(5), 14–19.

Margolis, H., & Tewel, K. (1988). Resolving conflict with parents: A guide for administrators. *NASSP Bulletin, 72*(506), 26–28.

Martinson, D. L. (1998). Vulgar, indecent, and offensive student speech: How should public school administrators respond. *Clearing House, 71*(6), 345–349.

Noguera, P. A. (1999). Confronting the challenge of diversity. *School Administrator, 56*(5), 16–19.

Sherman, R. (1990). Intergroup conflict on high school campuses. *Journal of Multicultural Counseling and Development, 18*(1), 11–18.

Stover, D. (1990). The new racism. *American School Board Journal, 177*(6), 14–18.

Stover, D. (1991). Racism redux. *Executive Educator, 13*(12), 35–36.

Zirkel, P. (1998). Boring or bunkum? *Phi Delta Kappan, 79*(10), 791–792.

Zirkel, P., & Gluckman, I. (1983). Stop, don't raise that curtain. *Principal, 62,* 45–46.

References

Miron, L. F., St. John, E. P, & Davidson, B. (1998). Implementing school restructuring in the inner city. *Urban Review, 30*(2), 137–166.

Zirkel, P. A. (2001). A gross over-order? *Phi Delta Kappan, 83*(3), 273–274.

Is the Devil Teaching Spelling?

Background Information

Over the past two decades, efforts to improve schools have exhibited tensions between popular reform strategies. For instance, both teacher empowerment and community involvement have been widely touted as effective reform strategies. These two objectives have some basic incongruities, however, making them difficult to implement simultaneously. The primary intention of empowerment is to provide professional practitioners ample discretion to make decisions that are appropriate to the needs of patients or clients. In the case of education, this means giving teachers greater discretion over curricular and instructional decisions (Barth, 2001). Community involvement is nested in an intricate mix of philosophical, political, and economic objectives. As an example, concepts such as school councils are congruous with life in a democratic society and they often build support necessary for acquiring scarce resources (Kowalski, 2003). Teachers and parents, however, do not always agree on educational priorities or on the parameters of effective teaching (Davis, 1997). Consequently, principals must determine how they will treat the inevitable tensions that exist between professionalism and democracy. How should a principal balance citizen participation in governance with teachers' rights to control professional practice in the classroom?

Democratic administration has proven to be an elusive concept for yet another reason. Principals are expected to maintain control of schools while involving teachers, parents, and students in decision making. Commenting on tensions between control and participation, Corwin and Borman (1988) wrote:

> District administrators are held accountable for things they cannot always control. This condition is a product of decentralization processes within formally centralized school districts. School districts are organized officially as hierarchies. Implementing educational policy is legally and politically the responsibility of high-level district administrators. However, in practice only certain decisions are centralized. Many others have been decentralized, and administrators can never fully control such responsibilities. (p. 212)

Modern reforms, such as site-based management, are accentuating the difficulties inherent in the simultaneous pursuit of professionalism and participation.

The selection of instructional materials is one area where conflict between parents and educators has been evident. Throughout much of the last century, for instance, there were multiple instances in which community pressure groups attempted to censor materials such as library books or textbooks. In this case, parents object to the use of materials used in a gifted education program. In addition to exhibiting tensions between teacher and parental rights, the case demonstrates difficulties experienced by administrators who are supposed to maintain control while empowering others.

Key Areas for Reflection

1. Parental objections to instructional materials
2. The parameters of professionalism and teacher empowerment
3. Delegating authority and accountability
4. Censorship in public schools
5. Relationship between district and school administration

The Case

"I really like this software program. It fits nicely with what we are trying to accomplish in this program. And besides, the students will like the content."

The evaluation came from Sandy Oberfeld, a second-grade teacher who was demonstrating the product to 17 colleagues in a meeting at Samuels Elementary School. The purpose of the meeting was to review instructional materials for use in the district's gifted and talented program.

"I agree with Sandy," said Beatrice Sachs. "My children like having an array of materials. They have so many toys and gadgets at home, it's hard to motivate them. I think 'Sorcerer' is a novel way to get them to work independently on their spelling. Our students have learned to think and process information by watching television and playing video games. Computer games usually capture their attention."

The elementary school gifted and talented program in the Maple Creek School District is clustered in three of the system's 10 elementary schools. Serving two affluent suburban communities in the Midwest, the district ranks in the top 2 percent of the state in per-pupil expenditures for instruction.

The teachers who participate in the gifted and talented program meet once every two months after school. They get together to discuss materials, share ideas, and coordinate curriculum. Sandy Oberfeld, who was demonstrating the product, was the group's coordinator. She had learned about "Sorcerer" while attending a gifted education conference.

After a few positive comments, Lucy McNeil, one of the teachers at the meeting, suggested that some parents might object to this product.

"You know in this day and age," she said, "one is never sure what standards parents will use in evaluating instructional materials. Some fundamentalist groups have criticized computer games similar to this one in the past. They think anything that has a magic or witchcraft theme is evil."

No one reacted to this cautionary comment. Three or four teachers said they wanted to purchase "Sorcerer." Hearing no objections, Mrs. Oberfeld announced she would requisition 60 copies of the product—20 for each of the three participating schools.

Since the early 1990s, teachers in this district have had considerable autonomy to select supplemental instructional materials. Typically, requisitions were approved by principals and forwarded to the district's business office. The elementary school gifted and talented program, however, operated differently. Located at three different sites, this program was given its own budget for supplies, equipment, and materials. The assistant superintendent for instruction was assigned supervisory responsibility for the program and its budget. Until four years ago, the principals in the three participating elementary schools attended the bimonthly gifted and talented staff meetings. The program was operating smoothly and they stopped attending the meetings.

As per established practice, the requisition to purchase 60 copies of "Sorcerer" was sent directly from Mrs. Oberfeld to the assistant superintendent for instruction, Dr. Wilbur Youngman. When he received the form, he did not question the recommended action nor did he contact any of the principals to determine if they had objections. He merely verified that sufficient funds were available to transact the purchase. He signed the requisition form, indicating approval, and forwarded it to the business office.

After the copies of "Sorcerer" were delivered, all 18 teachers involved with the program made them available to their students. They could be used in school or students could take them home for a period of one week. "Sorcerer" is constructed around a system of rewards and punishments given to students based on their spelling performance. As predicted, students liked the software.

About one month after "Sorcerer" was made available to students, the first parental complaint about the product was registered. Elizabeth Baker, the mother of a second-grade student at Lakeside Elementary School, called Principal Nancy Tannin.

"Miss Tannin, I'm calling you about a computer game one of the teachers gave to my daughter, Sally. She is in the gifted and talented program, and, as you know, students who are involved regularly bring home books and other supplementary materials. I became inquisitive about this game because Sally just couldn't leave it alone. And she was so intense when she was playing it. She told me the game was called "Sorcerer." I had never heard of it. Do you know what I'm talking about?"

The principal had never heard of the software game, and she admitted that fact to Mrs. Baker. She then told her that the teachers working in the program typically decide what materials to use.

"Well, don't you have to approve the purchase of instructional materials?" the mother asked.

"Normally, yes. But the gifted and talented program is not an individual school program. The assistant superintendent for instruction is responsible for approving purchases. I'm not certain why you are concerned. Do you think your daughter is spending too much time with this game? Or do you think that the product is not very good?"

"My concern is about the nature of the product. The theme deals with witchcraft and black magic. Now I realize that its purpose is to improve spelling skills, but why is it necessary to use controversial material? You may think I am overreacting—and maybe I am. But in this day and age, parents have to be especially sensitive about their children being exposed to undesirable values and beliefs."

Miss Tannin suggested that she would have to look into the matter before responding to the concern. The principal immediately assumed that Mrs. Baker was either overreacting or misinformed. She did not treat the telephone call as an urgent matter. Two days passed before Miss Tannin discussed Mrs. Baker's concern with one of the teachers involved with the gifted and talented program. The teacher told her that "Sorcerer" was very popular with the students and indicated that the teachers had approved of the product's purchase.

Based on this conversation, Miss Tannin telephoned Mrs. Baker and told her that she had discussed the concern with one of the gifted education teachers.

Mrs. Baker asked, "Did you look at the product? Did you actually sit at a computer and play the game?"

"Well, no. I didn't think that was necessary," Miss Tannin answered. "Our teachers are competent professionals. I trust them to make good decisions about instructional materials."

At this point, Mrs. Baker became angry. "Maybe the teachers are wrong this time. Don't you have a responsibility to oversee what they do? If you are not accountable for the instructional materials that are used in your school, who is? Telling me that the teachers think 'Sorcerer' is suitable for young children does alleviate my concerns. I'm not going to drop this matter."

After the conversation with Mrs. Baker, Miss Tannin telephoned the other two principals in the schools participating in the gifted and talented programs, Deloris Gragolis and Mitch Sancheck. She found out that they also had met with teachers after having received complaints about "Sorcerer." The three principals agreed that the teachers had the authority to purchase the materials but they also recognized that this issue could become a major problem. They met the next day and formulated the following strategy:

- They would send a memorandum to Dr. Youngman, alerting him to the situation and specifying the nature of the complaints they had received.
- All 18 teachers participating in the program would receive a copy of that memorandum.
- They would then contact the parents who had raised concerns and inform them that they should pursue the matter with Dr. Youngman, since he is responsible for approving gifted and talented program materials.

Just over two weeks after Mrs. Baker complained to Miss Tannin, a letter to the editor, signed by 16 parents, appeared in the local newspaper condemning the use of "Sorcerer."

> We are parents of elementary school children who participate in the gifted and talented program in the Maple Creek School District. Recently, our children have been exposed to a distasteful and evil computer game called "Sorcerer." This game is supposed to assist our children with their spelling skills, but in reality, it exposes them to witchcraft and other evil concepts.
>
> "Sorcerer" is yet another example that our public schools have become a pawn for those who wish to lower the standards and moral fiber of our society. Parents who financially support our public schools have every right to be concerned if they think the positive values taught at home are being eroded by school activities.
>
> The fact that the principals appear unwilling to deal with this matter is especially disconcerting. Our concerns have basically been ignored. As taxpayers and parents, we urge others to join us in a fight to keep control of our public schools. Let's keep our schools free of materials that promote witchcraft, devil worship, and other evil ideas. Call your school board member now and voice your objection!

The district's superintendent, Philip Montgomery, had not been briefed on this matter, and he learned about it when he read the newspaper. He immediately called Dr. Youngman, anticipating that school board members would be calling to inquire about "Sorcerer." Dr. Youngman told the superintendent that the principals had met with the teachers and neither the teachers nor the principals felt that the parents' objections were valid. The superintendent told him to contact the principals and Mrs. Oberfeld so that all of them could meet later that day. The meeting was held in the superintendent's conference room at 4:00 P.M. Dr. Montgomery indicated that since the letter to the editor was published that morning, he had been contacted by four of the school board members. He asked those present to answer three questions:

1. What are the parents' specific objections?
2. Why are these materials still being used if they are objectionable to some families?
3. Who made the decision to buy the materials in the first place?

"'Sorcerer' is similar to a popular video game that got some negative publicity recently," explained Mrs. Oberfeld. "At the time we decided to purchase it, we did not anticipate that some parents would object. And even if we knew that some might complain, I'm not sure we would have made a different decision. If we let right-wing religious groups dictate what we use in our schools, we'd be in big trouble. Now that they no longer think that communists are hiding under every desk, they think the devil is running the public schools. The fact of the matter is that this program motivates children to work on their spelling. Students are not required to use it. If some parents find it objectionable, all they have to do is tell their children not to use it. Why should other students be deprived just because a group of fundamentalist parents consider the software objectionable?"

Dr. Montgomery asked the principals if they had any comments. Miss Tannin spoke first.

"We have a great deal of confidence in Mrs. Oberfeld and the other teachers who work in this program. They all agreed to purchase these materials. When I received a complaint, I asked a teacher in my building to explain why it was purchased. When I told her about the concern, she said that students were not required to use 'Sorcerer.' She also said that she disagreed with the parent's judgment about the product."

"But did any of you actually use the material to see what was involved?" the superintendent asked.

The three principals and Dr. Youngman said that they had not done so. Mrs. Oberfeld pointed out that all of the teachers either had sampled the product or observed it in use.

"Who authorized this purchase?" the superintendent asked.

Miss Tannin answered, "The teachers recommended buying 'Sorcerer,' and the requisition was sent to Dr. Youngman."

"Well, technically, I approved the purchase," Dr. Youngman said. "But I can't be looking over every teacher's shoulder. My job, quite frankly, is simply to see that there is money in the budget and that the requisition has been processed properly. I don't think any of you want me deciding what you are going to use for instructional programs in your schools."

Mrs. Oberfeld became concerned by the defensive posture being taken by Dr. Youngman and the principals. "Before we start blaming each other, we ought to step back and think about what is at issue here. Are we going to allow a small group of parents to dictate what we use in our schools? I think these individuals would like to control every major decision we make. If they are successful in getting rid of "Sorcerer," they'll be back with more ridiculous demands. These people want to control what we read and how we think."

Miss Tannin spoke next. "Assume that any administrator would have blocked the purchase of this software. Wouldn't that have created a major political problem? How would the teachers respond if we told them that we will not approve requisitions because the material in question might be offensive to a few parents? I think we have to face up to what is at stake here. This is a censorship issue."

Mitch Sancheck then spoke. "We have a great deal of faith in our teachers. Quite frankly, I feel very comfortable having them rather than these parents decide what is best for students."

Dr. Montgomery pointed out that he did not want to unduly restrict instructional decisions made by teachers. Nevertheless, he was uncomfortable with a purchase process that bypassed principals. "When I was a principal, I had to sign every requisition that originated in my building," he told the others. "But I had no choice. Policy required my approval. Our current policy stipulates that one administrator with supervisory responsibility for the program in question and the business manager must sign each requisition. This problem clearly demonstrated that we can bypass principals and still be in compliance with the policy. We have two decisions to make. First, what do we do to resolve the current concerns? Second, what should be done to prevent this problem from recurring?"

Miss Tannin answered, "You may be in a better position to answer those questions. Maybe we should revise our policy so that principals cannot be bypassed."

Dr. Montgomery got up from his chair and said, "That certainly is one possibility; but before we move in that direction, we should weigh all possible consequences. For instance, what would occur in the gifted and talented program if one principal refused to sign a requisition? I want you to continue meeting until you have answers to my questions. I have to go to an awards program at the high school. I'll be back in about two hours. When I return, I hope to see recommendations regarding how we proceed with 'Sorcerer' and how we proceed with improving our policy."

The Challenge

Assume you are one of the principals in the meeting. What is your preferred recommendation for resolving the current problem? What is your recommendation for preventing this problem in the future?

Suggested Activities

1. Evaluate the process that was used to purchase materials for the gifted and talented program and make suggestions for improving the process.

2. Critique the argument that "Sorcerer" should not be removed because student usage is voluntary.

3. Evaluate the manner in which the three elementary principals handled this matter.

4. Evaluate the decision of the principals to quit attending the bimonthly meetings for the teachers involved in the gifted and talented program.

5. Discuss the rights of parents to control materials that are used in schools.

6. Complete the worksheet for Case 22.

Suggested Readings

Browder, L. H. (1998). The Religious Right, the Secular Left, and their shared dilemma: The public school. *International Journal of Educational Reform, 7*(4), 309–318.

Donelson, K. (1987). Censorship: Heading off the attack. *Educational Horizons, 65*(4), 167–170.

Donelson, K. (1987). Six statements/questions from the censors. *Phi Delta Kappan, 69*(3), 208–214.

Fege, A. F. (1993). The tug of war over tolerance. *Educational Leadership, 51*(4), 22–24.

Georgiady, N., & Romano, L. (1987). Censorship—Back to the front burner. *Middle School Journal, 18,* 12–13.

Jones, J. L. (1993). Targets of the right. *American School Board Journal, 180*(4), 22–29.

Kowalski, T. J., & Reitzug, U. C. (1993). *Contemporary school administration: An introduction.* New York: Longman (see Chapter 10).

Leahy, M. (1998). The religious right: Would-be censors of the state school curriculum. *Educational Philosophy & Theory, 30*(1), 18, 51.

McCarthy, M. (1985). Curriculum controversies and the law. *Educational Horizons, 64*(3), 53–55.

McCarthy, M. (1988). Curriculum censorship: Values in conflict. *Educational Horizons, 67*(1), 26–34.

Meadows, B. J. (1990). The rewards and risks of shared leadership. *Phi Delta Kappan, 71*(7), 545–548.

Pierard, R. (1987). The new religious right and censorship. *Contemporary Education, 58*(3), 131–137.

Rowell, C. (1986). Allowing parents to screen textbooks would lead to anarchy in the schools. *Chronicle of Higher Education, 33*(26), 34.

Smith, S. (1998). School by school. *American School Board Journal, 185*(6), 22–25.

Sullivan, P. (1998). Parent involvement. *Our Children, 24*(1), 23.

Weil, J. (1988). Dealing with censorship: Policy and procedures. *Education Digest, 53*(5), 23–25.

Zirkel, P., & Gluckman, I. (1986). Objections to curricular material on religious grounds. *NASSP Bulletin, 70*(488), 99–100.

References

Barth, R. S. (2001). Teacher leader. *Phi Delta Kappan, 82*(6), 443–449.

Corwin, R. G., & Borman, K. M. (1988). School as workplace: Structural constraints on administration. In N. J. Boyan (Ed.), *Handbook of research on educational administration* (pp. 209–238). New York: Longman.

Davis, O. L. (1997). Notes on the nature of power. *Journal of Curriculum and Supervision, 12*(3), 189–192.

Kowalski, T. J. (2003). *Contemporary school administration: An introduction.* Boston: Allyn and Bacon.

Decentralization and Inequality

Background Information

For much of the twentieth century, the governance structure of public education became increasingly centralized primarily for two reasons. First, policymakers concluded that fewer but larger school districts would increase the efficiency of public education; second, they believed that larger districts and schools would ensure adequate and reasonably equal education opportunities for all students in a given state (Kowalski, 2003). The trend toward centralized authority was obvious both among and within local school districts. Many states enacted consolidation laws requiring small schools and districts to merge; as a consequence, the number of school districts in the United States during the twentieth century declined from over 100,000 to less than 15,000. As school districts became larger, the number of personnel assigned to the superintendent's staff increased. New positions such as curriculum director were added, and the administration of individual schools became increasingly centralized.

Critics argue that economics and politics have been the primary motives for centralizing authority in public education. The emulation of business practices, especially the application of scientific management principles, made efficiency the primary objective in many local school districts, but centralization also was spawned by other factors. An increasing awareness of state responsibility for ensuring that students received adequate and equal educational opportunities was one of them. This consciousness prompted state governments to establish uniform curricula and standards. Centralization was a by-product, because district administrators were expected to ensure that individual schools were compliant (Kowalski, 1999). Legislation and subsequent litigation also played a major role in moving public education toward more centralized authority. Lawsuits in areas such as civil rights and special education exhibited that local schools were susceptible to prolonged legal battles, and this realization produced a compliance mentality (a state of mind that operating procedures needed to be uniform and controlled) (Tyack, 1990).

As the current school reform movement gained momentum during the 1980s, one of centralization's greatest flaws was magnified. Reformers concluded that highly centralized policies tended to be unresponsive to real student needs because conditions among districts in a state and among schools within a district were not uniform. Therefore, gearing reforms to an imaginary average student appeared to be myopic, and both state deregulation (relaxing state mandates for local districts) and district decentralization (reducing district control over individual schools) became popular school reform initiatives during the 1990s. Deregulation and decentralization have two primary motives: to promote the greater likelihood that school improvement efforts will reflect real student needs and to increase local support for reform by establishing governance structures that increase citizen participation.

Tensions between decentralization and centralization are persistent. Several scholars who have studied change in schools (e.g., Fullan, 2001) caution that neither approach is problem free. Whereas centralization tends to err in the direction of overcontrol, decentralization tends to err in the direction of chaos. Many superintendents and principals must wrestle with this reality as they attempt to employ popular decentralization strategies such as school-based management (SBM). Experience suggests that the major challenge facing them is not one of choosing between centralization and decentralization but rather one of creating an appropriate balance between the two organizational conditions—that is, they must determine which functions should be centralized and which functions should be decentralized.

In this case, a superintendent decentralizes budgets and requires schools to establish governance councils. In less than two years, several parents charge that the policy has resulted in resource and program disparities across the district's elementary schools. A parent, who is an attorney, questions the legality of the policy on the grounds that his children do not have access to educational opportunities equal to those provided in the district's other elementary schools. The conflict raises essential questions about major values that guide education policy—namely, *adequacy* (minimal level of educational opportunities), *liberty* (allowing individual schools to chart their own course), and *equality* (the responsibility of the school district to provide reasonably educational opportunities).

Key Areas for Reflection

1. Centralized and decentralized governance
2. Conflict between liberty and equality
3. Relationship between district and school administration under school-based management

4. Managing change in school districts
5. The role and responsibilities of school councils
6. The decentralization of budgets and effects on school spending and programs

The Case

Haver Ridge

Haver Ridge is the seat of government for Marvin County in central Illinois. With a population of approximately 16,000, the community has grown about 15 percent since the mid-1950s. Virtually all of the population increase occurred as a result of a new industrial park that was constructed on the edge of town in the early 1970s. The four new businesses that located in Haver Ridge resulted in nearly 400 new jobs.

Marvin County is predominately rural, with grain farms consuming about 80 percent of all the acreage. Haver Ridge and Fellington are the only two cities in the county, the latter having a population of approximately 10,000. Several small towns are scattered around the county, but each consists of little more than a grain elevator and a few stores. About 15 years ago, a new hospital and a municipal airport were built midway between Haver Ridge and Fellington.

River Valley Community College and the East Marvin Community School District are two of the largest employers in Haver Ridge. Collectively, they have about 950 employees. The college's primary service area is Marvin and two other counties.

School District

A number of years ago, the elementary and secondary public schools in Marvin County were reorganized into two districts. Their boundaries were established by drawing a line down the center of the county from north to south; as a result, both districts are large geographically. The East Marvin County School District, the larger of the two in terms of enrollment, has its district offices in Haver Ridge, where the district's high school, middle school, and three of its five elementary schools are also located.

The three elementary schools in Haver Ridge are Adams, Clark, and Lincoln. Among them, Clark is clearly the most unique. It is housed in an old building in the downtown area. Both the site and the size of the instructional spaces are very small in terms of modern standards. Previous efforts to replace the facility, however, have been thwarted by taxpayers who consider the building to be a landmark. By comparison, Adams and Lincoln, both in residential areas, are more modern and spacious buildings erected in the last two decades. Clark also has a different personnel profile than do the other two elementary schools; the average age of the teaching staff there is 53, about 10 years more than the averages at the other two elementary schools.

School Board

Farmers once dominated the school board in the East Marvin County School District but that no longer is true. A list of the board members, their occupations, and years of service on the school board are listed here:

Board Member	Occupation	Years on the Board
Delbert Daniels	Bank loan officer	3
Sheila Edell	Housewife (married to a farmer)	10
George Grogan	Dean of instruction at Marvin County Community College	
Bill Lucas	Owner of a local restaurant	7
Victoria Price	English instructor at Marvin County Community College	1
Ned Sustanit	Plant manager, truck trailer factory	5
Joe Wildman	High school counselor in another school district	1

Mr. Lucas has been president of the school board for the past two years.

Occasionally, votes cast by the board members are not unanimous, but such outcomes are issue related and not the product of political factions. The board members respect and like each other. In general, the school board's relationship with the local teachers' union has been positive, and in the last election, the union endorsed two incumbents who were reelected.

Administration

When a long-term superintendent retired three years ago, the board employed Burton Packard to replace him. Dr. Packard had been working as an assistant superintendent for instruction in a suburb of Chicago. He is a mid-career administrator with a reputation as a strong instructional leader. During his interview for the superintendency, he told the board that he believed in democratic schools and teacher empowerment. When asked to explain these beliefs, he told the board members, "I think teachers and parents should be our partners, and that includes collaborating with us when we make important decisions about our schools. If you are looking for a dictator, I'm not the person you want to hire." That philosophy also was embraced by most of the board members.

Ryan Fulton is the district's assistant superintendent for instruction. He moved to his present position 6 years ago after having served as principal of Haver Ridge High School for 8 years. Jane Westman, the assistant for business, moved to her present position 4 years ago after having served as principal at Lincoln Elementary for 13 years.

Two of the district's seven principals have been employed while Dr. Packard has been superintendent. They are Dr. Elaine Byers at the middle school and Mrs. Norene Vidduci at Adams Elementary School. Both had been employed by other school districts. Only two of the district's five elementary schools, Adams and Lincoln, have assistant principals.

Implementing SBM

Shortly after arriving in Haver Ridge, Dr. Packard announced that he wanted to decentralize authority in the school district. He announced that the changes would begin with the elementary schools the following school year and he identified three objectives:

1. The schools would have greater freedom to determine instructional priorities. Variance in curriculum and instructional materials would be allowed but students and teachers would be held to the same accountability standards.
2. Each elementary school was to establish a governance council composed of administrators, teachers, and parents. The councils would have considerable authority to determine instructional priorities and strategies for meeting the needs associated with those priorities.
3. The district's budgeting and fiscal management practices would be changed to allow individual schools to determine how the resources could best be used.

The seven school board members publicly applauded the superintendent's ideas but reactions from the elementary school principals were mixed. The two assigned to the district's rural schools, Milltown and Wild Creek, were supportive of two of the three objectives. These two schools had long-standing traditions of parental involvement and creating a council would only formalize what they had been doing. The two principals, however, were troubled by the prospect of having to manage a school budget. The principal at Clark, Mrs. Simpson, was even more apprehensive. She and most of her staff did not think a school council would work well for them. In addition, they feared that allocations for school budgets would be done solely on a per-pupil basis, an action that could place them at a disadvantage, given Clark's high percentage of students with special needs. The remaining two elementary school principals at Adams and Lincoln were highly supportive of all three of Dr. Packard's objectives.

The elementary principals were given five months to develop a plan to meet the three objectives. They were told that the plans had to include the following information:

- The composition of the school's council
- Methods for selecting council members
- Details about how the school budget would be planned and managed

After the plans were developed, Dr. Packard reviewed them and met with each principal. He discussed facets of the plans and sought clarifications but he did not require modifications to any of the documents.

First Two Years SBM

During the first two years of implementation, differences that were not that evident in the plans became apparent. As an example, cooperative learning became the centerpiece of the instructional program at Adams Elementary School even though none of the other districts had embraced this model. A considerable portion of that school's resources had been used for teacher staff development, the purchase of microcomputers, and the purchase of materials used to implement cooperative learning activities. The following is a summary of the conditions at the five elementary schools after the second year of implementation:

School	Council Membership	Primary Foci
Adams	6 teachers, 6 parents, and principal	Cooperative learning, investment in computers, staff development, and instructional materials
Clark	6 teachers, 4 parents, and principal	Strengthening traditional programs, remedial materials, investment in basic textbooks
Lincoln	4 teachers, 8 parents, and principal	Infusion of technology, increasing time on task, remodeling the media center, and individualized instruction
Milltown	4 teachers, 4 parents, and principal	Investment in computers, strengthening materials for current programs
Wild Creek	4 teachers, 4 parents, and principal	Mastery learning, investment in computers, staff development

The school councils functioned differently in the five schools. At Adams and Lincoln, teachers and parents frequently assumed the responsibility of suggesting agenda items. This was also true, but to a lesser degree, at Milltown and Wild Creek. At Clark, teachers and parents never asked to put items on the agenda, and they were largely passive during council meetings. The council meetings at Clark, which were held once each month, were highly predictable. Mrs. Simpson would construct the agenda, do most of the talking, and the members would vote to support whatever she recommended. Often, only one or two of the four parent members would attend a council meeting. The teachers on the Clark council basically viewed the meetings as a waste of time.

Problem

Each year, students in grades 2, 4, and 6 are required to take standardized achievement tests. Students receive individual results and schools receive an average score for each grade level. For at least the last seven years, Lincoln has had the highest average test scores in the district, and Clark has had the lowest. Following are the results for sixth-grade students for the past three years. Years 2 and 3 are years under the decentralization plan.

School Average	*Test Scores*			*Rank in District*		
	Yr 1	*Yr 2*	*Yr 3*	*Yr 1*	*Yr 2*	*Yr 3*
Adams	57.3	58.2	58.3	2	2	2
Clark	48.7	48.3	48.1	5	5	5
Lincoln	59.2	60.1	61.2	1	1	1
Milltown	55.2	55.3	55.3	3	4	4
Wild Creek	54.6	55.4	55.7	4	3	3

In past years, the local newspaper paid little attention to these scores, but that changed because of Dr. Packard's decentralization program. The editor had a reporter write a series of articles trying to connect test scores with the superintendent's decentralization plan. The articles suggested that increases in test scores at Lincoln might be the result of the school's investment in technology, and hinted that poor performance of Clark's students might be tied to the school's continued emphasis on remedial work. In essence, the stories gave the impression that the decisions made by the school councils affected student test performance.

Dr. Packard reacted to the articles in a meeting with Janice Bell, the reporter who had written them. He told her that it was premature to make the connections suggested by her articles. He also expressed confidence that Principal Simpson and the Clark school council were making appropriate decisions for the students at that school. He added that many factors affected student performance on standardized tests, including some that were beyond the school's control. He cited the social and economic conditions of a student's home life as examples. Ms. Bell took many notes during the meeting but did not take issue with any of the superintendent's statements. She also met with several school board members and discovered that Dr. Packard had made these same comments about the test scores to them. The board members said that they agreed with the superintendent's views. However, the board president, Mr. Lucas, added that he expected test scores to improve even more as a result of the decentralization initiatives.

Several parents of Clark students who were unhappy with the decentralization concept concurred with Ms. Bell that there was a possible nexus between student test performance and budgetary decisions. The most vocal of them was Anthony Bacon, an attorney and director of employee relations at the community college. He objected to the idea of allowing schools to have so much fiscal and instructional independence. After the newspaper articles written by Ms. Bell had been published, he attended a school board meeting and voiced his misgivings to the board and superintendent publicly.

Mr. Bacon knew only two of the school board members, Dr. Grogan and Mrs. Price, both of whom were employees of the community college. He had never met Dr. Packard prior to the board meeting. After being recognized by the board president, Mr. Bacon read a prepared statement:

> Ladies and gentlemen, Dr. Packard, and members of the school staff: I appear here today as a concerned parent of two children who attend Clark Elementary School. When we moved to this community four years ago, my wife and I bought an older home in the downtown area. One of our hobbies is remodeling older homes. We were concerned initially about our children attending Clark Elementary School, largely because the other elementary schools in Haver Ridge are newer and have more positive reputations. Before purchasing the house, I called the former superintendent and he assured me that, programmatically, all the elementary schools offered the same curriculum and opportunities to students. His assurance played a major part in our decision to purchase the house.
>
> It appears that conditions in the school district changed two years ago when Dr. Packard became superintendent and initiated his decentralization plan. That is why I am here today. I realize that decentralizing governance is a popular idea, but letting schools have considerable independence also creates problems. I have not objected to decentralization previously, because I did not realize until the recent newspaper articles just how different the elementary schools in this district have become.
>
> I am here to share several specific concerns. First, it is obvious to me that the school councils do not operate uniformly. A parent on the Clark council told me that her role essentially involved rubber stamping decisions already made by the principal. But at Lincoln, the parents and teachers appear to have a much broader role—one that permits them to introduce agenda items and speak freely about their concerns. For example, Mary Burgess, the director of instructional technology at our college, is a member of the Lincoln Elementary School council. She played a pivotal role in getting the school to invest so heavily in technology.
>
> Second, and more importantly, I believe that decentralization will not only fail to narrow gaps in resources and student performance, but it will actually widen them. Each school received the same amount of money per student. But the needs of students at Clark are generally greater than at the other elementary schools. And this fact apparently was ignored. The principal at Clark, Mrs. Simpson, told me that she devoted more resources to remedial activities because so many students at the school needed the extra help. As a result, Mrs. Simpson said that she had limited resources for purchasing technology.

I believe resources should be shared equally across all schools—and this includes human resources. Mrs. Burgess could have shared her technology expertise with all principals. Why should Lincoln be the only school that benefits just because her children attend that school? At what point do board members and the superintendent intervene when resources being provided to schools are clearly unequal? Imagine where we would be today if the federal government took a "hands off" approach to dealing with racial segregation decades ago. In essence, the school board and superintendent are the federal government. You must step in and ensure equal opportunity for all students. I respectfully request that you reexamine your decentralization plan and take immediate actions restore uniform programs and resources across our district's schools.

Mr. Bacon then distributed copies of his statement to the board members and media representatives. The board president thanked him for his comments and then asked the superintendent if he wanted to respond to Mr. Bacon. The superintendent indicated that he would look into the matter and reply in the next two weeks.

Mr. Bacon's statement surprised two of the board members and they began to have second thoughts about supporting decentralization. They telephoned Dr. Packard in the days following the meeting, advising him not to take this matter lightly and suggesting that he respond thoroughly to Mr. Bacon's concerns.

One week after the April board meeting, the board president convened an executive session and asked Dr. Packard to share his reply to Mr. Bacon before it was issued publicly. The board's attorney also was asked to attend the meeting. During this session, the superintendent made the following points:

- Mr. Bacon's claims about the school councils were only partially correct. Although it is true that the school councils are not uniform either in membership or operating procedures, such differences were not by design. Mrs. Simpson tried repeatedly to increase the level of parental involvement in the Clark Elementary School council. The council members at Clark have had opportunities to place items on the agenda and they have never been discouraged from speaking openly. They have chosen to do neither.
- When the Clark Elementary School council was first formed, Mr. Bacon received an invitation from Mrs. Simpson to be a member. He declined.
- Budget allocations to the schools are made on a per-pupil basis. No exceptions, such as providing additional funding for special needs students, are made because doing so would be difficult and the action would be controversial. Thus, differences in technology acquisitions are attributable to school council decisions and not to district policy or regulations.
- Although it is true that the decision to invest heavily in remedial materials at Clark was recommended by the principal, the decision was made by the school council and supported by the school's faculty.

- The number of students from low-income families enrolled at Clark is increasing. For example, the number of free and reduced lunches has increased by approximately 7 percent over the past two years. This factor, more than any other, may be responsible for slight declines in test scores.
- All students in the school district receive the same basic education prescribed by the state department of education. If Mr. Bacon's arguments about inequities were taken at face value, virtually every school district with more than one elementary school would be guilty of not offering identical learning experiences.

In the summary section of his report, Dr. Packard recommended that the board not alter its decentralization policy, including that which pertains to budgetary allocations. He added that Mrs. Simpson would be directed to allocate at least 25 percent of next year's equipment and supply funds to purchase additional computers and/or software for her school to ensure that technology gaps among the schools would not widen.

After listening to Dr. Packard's comments and reading the report in its entirety, the board's attorney advised them that the superintendent's response to Mr. Bacon was appropriate. After discussing the matter, the board directed Dr. Packard to send the response, as written, to Mr. Bacon.

After receiving the official response from the superintendent, Mr. Bacon called Dr. Grogan, one of the board members. He told him, "I don't think the superintendent's perception of equal opportunity is legally correct. Providing the prescribed state curriculum is a matter of adequacy, not equity. If students at Lincoln spend eight hours a week working with computers, and students at Clark spend only two, does that constitute equal educational opportunity? Just for a moment, George, you are an educator. Answer the equity question as a professional. Is it ethical or moral to determine educational opportunities on a school-by-school basis?"

Dr. Grogan responded, "Our attorney looked at Dr. Packard's response, and he feels the superintendent is correct about the equity issue. School districts across this country are giving individual schools greater freedom over curriculum and instruction. If equity were a legal concern as you indicate, don't you think this issue would have been litigated?"

Dr. Grogan urged Mr. Bacon to consider if his concerns could be addressed without the school board having to abandon its commitment to decentralization. He also urged him to meet with the superintendent privately. Mr. Bacon said he would do both. The following day, he met with Dr. Packard, but instead of offering a compromise, he continued to argue that the superintendent's perception of equal treatment was incorrect legally.

Dr. Packard responded to the comment. "The differences among our schools are not great. For example, the number of computers at Milltown is essentially the same as it is at Clark. There are many ways to educate children. Computers are not the only tool, nor are they the only measure of educational opportunity. If schools did not have an opportunity to make decisions based on specific school needs, Clark may not have been appropriately responsive to the need for more remedial work. Schools can never be totally equal—nor should they be. I believe schools are most effective when they are responsive to the real needs of their clients."

The conversation went on for about an hour, but the differences between the two men were not resolved. Over the course of the next few weeks, Mr. Bacon enlisted the support of five other Clark Elementary School families. In mid-May, this group retained the services of a prestigious law firm with the intention of challenging the school district's decentralization plan in court. The lead attorney representing the group wrote a letter to Dr. Packard and the school board president threatening a suit unless actions were taken to reverse the inequities created by decentralization.

Concern among the board members intensified, but no member publicly denounced the decentralization plan. The day after receiving the attorney's letter, the board president, Mr. Lucas, again summoned the board, Dr. Packard, and the school attorney to an executive session. The attorney was asked to comment about the potential lawsuit.

He said, "As I told you before, I think that Dr. Packard's response is reasonable. I cannot predict how a lawsuit would turn out. If you are asking me if we can win in court, my answer is yes. But as you know, litigation is expensive, time consuming, and there is never any guarantee of the outcome. Besides, the families filing the lawsuit would have big legal bills. I know the lawyers they have retained and they are expensive."

The board members were not united in their reactions to a lawsuit. Two said that they would reverse their position on decentralization if the suit was actually filed, and two others said they might reverse their position if one was filed. The board president asked Dr. Packard if he had changed his position. He responded, "In light of the differences expressed today, I would like to think this over. Let's meet again in one week and I'll be prepared to give you my answer."

The Challenge

Assume you are the superintendent. What factors would you consider before providing the school board with an answer?

Suggested Activities

1. Discuss the tensions that exist among three values that guide education policy: adequacy, equity, and liberty.

2. Identify the intended purposes, strengths, and weaknesses of decentralization.

3. Evaluate the manner in which this superintendent introduced and then pursued decentralization.

4. Identify and discuss the legal, political, and professional issues that are embedded in this case.

5. Invite a principal or superintendent involved with SBM to discuss this case with the class.

6. Complete the worksheet for this case.

Suggested Readings

Bauer, S. C. (1998). Designing school-based systems: Deriving a theory of practice. *International Journal of Educational Reform, 7*(2), 108–121.

Brick, B. H. (1993). Changing concepts of equal educational opportunity: A comparison of the views of Thomas Jefferson, Horace Mann, and John Dewey. *Thresholds in Education, 19*(1–2), 2–8.

Candoli, I. C. (1995). *School-based management in education: How to make it work in your school.* Lancaster, PA: Technomic (see Chapter 3).

Dempster, N. (2000). Guilty or not: The impact and effects of site-based management on schools. *Journal of Educational Administration, 38*(1), 47–63.

Florestal, K., & Cooper, R. (1997). *Decentralization of education: Legal issues.* (ERIC Document Reproduction Service No. ED 412 616)

Holloway, J. H. (2000). The promise and pitfalls of site-based management. *Educational Leadership 57*(7), 81–82.

Hughes, L. W. (1993). School-based management, decentralization, and citizen control—A perspective. *Journal of School Leadership, 3*(1), 40–44.

Kowalski, T. J. (2003). *Contemporary school administration: An introduction* (2nd ed.). Boston: Allyn and Bacon (see Chapter 8).

Leithwood, K., Jantzi, D., & Steinbach, R. (1998). *Do school councils matter?* (ERIC Document Reproduction Service No. ED 424 644)

Leonard, L. J. (1998). Site based management and organizational learning: Conceptualizing their combined potential for meaningful reform. *Planning & Changing 29*(1), 24–46.

Lifton, F. B. (1992). The legal tangle of shared governance. *School Administrator, 49*(1), 16–19.

Mitchell, J. K., & Poston, W. K. (1992). The equity audit in school reform: Three case studies of educational disparity and incongruity. *International Journal of Educational Reform, 1*(3), 242–247.

Myers, J. A. (1997). Schools make the decisions: The impact of school-based management. *School Business Affairs, 63*(10), 3–9.

Peternick, L., & Sherman, J. (1998). School-based budgeting in Fort Worth, Texas. *Journal of Education Finance, 23*(4), 532–556.

Polansky, H. B. (1998). Equity and SBM: It can be done. *School Business Affairs, 64*(4), 36–37.

Reyes, A. H. (1994). The legal implication of school-based budgeting. (ERIC Document Reproduction Service No. ED 379 753)

Wilson, S. M., Iverson, R., & Chrastil, J. (2001). School reform that integrates public education and democratic principles. *Equity & Excellence in Education, 34*(1), 64–70.

References

Fullan, M. (2001). *Leading in a culture of change.* San Francisco: Jossey-Bass.

Kowalski, T. J. (1999). *The school superintendent: Theory, practice, and cases.* Upper Saddle River, NJ: Merrill, Prentice Hall.

Kowalski, T. J. (2003). *Contemporary school administration: An introduction* (2nd ed.). Boston: Allyn and Bacon.

Tyack, D. (1990). Restructuring in historical perspective: Tinkering towards Utopia. *Teachers College Record, 92*(2), 170–191.

Who Creates the School's Vision?

Background Information

Visioning and long-range planning have become increasingly important administrative responsibilities for several reasons. One is that the pace of societal change continues to accelerate requiring organizations to engage in constant renewal. Another is the belief that meaningful reform is much more likely to be achieved if it is pursued at the district and individual school levels. These and related conditions have prompted superintendents and school board members to find "visionary" principals. But what is the essence of this desired attribute? Consider the following perceptions of visionary leaders that have been applied to public education:

- Administrators who possess knowledge about society and education enhancing their ability to predict the future
- Administrators who are identified with a specific reform agenda that requires substantial change in schools (e.g., site-based management)
- Administrators who understand the dynamics of change and who earned reputations as change agents

Such images often lead employing officials to believe that some principals can single-handedly transform a failing school in a brief period of time.

Whereas a school's mission statement focuses on the present and details what the school is expected to accomplish, its vision statement describes a desired future. A vision statement, however, should be more than a dream and more than the agenda of power elites (select individuals who hold either legitimate or political power). Properly construed, it is established using accurate data and reliable forecasts about society and education (Kowalski, 1999); it is developed by melding the collective visions of individuals and groups in the community being served (Fullan,

2003). Public schools in the United States should personify the foundational values of a democratic society.

When visioning is conceived as a collective responsibility, the ideal principal role is largely facilitative. That is, he or she collects pertinent data, identifies trends, shares information, and builds consensus. One should not conclude that this process nullifies the importance of administrators having a vision of the future. Principals are expected to be both leaders and managers. As leaders, they should be visionaries, because leadership entails decisions about what needs to be done (Kowalski, 2003). A principal's knowledge about education and administration, however, should be treated as a resource and not as a justification for making dictatorial decisions.

In this case, a new principal in a rural middle school attempts to create a broad-based committee to develop a school vision. Several influential teachers believe the principal should determine the school's future and they thwart her efforts to prepare the statement democratically. As you read this case, consider conditions that contributed to the opposing philosophies and the resulting conflict.

Key Areas for Reflection

1. Visioning
2. School culture
3. Principal leadership style
4. Professionalism versus democracy
5. Principal role expectations

The Case

Community and School District

The Lightville Community School District serves two predominately rural townships in a southwestern state. Lightville, the only town of any size in the district, is a typical small farming community with two grain elevators and a handful of other small businesses. Nearly 75 percent of the residents live on farms. There are three schools that collectively enroll just under 1,000 students. All of the facilities are relatively new and located on a single rural campus about two miles from Lightville. The elementary school, opened 12 years ago, was the first building erected on this 93-acre site. Last year, construction was completed on the new middle school and new high school. Previously, secondary-level students had attended Lightville Junior-Senior High School, a 65-year old building that was razed after the new schools were opened.

The seven school board members are elected to serve four-year terms. Three of them have been in office for more than three terms, and three others have been in office for more than two terms. The superintendent, Stan Rawlings, started teaching in Lightville 32 years ago; this is his eighteenth year as superintendent.

Middle School and the New Principal

Physically separating the middle grades from the high school was a recommendation advanced by Superintendent Rawlings. When he first proposed the idea, there was division among the taxpayers. Three alternatives had been studied by the architects: renovating the Jr.-Sr. High School; replacing the Jr.-Sr. high school; or building separate schools. Only a handful of residents supported the first alternative, even though it was the least expensive. Support for the second option was greater but, in general, most taxpayers did not voice a strong opinion on this matter. The school board voted unanimously to accept the superintendent's recommendation to build separate schools.

The new middle school enrolls 268 pupils. The design was influenced by the intention to use both teacher teaming and block scheduling. Edgar Findley, who had been principal of the Lightville Jr.-Sr. High School, became principal of the new high school. His assistant principal retired about two months before the two new secondary schools opened. The superintendent and school board decided to look outside the school district for an innovative principal who would shape a model middle school.

Susan Potter was an experienced teacher and middle school assistant principal in a suburban Dallas school district when she applied for the vacancy in Lightville. She was looking for a new challenge and she was excited about the prospect of being able to build a middle school program from the ground floor. Her positive feelings were reinforced after interviewing for the job; she was impressed with the experience of the faculty and the community's apparent support for education.

Prior to conducting the search for a new principal, Superintendent Rawlings had convinced the school board that this administrator should be employed at least one semester before the new school actually opened. Again, the board agreed. Principal Potter's employment with Lightville started officially on January 5—six and one-half months before the school became operational. The superintendent told her that she had three primary responsibilities during this period: make final staffing decisions, organize the school's programs, and complete the schedule. Despite the decision to use teaming and block scheduling, no actual instructional planning had occurred before the architects designed the middle school. The superintendent merely had instructed the designers to shape a building that accommodated these two strategies.

The staffing assignment proved to be the easiest task. Working with the superintendent and high school principal, Ms. Potter identified teachers and support staff who were assigned to the middle school by mid-March. Once that was done, she took action to create a visioning and planning committee.

The Committee

With input from Superintendent Rawlings and the school board members, Susan appointed four teachers and four parents to the visioning and planning committee. Five of the members were females, and the four teachers represented different areas of the school's curriculum.

At the committee's first meeting, Principal Potter outlined her philosophy and objectives regarding the committee's responsibilities:

- The committee should operate democratically.
- Consensus should be the preferred method for making decisions.
- The principal (Potter) should be a voting member of the committee but not its chair.
- The committee's first task should be to develop a vision statement that would provide directions for the planning phases.
- The vision statement should reflect the collective values and beliefs of the committee members.
- The broader community, including the middle school's faculty, should have an opportunity to react to the proposed vision statement before it is adopted.

The members agreed with her preferences except with one pertaining to the committee chairmanship. Most members commented that they expected and wanted her to assume this role. She convinced them to select another person.

Helen Burke, an English and social studies teacher, was chosen as the committee's chair. At the time, she was chairperson of the English Department at the high school and married to one of the school board members. Her husband, a farmer, is a highly respected community leader and one of the most influential board members. Helen surprised many of her colleagues when she asked to be assigned to the new middle school. She had persuaded her husband to support the two-school option and she felt some responsibility to ensure that the new middle school would be effective.

Conflict

Helen and Susan worked well together and they quickly became friends. They were about the same age, and Helen was delighted that the school district had finally employed a female principal. Two days after the initial committee meeting, the two women met to discuss the agenda for the committee's next meeting.

Helen began the conversation by saying, "Susan, I want you to know that I will do anything I can to help you develop a quality school. We are looking to you to provide the leadership we need. So don't ever hesitate to call on me to help you get things done. We have an excellent committee, and I am certain that the members will support your ideas."

"I appreciate that, Helen, and I am grateful that you have agreed to be the chair. Obviously, the other members see you as a leader," Susan responded. "We have a great deal of work to do in the next two months, and virtually everything depends on the committee's ability to finish its work on time."

Susan then reiterated that the committee's first task was to fashion a vision statement. She explained that the statement would provide a reference point for making both organizational and instructional decisions.

Helen then told her, "After you interviewed with the school board, my husband told me that you were a visionary leader—just the type of person we needed to direct our new school. I think we should spend most of the next meeting having you share your middle school philosophy. This community respects administrators, and our superintendent and principals are expected to shape important educational decisions. You are going to find that the committee is going to be highly supportive of your ideas."

Susan was surprised by Helen's comments. It sounded as if she was to develop the vision and the committee would merely rubber stamp it.

"Helen, I really appreciate your kind words; however, I don't think having me dictate the vision is a good way to begin. As I noted in our first committee meeting, a vision statement should reflect the collective thinking of the school and the community. Every committee member should have an opportunity to reflect on what they believe the new middle school should become in the next decade. I'm new here. I don't really feel comfortable dictating the future."

"But Susan," Helen said, "you're the expert. You're the person who is supposed to lead us and our new school. I really think the committee members expect you to tell us what the new school should become."

"I don't have a problem being a facilitator. For example, I can provide information about the middle school philosophy and answer questions. I can tell you about effective practices. And I don't have a problem participating in discussions—even when it is clear that we have different ideas. But if we begin by having me propose the school's vision statement, I'm afraid committee members will fall victim to 'groupthink,'" Susan commented.

"What do you mean?"

"Groupthink is basically a process that causes individuals to agree to positions that appear to be supported by key individuals or a majority of the group—even when the individuals do not personally agree with the positions. More simply, it's going along to get along," Susan explained.

Helen thought for moment and then said, "I don't think we need to worry about groupthink with this committee. If a committee member doesn't agree with something, he or she will let you know. They are not bashful. But on the other hand, I'm not sure how much the committee members, including the teachers, know about middle schools. If we start by having members state personal visions, we may not have a vision statement by the time school opens in August. Given our time constraints, I don't think this approach will work."

Sensing that she and Helen were not going to agree on this key issue, Susan suggested that the matter be discussed by the entire committee. She asked Helen to place the matter at the top of the next meeting's agenda.

Helen answered, "Fine, but I think you'll find that the other committee members feel pretty much as I do. We may just be wasting more time."

At the next meeting, Helen explained that she and Susan had met to discuss how the committee would proceed with developing the vision statement. She explained her position to the group and indicated that Susan held a different view.

"I want Susan to explain her feeling on this matter," Helen told the members. "After she finishes, we can discuss how we want to proceed."

Susan explained that vision statements should reflect the collective thoughts of those who belonged to a school's broader community. "Sure, I can give you a boilerplate vision statement that reflects common elements of the middle school philosophy. But some of those elements may not be appropriate for this community and this district. Let me give you an example. Not all middle schools treat social activities in the same way. Should sixth-grade students be allowed to attend dances? Should the sixth grade be fully integrated academically with other grades? Often, community values and beliefs influence the answers to such questions. I would like to hear your views on these and related matters. Such discussion ensures that each person has an opportunity to dream about creating a model middle school."

Dan Kelby, a physical education teacher, was the first committee member to respond to Susan's comments. "I have several thoughts about the new school, especially related to athletic programs. But if we all start sharing our ideas, we may be here dreaming for months. I think things would proceed more quickly if we follow Helen's suggestion that you provide an initial vision statement and we react to it. Chances are we are going to agree with your ideas."

Two other committee members, both parents, said they agreed with Dan.

Susan then replied, "Several days ago when I met with Helen, I told her why I was apprehensive about proceeding in the manner suggested. If I provide the initial vision statement, you automatically become a reactor. You know this community much better than I do. I can provide information about effective middle schools, but this information needs to be considered in light of community culture."

Helen then asked Susan, "Would you be specific about the process you prefer?"

"Each member of the committee should share his or her beliefs about what the school should look like in 5 or 10 years. Then we would ask questions and discuss the individual visions. The objective is to reach consensus. I participate and facilitate, but my views are not treated any differently than any other member's views."

"Susan, we all appreciate your sensitivity to community values," Helen said. "And I know that you believe in collaboration. However, you are the principal and we expect you to lead. Your knowledge and experience with middle school education are primary reasons why you were selected for this job. Just because we begin with 'your' vision doesn't mean that we will not end with 'our' vision."

After about 10 minutes of additional discussion, a motion was made to have the principal craft a vision statement as a starting point for the committee's work. Seven members of the committee voted to support the motion, one abstained, and Susan voted against the motion. Helen met with Susan after the others left.

"I hope you don't feel discouraged by this meeting, Susan. You said you didn't know our culture. Well, part of our culture is that we believe that administrators should lead. We are accustomed to principals telling us what needs to be done. Trust me on this matter. When the committee is finished, we will have a vision statement that we and the entire community can support."

Helen's words did not make Susan feel better. She concluded that Helen had probably discussed this issue with most if not all of the other committee members prior to the meeting; and it was apparent that Helen could influence them. Susan was convinced that the committee would support her position. If that happened, the new school would open without her really knowing the true feelings of the community and faculty. Even worse, the committee members might treat the vision statement as being "her agenda."

The next committee meeting was scheduled for the following week. Susan tried to identify and evaluate her options.

The Challenge

Put yourself in Susan's position. What would you do?

Suggested Activities

1. Discuss the purpose of having a vision statement and distinguish a *vision statement* from a *mission statement.*

2. Identify and evaluate alternative approaches to developing a school vision.

3. Identify and discuss the advantages and disadvantages of developing a collaborative vision.

4. Assume you are the principal in this case. Evaluate the fact that Helen's husband is on the school board.

5. Complete the worksheet for Case 24.

Suggested Readings

Brouillette, L. (1997). Who defines 'democratic leadership?' Three high school principals respond to site-based reforms. *Journal of School Leadership, 7*(6), 569–591.

Fullan, M. (2003). *Change forces with a vengeance.* Philadelphia: Taylor and Francis.

Fullan, M., & Hargreaves, A. (1997). 'Tis the season. *Learning, 26*(1), 27–29.

Keedy, J. L., & Finch, A. M. (1994). Examining teacher-principal empowerment: An analysis of power. *Journal of Research and Development in Education, 27*(3), 162–175.

Krajewski, B., & Matkin, M. (1996). Community empowerment: Building a shared vision. *Principal, 76*(2), 5–6, 8.

Smith, S. C., & Stolp, S. (1995). Transforming a school's culture through shared vision. *OSSC Report, 35*(3), 1–6.

Starratt, R. J. (1995). *Leaders with vision: The quest for school renewal.* Thousand Oaks, CA: Corwin.

Yearout, S., Miles, G., & Koonce, R. H. (2001). Multi-level visioning. *Training & Development, 55*(3), 7, 30.

References

Fullan, M. (2003). *Change forces with a vengeance.* Philadelphia: Taylor and Francis.

Kowalski, T. J. (1999). *The school superintendent: Theory, practice, and cases.* Upper Saddle River, NJ: Merrill, Prentice-Hall (see Chapter 8).

Kowalski, T. J. (2003). Contemporary school administration: An introduction (2nd ed.). Boston: Allyn and Bacon.

Worksheet for Case 1

1. Superintendent Pratt sees federal intervention into public elementary and secondary education as a violation of local control. Do you agree or disagree with him? Why?

   _____

   _____

   _____

2. Both superintendents in this case have serious concerns about implementing the NCLB Act, yet they respond very differently to the task. What factors do you think affect their behavior?

   _____

   _____

   _____

3. What are the advantages and disadvantages of Superintendent Barstow's strategy for implementing the NCLB Act?

   _____

   _____

   _____

4. If you were a principal in Marcum County, how would you react to the superintendent's suggestion that the principals separate into two groups and work with their respective assistant superintendents?

   _____

   _____

   _____

5. The NCLB Act includes rewards and penalties based on school performance. Potentially, personnel, including principals, could be affected negatively if the schools they lead fail to make satisfactory progress. Do you support or oppose this provision of the law? State a reason for your position.

   _____

   _____

   _____

Worksheet for Case 2

1. What are some possible reasons why educators, including administrators, oppose alternative schools?

   _____

   _____

   _____

2. If you were Sharon, what would you have done differently to pursue an alternative school?

   _____

   _____

   _____

3. What are the advantages and disadvantages of creating the type of alternative school favored by most of the committee members?

   _____

   _____

   _____

4. The superintendent appears reluctant to create the type of alternative school he and Sharon favor because the school board may not approve it. Does a superintendent have a professional obligation to recommend what he believes to be best policy or should he avoid political conflict? Defend your position.

   _____

   _____

   _____

5. To what extent do alternative schools pose a threat to traditional schools? What is the basis of your response?

   _____

   _____

   _____

   _____

Worksheet for Case 3

1. To what extent are the racial, social, and economic characteristics of the school district relevant to the problem presented in the case?

    _____

    _____

    _____

2. If you were the principal, would you consider Carl Turner's record of fighting relevant to reaching a decision on this matter? Why or why not?

    _____

    _____

    _____

3. What are the possible disadvantages?

    _____

    _____

    _____

4. To what extent is the principal's reputation as a disciplinarian and his popularity in the Memorial Park area of the city relevant to this case?

    _____

    _____

    _____

    _____

5. When the principal tries to find Carl, he discovers that he is not in his fourth-period class. How do you evaluate his absence from school after three periods with respect to making a decision in this case?

    _____

    _____

    _____

    _____

Worksheet for Case 4

1. What are the possible benefits and possible pitfalls of faculty having diverse preferences for a principal's leadership style?

   _____

   _____

   _____

2. Do you think that Dr. Werner should try to improve her relationship with teachers by having more contact with them outside the classroom settings (e.g., conversing with them in the faculty lounge)? Why or why not?

   _____

   _____

   _____

3. Should teachers expect to be paid for chaperoning activities such as the camping trip described in the case? Why or why not?

   _____

   _____

   _____

4. What steps might Dr. Werner take to change the attitudes of her critics?

   _____

   _____

   _____

   _____

5. As described in this case, do you consider Dr. Werner's behavior to be closer to a transactional or a transformational leadership style? Support your answer.

   _____

   _____

   _____

   _____

Worksheet for Case 5

1. Is the community environment an important variable in this case? Explain your response.

   _____

   _____

   _____

2. Why do you believe the superintendent and associate superintendent placed so much emphasis on the assistant principal's personal appearance?

   _____

   _____

   _____

3. What values and beliefs contribute to organizational dress norms for executives?

   _____

   _____

   _____

   _____

4. Do you believe that there is a relationship between administrative appearance and job performance? Why or why not?

   _____

   _____

   _____

   _____

5. What are some possible reasons why the assistant principal was not socialized to dress like other administrators in the district, including the principal who is his direct supervisor?

   _____

   _____

   _____

   _____

Worksheet for Case 6

1. Is it common for principals to react negatively to centralized controls? What information supports your conclusion on this matter?

_____

_____

_____

2. Duties and responsibilities in school districts are commonly divided into distinct divisions. In this case, two divisions—curriculum and business—compete for jurisdiction over a decision on petty-cash funds. What are the possible advantages of dividing administrative functions into organizational divisions?

_____

_____

_____

3. What are the possible disadvantages?

_____

_____

_____

_____

4. What are the possible advantages of using committees to make administrative decisions?

_____

_____

_____

5. What are the possible disadvantages of using committees to make administrative decisions?

_____

_____

_____

_____

Worksheet for Case 7

1. Do you consider Mr. Lattimore to be dictatorial? Why or why not?

   _____

   _____

   _____

2. Assume that the principal changes his mind and accepts the offer to be reassigned to the central office. Is this an acceptable resolution to the conflict? Why or why not?

   _____

   _____

   _____

   _____

3. Did the teachers act ethically in asking parents to sign the petition? Did they act ethically in signing the letter? Support your answers.

   _____

   _____

   _____

   _____

4. Do you think the principal is being prudent with respect to rejecting the offer to transfer to a central office position? Why or why not?

   _____

   _____

   _____

   _____

5. What positive actions might bring the parents, teachers, and principal together to address this problem?

   _____

   _____

   _____

   _____

Worksheet for Case 8

1. Do you think that the superintendent did an adequate job of educating his staff about school-based management? Why or why not?

_____

_____

_____

2. If you were a principal in this school district, would you have signed the petition? Why or why not?

_____

_____

_____

_____

3. What are the advantages and disadvantages of the superintendent withdrawing his recommendation?

_____

_____

_____

_____

4. Was it ethical for the principal at South High School to convene the meeting and compose the petition? Why or why not?

_____

_____

_____

_____

5. Should Dr. Pisak take action against the principals who signed the petition? Why or why not?

_____

_____

_____

_____

Worksheet for Case 9

1. If you were the principal in this case, what would you have done differently after receiving the first complaints from parents in October?

   _____

   _____

   _____

2. What, if any, relevance do you assign to the facts that relatively few parents attended the meeting with the principal and that some of the parents who attended supported the teacher?

   _____

   _____

   _____

3. What values and beliefs might contribute to a superintendent isolating himself from other administrators?

   _____

   _____

   _____

4. The principal did not disclose to the parents the reason why Mrs. Comstock was assigned to teach third grade. Given the nature of this case, do you believe that the principal had an ethical responsibility to divulge this information? Why or why not?

   _____

   _____

   _____

   _____

5. Was Mr. Carlsburg acting in his own interests or the school's interests? Explain your response.

   _____

   _____

   _____

Worksheet for Case 10

1. Why do you believe the teacher (Mrs. Durnitz) is being inflexible with regard to enforcing the policy on plagiarism?

_____

_____

_____

2. Do you believe that the principal (Mr. Furtoski) is being rational and objective in dealing with the plagiarism case? Why or why not?

_____

_____

_____

3. Assume you were the principal in this case. To what extent would your decision be influenced by the advice offered by the school board's attorney?

_____

_____

_____

4. Do you believe the superintendent and school board are acting appropriately by allowing the principal to essentially make the final decision? Why or why not?

_____

_____

_____

5. If you were the principal, what factors would you weigh in deciding whether to accept the proposed compromise offered by the student's attorney?

_____

_____

_____

_____

Worksheet for Case 11

1. Is it possible for a superintendent to spend most of his or her time away from the school district and still be highly effective? What evidence do you have to support your response?

   _____

   _____

   _____

2. What alternatives does Dr. Myers have to resolve this matter?

   _____

   _____

   _____

3. What values and beliefs might contribute to a superintendent isolating himself from other administrators?

   _____

   _____

   _____

   _____

4. In anticipation of his absences from the district, Dr. Sagossi tells the administrators that Dr. Yanko will be in charge during his absence. Based on the case, how do you evaluate this arrangement?

   _____

   _____

   _____

   _____

5. Are superintendents ever justified spending a majority of their time outside the school district? Why or why not?

   _____

   _____

   _____

   _____

Worksheet for Case 12

1. What factors may influence the principal to believe that corporal punishment is effective?

   _____

   _____

   _____

2. If law permits corporal punishment, should local districts have specific policies regarding its use? Why or why not?

   _____

   _____

   _____

   _____

3. In your opinion, has Mr. Carson acted professionally? Why or why not?

   _____

   _____

   _____

   _____

4. What factors should the superintendent consider in deciding whether to recommend a policy change in the area of corporal punishment?

   _____

   _____

   _____

5. Based on the evidence in the case, do you believe that Mr. Sanchez is an effective principal? Why or why not?

   _____

   _____

   _____

   _____

Worksheet for Case 13

1. Why do you think the assistant principal is looking for a different position?

   _____

   _____

   _____

2. Did the assistant principal (Raymond) promise to remain at the high school for at least five years? What evidence do you have to support your response?

   _____

   _____

   _____

   _____

3. Should Raymond have told the principal that he was applying for another job? Why or why not?

   _____

   _____

   _____

   _____

4. Do you believe that the principal has acted appropriately in this case? Why or why not?

   _____

   _____

   _____

   _____

5. Assume that Raymond does not get the job in suburban Chicago. Should he stay at Bentonville High School? Why or why not?

   _____

   _____

   _____

   _____

Worksheet for Case 14

1. Do you believe that the Principal Farley's behavior is ethical? Why or why not?

   _____

   _____

   _____

2. Do you believe that Associate Principal Howard's behavior is ethical? Why or why not?

   _____

   _____

   _____

3. Based on your knowledge and experiences, do you believe it is possible for a principal in a large high school to be effective if he or she is away from the school campus 40 percent or more of the time? Explain your response.

   _____

   _____

   _____

4. Do you believe that the associate principal addressed her concerns appropriately? If so, why? If not, how should she have addressed them?

   _____

   _____

   _____

   _____

5. Should the mayor in this case have been involved in selecting Principal Farley? Why or why not?

   _____

   _____

   _____

   _____

Worksheet for Case 15

1. Instead of reprimanding the board member, what other actions might be taken?

   _____

   _____

   _____

2. Do you believe that the superintendent acted appropriately in taking this problem directly to the board president? Would it have been better to talk to Elmer Hodson first to get his side of the story? Why or why not?

   _____

   _____

   _____

3. What constitutes a conflict of interest for a school board member? Does your state have laws addressing conflicts of interest for public officials?

   _____

   _____

   _____

4. In your opinion, is it more important for the superintendent to insist on ethical board behavior or to maintain his relationship with Mr. Hodson? Why?

   _____

   _____

   _____

   _____

5. Is it possible that the conflict presented in this case can be used to improve conditions in the school district? If so, how?

   _____

   _____

   _____

   _____

Worksheet for Case 16

1. Rev. James cited a case in which a white student had been expelled for just one year for a bomb threat. Do you agree with him that the fistfight was a lesser offense? Do you agree with him that the lesser penalty given to the white student was evidence of discriminatory discipline practices? Why or why not?

   _____

   _____

   _____

2. Should a student's cumulative record be considered in an expulsion hearing? Why or why not?

   _____

   _____

   _____

3. Do you agree with the superintendent's statement that achievement test scores over the past two years probably were not influenced by any actions related to decentralization? Explain your answer.

   _____

   _____

   _____

4. The one student recommended for expulsion requested that he be permitted to withdraw from school instead of being expelled. The hearing officer, superintendent, and school board concurred. Do you think this was a good decision? Why or why not?

   _____

   _____

   _____

5. Was Rev. James's claim of unequal treatment of black students nullified when the school board reduced the expulsion period? Why or why not?

   _____

   _____

Worksheet for Case 17

1. Do you agree with the principal's decision to permit council members to be elected? What other options could he have used to select council members?

   _____

   _____

   _____

2. One possible solution to this situation would be to remove the four teachers who are members of the competing factions from the council. Would you support this action? Why or why not?

   _____

   _____

   _____

3. Are teachers adequately prepared to be members of school governance councils? Defend your response.

   _____

   _____

   _____

   _____

4. What do you believe are the positive effects of SBM on the school principal's role?

   _____

   _____

   _____

   _____

5. What do you believe are the negative effects of SBM on the school principal's role?

   _____

   _____

   _____

   _____

Worksheet for Case 18

1. Amber believes principals and assistant principals should spend some of their time working with teachers. Although instructional supervision is clearly an ideal role for building-level administrators, is it a real role? What evidence do you have to support your response?

   _____

   _____

   _____

2. Assume that Amber remains at Polk but openly criticizes beliefs that many students are doomed to fail. What are the possible consequences?

   _____

   _____

   _____

3. The principal in this case indicates that there are considerable differences between the ideals expressed in textbooks and college classrooms and the real conditions in schools. Based on your own experiences, do you agree with him? Why or why not?

   _____

   _____

   _____

4. Amber must make two important decisions: Should she stay at Polk? Should she remain in administration? What factors should be weighed in answering these questions?

   _____

   _____

   _____

5. What are the advantages and disadvantages for Amber if she decides to remain at Polk Middle School?

   _____

   _____

   _____

Worksheet for Case 19

1. When Principal Emmons assumed the principalship of the vocational school, he presented a list of problems to the board members (superintendents). The majority did not want to deal with the issues. If you were principal of the vocational school, would have dropped the matter (as did Principal Emmons), or would you pursue a different approach? If so, explain your approach.

   _____

   _____

   _____

2. What are the primary variables producing conflict in this case?

   _____

   _____

   _____

3. What are the advantages and disadvantages of Principal Emmons attempting to mount political support for the consultant's report?

   _____

   _____

   _____

4. In your opinion, do the superintendents on the governing board have a moral obligation to protect the confederation? Why or why not?

   _____

   _____

   _____

5. In this case, the vocational school students attend half-day and are officially enrolled in and receive diplomas from their "home" high school. Is this a good arrangement? Why or why not?

   _____

   _____

   _____

   _____

Worksheet for Case 20

1. Do you think Dr. Tatum was prepared adequately to become principal of a large high school? Why or why not?

   _____

   _____

   _____

2. What is your impression of the behavior of the three assistant principals in this case? Were they behaving appropriately? Explain your answer.

   _____

   _____

   _____

3. What are the arguments for and against zero-tolerance policies?

   _____

   _____

   _____

   _____

4. Does your state have laws stipulating what must be done to students in public schools if they are caught using or selling illegal drugs? If so, what are these laws?

   _____

   _____

   _____

   _____

5. Do you agree with the superintendent's directive that every student who receives in-school suspension must complete a substance abuse program? Why or why not?

   _____

   _____

   _____

   _____

Worksheet for Case 21

1. Did the assistant principal do an adequate job of checking with administrators in other schools that had convocations featuring the same group? Why or why not?

   _____

   _____

   _____

2. The superintendent in this case allows the principal to make a decision. If you were the principal, would you prefer to have had a superintendent who would have told you what to do? Why or why not?

   _____

   _____

   _____

3. To what extent should high schools provide a forum for controversial ideas?

   _____

   _____

   _____

4. When the principal met with the three assistants, she allowed them to present alternative solutions. The outcome was three different proposals. If you were the principal, would you have conducted this meeting differently? If so, how?

   _____

   _____

   _____

5. Is it possible to involve community leaders in making the convocation decision? If so, how?

   _____

   _____

   _____

   _____

Worksheet for Case 22

1. Should teachers have the freedom to select the instructional materials they use? Why or why not?

   _____

   _____

   _____

2. Assume that "Sorcerer" is removed from the schools as demanded by the group of parents. How do you think the teachers would respond?

   _____

   _____

   _____

3. The case provides some information about the meeting at which the teachers decided to purchase the software. Based on this information, what is your evaluation of the decision-making process that was used?

   _____

   _____

   _____

4. In what ways are professionalism and democracy compatible and incompatible?

   _____

   _____

   _____

   _____

5. Would it have been possible for the principals to maintain control while allowing the teachers considerable authority to select instructional materials? If yes, how could this have been done?

   _____

   _____

   _____

   _____

Worksheet for Case 23

1. What are the advantages and disadvantages of Dr. Packard deciding to stand firm and not alter the decentralization program?

   _____

   _____

   _____

2. Based on what you read, do you think the administrative staff was adequately prepared to implement the changes required by the superintendent? Why or why not?

   _____

   _____

   _____

3. Do you agree with the superintendent's statement that achievement test scores over the past two years probably were not influenced by any actions related to decentralization? Provide a rationale for your answer.

   _____

   _____

   _____

4. Ideally, what should the superintendent have done to build political support in the community for decentralization?

   _____

   _____

   _____

   _____

5. The superintendent suggested that inequities exist across all public schools. Do you agree or disagree? What is the basis of your response?

   _____

   _____

   _____

   _____

Worksheet for Case 24

1. What is your definition of a visionary leader? What is the basis of your definition?

   _____

   _____

   _____

2. In this case, Susan alludes to a community culture. What does this mean?

   _____

   _____

   _____

3. What is the nature of the potential conflict between professionalism and democracy?

   _____

   _____

   _____

   _____

4. Based on your knowledge of school administration, what role should the principal play in building the school's vision?

   _____

   _____

   _____

5. Is it possible that Susan can capitalize on the conflict to produce some positive results for the district and new middle school? If so, what are these opportunities?

   _____

   _____

   _____

   _____

Index

This index is designed to assist you in locating subject areas in the cases. The subjects listed here include both major and minor topics included in the cases.

Topic	Relevant Cases
Administrator-Teacher Relationships	3, 4, 5, 6, 7, 9, 10, 12, 14, 17, 18, 22, 24
Alternative Schools/Programs	2, 20
Assistant Principals	3, 5, 12, 13, 14, 16, 18, 20, 21
Assistant Superintendents/Central Office	1, 2, 5, 6, 7, 8, 11, 14, 16, 20, 22, 23
Budgeting, Fiscal Issues	6, 11, 14, 17, 19, 22, 23
Business Manager	6, 11
Career Development	4, 5, 7, 8, 11, 13, 14, 18, 20
Change Process	1, 2, 4, 6, 7, 8, 9, 13, 17, 20, 23, 24
Communication Problems	3, 4, 5, 6, 7, 8, 9, 10, 11, 12, 13, 14, 15, 16, 17, 18, 20, 21, 22, 23
Community Relations (*see* Public Relations)	
Curriculum and Instruction	3, 6, 7, 8, 9, 10, 17, 18, 19, 21, 22, 23
Decision-Making Procedures	1, 2, 5, 6, 7, 8, 9, 10, 11, 12, 13, 14, 15, 16, 17, 20, 21, 22, 23, 24
Educational Outcomes	1, 7, 9, 10, 20, 21, 22, 23
Elementary Schools	7, 8, 9, 17, 22, 23
Employment Practices	4, 5, 7, 9, 17, 20, 23
Employment Security/Stress	5, 7, 11, 12, 13, 14, 15, 16, 18, 20, 23
Ethical/Moral Issues	3, 4, 5, 7, 8, 9, 10, 11, 12, 13, 14, 15, 16, 17, 18, 19, 20, 21, 22
Evaluation	1, 4, 5, 6, 7, 9, 10, 22, 23
Federal Programs	1
High Schools	2, 3, 4, 5, 10, 13, 14, 16, 19, 20, 21

Leadership Style/Theory	1, 2, 3, 4, 5, 6, 7, 8, 9, 10, 11, 12, 13, 14, 17, 18, 20, 22, 23, 24
Legal Issues	3, 5, 6, 10, 12, 13, 15, 16, 19, 20, 21, 23
Middle Schools	12, 13, 18, 24
Multicultural Issues	3, 7, 10, 12, 16, 20, 21
Organizational Theory	4, 5, 6, 7, 8, 9, 11, 12, 13, 14, 17, 18, 23, 24
Philosophical Issues	2, 3, 4, 5, 6, 7, 8, 9, 10, 11, 12, 13, 14, 16, 17, 18, 20, 21, 22, 23, 24
Policy Development/Analysis	2, 3, 6, 7, 10, 12, 13, 15, 16, 17, 19, 20, 21, 22, 23
Political Behavior	1, 2, 3, 4, 5, 6, 7, 8, 9, 10, 12, 13, 14, 15, 16, 17, 19, 20, 21, 22, 23
Power, Use by Administrators	2, 3, 4, 5, 6, 7, 8, 10, 11, 12, 13, 14, 16, 17, 18, 19, 20, 23
Principals	1, 2, 3, 4, 5, 6, 7, 8, 9, 10, 12, 13, 14, 16, 17, 18, 19, 20, 21, 22, 23, 24
Public Relations	3, 5, 7, 9, 10, 12, 13, 14, 16, 19, 20, 21, 22, 23
Rural, Small-Town Schools	8, 13, 15, 23, 24
School Boards	3, 8, 10, 13, 14, 15, 16, 17, 23
School Reform	1, 2, 8, 17, 19, 23
Site-Based Management	8, 17, 23
Student Discipline (Student Services)	3, 7, 10, 12, 16, 20, 21
Suburban Schools	5, 9, 11, 22
Superintendents	3, 5, 6, 8, 10, 11, 15, 16, 18, 19, 23
Teacher Professionalization	4, 7, 9, 10, 17, 22, 24
Teacher Unions (Collective Bargaining)	10, 16
Urban/Larger City Schools	3, 7, 10, 12, 14, 16, 17, 20, 21
Visioning/Planning	1, 7, 19, 24
Violence	3, 12, 16
Vocational Schools	19
Women Administrators	2, 4, 5, 6, 11, 14, 16, 17, 18, 19, 20, 21, 23, 24